S0-BZW-724

Mobil ★★
Travel Guide

Boston

ExxonMobil
Travel Publications

Maps by
✸ RAND M^cNALLY

Acknowledgements

We gratefully acknowledge the help of our representatives for their efficient and perceptive inspections of the lodging and dining establishments listed; the establishments' proprietors for their cooperation in showing their facilities and providing information about them; and the many users of previous editions who have taken the time to share their experiences.

Mobil Travel Guide is also grateful to all the highly talented writers who contributed entries to this book.

Mobil, Exxon, and Mobil Travel Guide are trademarks of Exxon Mobil Corporation or one of its subsidiaries. All rights reserved. Reproduction by any means including but not limited to photography, electrostatic copying devices, or electronic data processing is prohibited. Use of information contained herein for solicitation of advertising or listing in any other publication is expressly prohibited without written permission from Exxon Mobil Corporation. Violations of reserved rights are subject to prosecution.

Copyright © 2004 EMTG, LLC. All rights reserved. Except for copies made by individuals for personal use, this publication may not be reproduced in whole or in part by any means whatsoever without written permission from the Mobil Travel Guide, 1460 Renaissance Drive, Suite 401, Park Ridge, IL 60068; 847/795-6700; info@mobiltravelguide.com.

Maps Copyright © 2004 Rand McNally & Company

Printing Acknowledgement: North American Corporation of Illinois

www.mobiltravelguide.com

The information contained herein is derived from a variety of third-party sources. Although every effort has been made to verify the information obtained from such sources, the publisher assumes no responsibility for inconsistencies or inaccuracies in the data or liability for any damages of any type arising from errors or omissions.

Neither the editors nor the publisher assumes responsibility for the services provided by any business listed in this guide or for any loss, damage, or disruption in your travel for any reason.

ISBN: 0-7627-2897-3

Manufactured in the United States of America.

10 9 8 7 6 5 4 3 2 1

Contents

Side Trips—Overnight Stays

Index

MAP SYMBOLS

Free limited-access highway	Interstate highway
New — under construction	U.S. highway
Toll limited-access highway	State or provincial highway
New — under construction	Other highway
Other multilane highway	Miles between arrows One mile or less not shown
Principal highway	
Other through highway	Interchanges and interchange numbers
Other road	
Unpaved road	Time zone boundary
Ferry	

Urbanized area in state maps; in city maps
Separate cities within metro area

National capital; state capital; cities; towns
(size of type indicates relative population)

U.S. or Canadian National Park

State/Provincial Park or Recreation Area

National Forest or Grassland, city park

Point of interest

Hospital, medical center

Continental divide

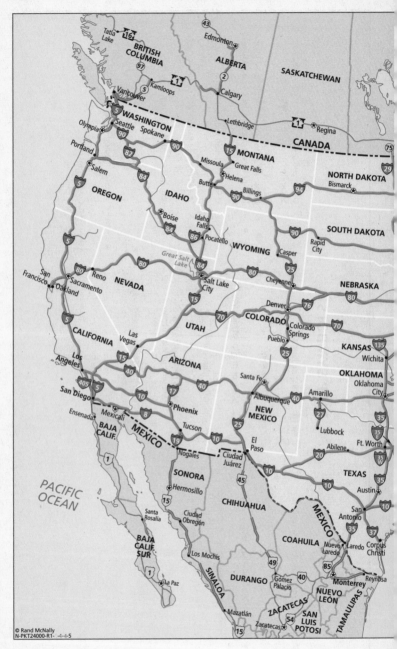

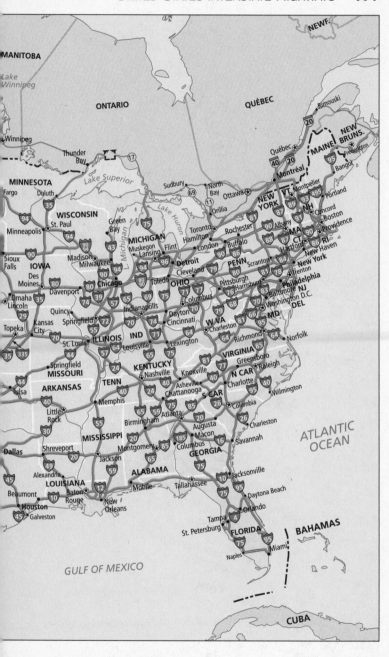

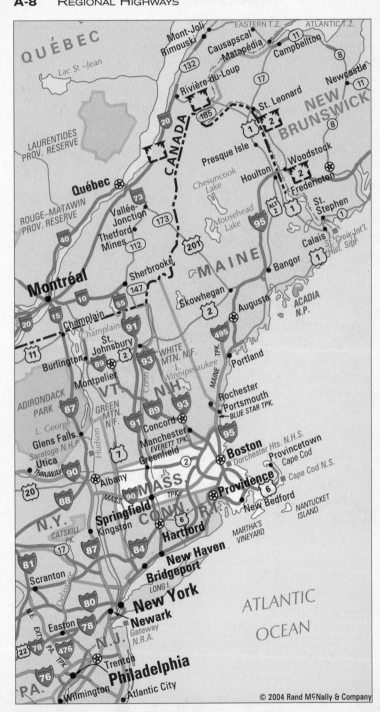

© 2004 Rand McNally & Company

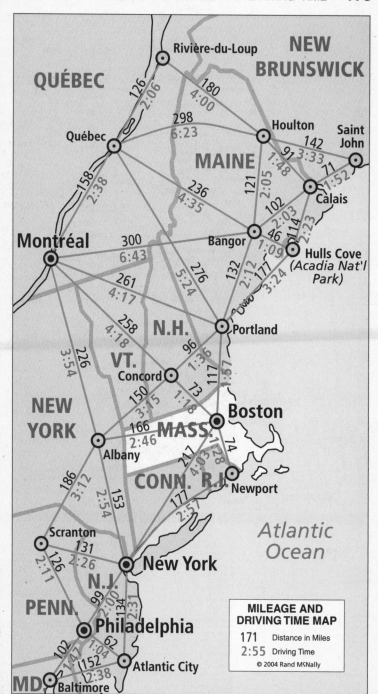

QUÉBEC

Rivière-du-Loup

126
2:06

180
4:00

NEW BRUNSWICK

Québec

298
6:23

Houlton

142

Saint John

158
2:38

MAINE

236
4:35

121

91 3:33
1:48

71
1:52

102
2:03

Calais

114
2:23

Montréal

300
6:43

Bangor

46
1:09

Hulls Cove
(Acadia Nat'l Park)

261
4:17

276
5:24

132

177
3:24

2:12

258
4:18

N.H.

Portland

226
3:54

VT.

96
1:36

Concord

150
3:15

73
1:18

117
1:57

NEW YORK

166
2:46

Boston

Albany

217
4:03

128

74

186
3:12

CONN. R.I.

153
2:54

Newport

177
2:57

Atlantic Ocean

Scranton

131
2:26

126
2:11

New York

N.J.

PENN.

99
2:00

134
2:31

Philadelphia

102
1:47

62
1:04

152
2:38

Atlantic City

MD. Baltimore

MILEADGE AND DRIVING TIME MAP

171   Distance in Miles
2:55 Driving Time
© 2004 Rand McNally

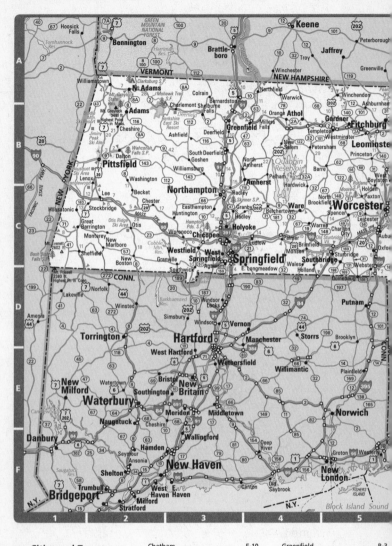

Cities and Towns

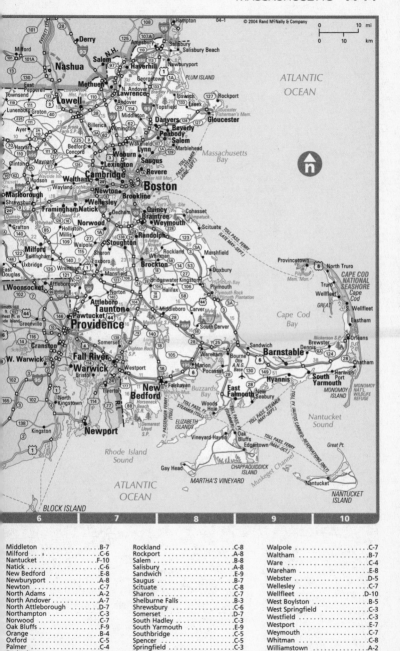

© 2004 Rand McNally & Company

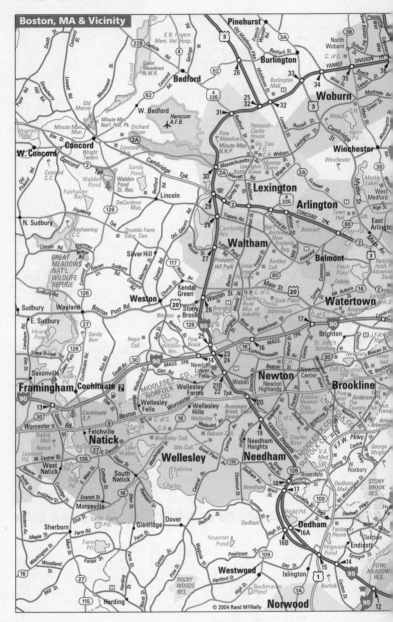

Boston, MA & Vicinity

© 2004 Rand McNally

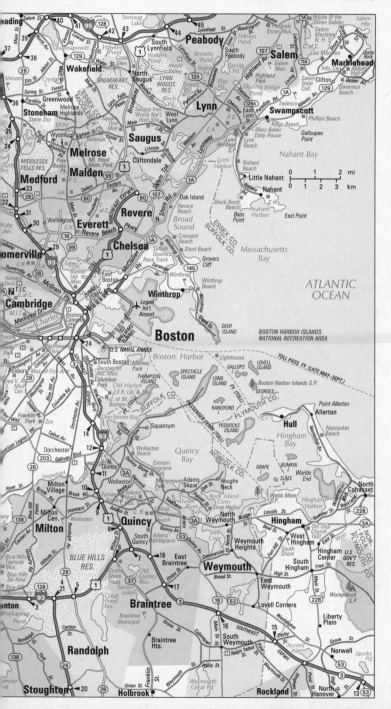

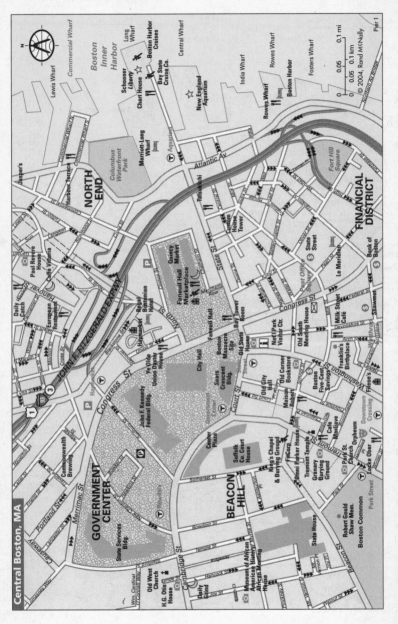

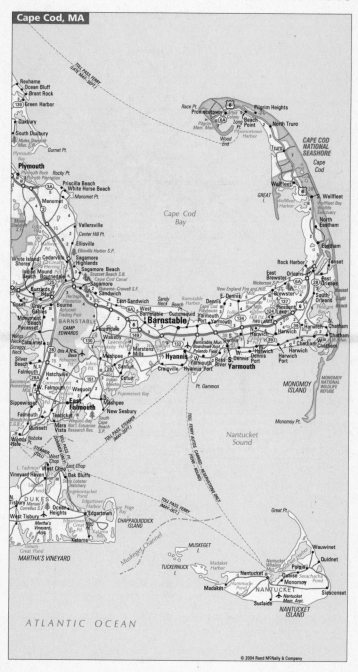

Cape Cod, MA

© 2004 Rand McNally & Company

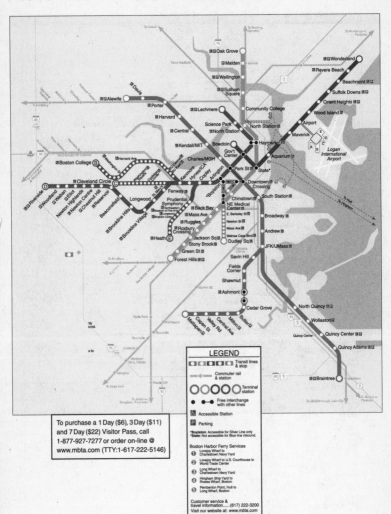

To purchase a 1 Day ($6), 3 Day ($11) and 7 Day ($22) Visitor Pass, call 1-877-927-7277 or order on-line @ www.mbta.com (TTY:1-617-222-5146)

Making road trips easy is our driving ambition.

Come and see how easy and convenient our Exxon and Mobil locations are. Before you head off for your next road trip, stop into your local Exxon or Mobil retailer and fill up on the essentials: film, batteries, cold soda for your thirst, salty snacks and candy for your hunger and, of course, automotive services and quality fuels. With over 16,000 locations nationwide, we make it effortless.

And don't forget to use your *Speedpass*™ to get back on the road even faster. After all, getting there is half the fun. How do we know? We're drivers too.

Speedpass is FREE. Visit speedpass.com or call toll free 1-87-SPEEDPASS (1-877-733-3727). Available at Exxon and Mobil locations that accept *Speedpass*. Service offerings vary by Exxon and Mobil location. Film and batteries only available at participating Exxon and Mobil convenience stores. ©2003 Exxon Mobil Corporation. All rights reserved.

EXXON   **Mobil**

We're drivers too.

I know the long way home is shorter today.

2003 AT&T Wireless. All rights reserved. Compatible device and active voice plan required. Monthly and usage charges apply for mMode service. Accuracy, availability, speed of delivery and timeliness are not guaranteed and are subject to transmission limitations. Not available for purchase or use in all areas. Geographic limitations and other charges and restrictions apply. All marks are property of their respective owners.

You no longer have to listen to traffic reports telling you you're stuck in traffic. With mMode only from AT&T Wireless, you can see the real-time traffic data the radio stations use right on the screen of your phone. And if you want to take another route, getting driving directions with mMode is just as easy.

Call 1 866 reachout®, go to attwireless.com/mMode, or visit any AT&T Wireless Store for more information.

reachout® with mMode™

on the wireless service America trusts™

Meet The Stars

Mobil 2004 Five-Star Award Winners

LODGINGS

California

The Beverly Hills Hotel, *Beverly Hills*

Chateau du Sureau, *Oakhurst*

Four Seasons, San Francisco, *San Francisco*

Hotel Bel-Air, *Los Angeles*

The Peninsula Beverly Hills, *Beverly Hills*

Raffles L'Ermitage Beverly Hills, *Beverly Hills*

The Ritz-Carlton San Francisco, *San Francisco*

Colorado

The Broadmoor, *Colorado Springs*

The Little Nell, *Aspen*

Connecticut

The Mayflower Inn, *Washington*

Florida

Four Seasons Resort Palm Beach, *Palm Beach*

The Ritz-Carlton, Naples, *Naples*

The Ritz-Carlton, Palm Beach, *Palm Beach*

Georgia

Four Seasons Hotel Atlanta, *Atlanta*

The Lodge at Sea Island Golf Club, *Sea Island*

Illinois

Four Seasons Hotel Chicago, *Chicago*

Peninsula Chicago, *Chicago*

The Ritz-Carlton, A Four Seasons Hotel, *Chicago*

Massachusetts

Four Seasons Hotel Boston, *Boston*

Blantyre, *Lenox*

New York

Four Seasons Hotel New York, *Manhattan*

The Point, *Saranac Lake*

The Ritz-Carlton New York Central Park, *Manhattan*

The St. Regis, *Manhattan*

North Carolina

Fearrington House, *Pittsboro*

South Carolina

Woodlands Resort and Inn, *Summerville*

Texas

The Mansion on Turtle Creek, *Dallas*

Vermont

Twin Farms, *Woodstock*

Virginia

The Inn at Little Washington, *Washington*

The Jefferson Hotel, *Richmond*

RESTAURANTS

California

The Dining Room at The Ritz-Carlton San Francisco, *San Francisco*

The French Laundry, *Yountville*

Gary Danko, *San Francisco*

Georgia

The Dining Room, *Atlanta*

Seeger's, *Atlanta*

Illinois

Charlie Trotter's, *Chicago*

Trio, *Evanston*

New York

Alain Ducasse, *Manhattan*

Jean Georges, *Manhattan*

Ohio

Maisonette, *Cincinnati*

Pennsylvania

Le Bec-Fin, *Philadelphia*

South Carolina

The Dining Room at Woodlands, *Summerville*

Virginia

The Inn at Little Washington, *Washington*

The Mobil Travel Guide has been rating establishments since 1958. Each establishment awarded the Mobil Five-Star rating is "one of the best in the country."

Welcome

Dear Traveler,

Since its inception in 1958, Mobil Travel Guide has served as a trusted advisor to auto travelers in search of value in lodging, dining, and destinations. Now in its 46th year, the Mobil Travel Guide is the hallmark of our ExxonMobil family of travel publications, and we're proud to offer an array of products and services from our Mobil, Exxon, and Esso brands in North America to facilitate life on the road.

Whether you're looking for business or pleasure venues, our nationwide network of independent, professional evaluators offers their expertise on thousands of travel options, allowing you to plan a quick family getaway, a full-service business meeting, or an unforgettable Five-Star celebration.

Your feedback is important to us as we strive to improve our product offerings and better meet today's travel needs. Whether you travel once a week or once a year, please take the time to contact us at www.mobil travelguide.com. We hope to hear from you soon.

Best wishes for safe and enjoyable travels.

Lee R Raymond

Lee R. Raymond
Chairman and CEO
Exxon Mobil Corporation

A Word to Our Readers

Travelers are on the roads in great numbers these days. They're exploring the country on day trips, weekend getaways, business trips, and extended family vacations, visiting major cities and small towns along the way. Because time is precious and the travel industry is ever-changing, having accurate, reliable travel information at your fingertips is critical. Mobil Travel Guide has been providing invaluable insight to travelers for more than 45 years, and we are committed to continuing this service well into the future.

The Mobil Corporation (known as Exxon Mobil Corporation since a 1999 merger) began producing the Mobil Travel Guide books in 1958, following the introduction of the US highway system in 1956. The first edition covered only five southwestern states. Since then, our books have become the premier travel guides in North America, covering the 48 contiguous states and Canada. Now, ExxonMobil presents the newest editions to our travel guides: city travel planners. We also recently introduced road atlases and specialty publications, a robust new Web site, as well as the first fully integrated, auto-centric travel support program called MobilCompanion, the driving force in travel.

Since its founding, Mobil Travel Guide has served as an advocate for travelers seeking knowledge about hotels, restaurants, and places to visit. Based on an objective process, we make recommendations to our customers that we believe will enhance the quality and value of their travel experiences. Our trusted Mobil One- to Five-Star rating system is the oldest and most respected lodging and restaurant inspection and rating program in North America. Most hoteliers, restaurateurs, and industry observers favorably regard the rigor of our inspection program and understand the prestige and benefits that come with receiving a Mobil star rating.

The Mobil Travel Guide process of rating each establishment includes:
- Unannounced facility inspections
- Incognito service evaluations for Mobil Four- and Five-Star properties
- A review of unsolicited comments from the general public
- Senior management oversight

For each property, more than 450 attributes, including cleanliness, physical facilities, employee attitude, and courtesy, are measured and evaluated to produce a mathematically derived score, which is then blended with the other elements to form an overall score. These quantifiable scores allow comparative analysis among properties and form the basis that Mobil Travel Guide uses to assign its Mobil One- to Five-Star ratings.

This process focuses largely on guest expectations, guest experience, and consistency of service, not just physical facilities and amenities. It is fundamentally a relative rating system that rewards those properties that continually strive for and achieve excellence each year. Indeed, the very best properties are consistently raising the bar for those that wish to compete with them. These properties proactively respond to consumers' needs even in today's uncertain times.

Only facilities that meet Mobil Travel Guide's standards earn the privilege of being listed in the guide. Deteriorating, poorly managed establishments are deleted. A Mobil Travel Guide listing constitutes a positive quality recommendation; every listing is an accolade, a recognition of achievement. Our Mobil One- to Five-Star rating system highlights its level of service. Extensive in-house research is constantly underway to determine new additions to our lists.

- The Mobil Five-Star Award indicates that a property is one of the very best in the country and consistently provides gracious and courteous service, superlative quality in its facility, and a unique ambience. The lodgings and restaurants at the Mobil Five-Star level consistently and proactively respond to consumers' needs and continue their commitment to excellence, doing so with grace and perseverance.

- Also highly regarded is the Mobil Four-Star Award, which honors properties for outstanding achievement in overall facility and for providing very strong service levels in all areas. These award-winners provide a distinctive experience for the ever-demanding and sophisticated consumer.

- The Mobil Three-Star Award recognizes an excellent property that provides full services and amenities. This category ranges from exceptional hotels with limited services to elegant restaurants with a less-formal atmosphere.

- A Mobil Two-Star property is a clean and comfortable establishment that has expanded amenities or a distinctive environment. A Mobil Two-Star property is an excellent place to stay or dine.

- A Mobil One-Star property is limited in its amenities and services but focuses on providing a value experience while meeting travelers' expectations. The property can be expected to be clean, comfortable, and convenient.

Allow us to emphasize that we do not charge establishments for inclusion in our guides. We have no relationship with any of the businesses and attractions we list and act only as a consumer advocate. In essence, we do the investigative legwork so that you won't have to.

Keep in mind, too, that the hospitality business is ever-changing. Restaurants and lodgings—particularly small chains and standalone establishments—change management or even go out of business with surprising quickness. Although we make every effort to double-check information during our annual updates, we nevertheless recommend that you call ahead to make sure the place you've selected is still open and offers all the amenities you're looking for. We've provided phone numbers; when available, we also list fax numbers and Web site addresses.

We hope that your travels are enjoyable and relaxing and that our books help you get the most out of every trip you take. If any aspect of your accommodation, dining, or sightseeing experience motivates you to comment, please drop us a line. We depend a great deal on our readers' remarks, so you can be assured that we will read your comments and assimilate them into our research. General comments about our books are also welcome. You can write to us at Mobil Travel Guide, 1460 Renaissance Dr, Suite 401, Park Ridge, IL 60068, or send an e-mail to info@mobiltravelguide.com.

Take your Mobil Travel Guide books along on every trip you take. We're confident that you'll be pleased with their convenience, ease of use, and breadth of dependable coverage.

Happy travels!

How to Use This Book

The Mobil Travel Guide City Guides are designed for ease of use. The book begins with a general introduction that provides a geographical and historical orientation to the state and gives basic statewide tourist information, from climate to highway information to seatbelt laws. The remainder is devoted to the featured city, as well as neighboring towns and nearby tourist destinations.

The following sections explain the wealth of information you'll find in this book: information about the city and its neighborhoods, things to see and do there, and where to stay and eat.

Maps

At the front of this book in the full-color section, we have provided a US and a state map as well as detailed city maps to help you find your way around. You'll find a key to the map symbols following the Contents page at the beginning of the map section.

Driving and Walking Tours

The driving tours that we include are usually day trips that make for interesting side excursions, although they can be longer. They offer you a way to get off the beaten path and visit an area that travelers often overlook. These trips frequently cover areas of natural beauty or historical significance.

Each walking tour focuses on a particularly interesting area of the city. Again, these tours can provide a break from everyday tourist attractions, and they often include places to stop for meals or snacks.

What to See and Do

The Mobil Travel Guide offers information about nearly 20,000 museums, art galleries, amusement parks, historic sites, national and state parks, ski areas, and many other types of attractions. A white star on a black background ★ signals that the attraction is a must-see—one of the best in the area. Because municipal parks, public tennis courts, swimming pools, and small educational institutions are common to most cities, they generally are not mentioned.

In an attraction's description, you'll find the months, days, and, in some cases, hours of operation; the address/directions, telephone number, and Web site (if there is one); and the admission price category. We use the following ranges for admission fees:

⊙ FREE
- ⊙ **$** = Up to $5
- ⊙ **$$** = $5.01-$10
- ⊙ **$$$** = $10.01-$15
- ⊙ **$$$$** = Over $15

Special Events

Special events are either annual events that last only a short time, such as festivals and fairs, or longer, seasonal events such as horseracing, summer theater and concerts, and professional sports. The Mobil Travel Guide Special Events listings also include infrequently occurring occasions that mark certain dates or events, such as centennials and other commemorative celebrations.

Side Trips

We recognize that your travels don't always end where a city's boundaries fall, so we've included some side trips that technically fall outside the scope of this book but that travelers frequently visit when they come to this city. Nearby national parks, other major cities, and major tourist draws fall into this category. We have broken the side trips into three categories: day trips (less than a three-hour drive); overnight stays (between a three- and five-hour drive); and weekend excursions (more than a five-hour drive). You'll find the side trips at the end of the listings.

Lodging and Restaurant Listings

Lodgings and restaurants are listed under the city or town in which they are located. Lodgings and restaurants located within 5 miles of a major commercial airport are listed under a separate "Airport Area" heading that follows the city section.

LODGINGS

Travelers have different wants and needs when it comes to accommodations. To help you pinpoint properties that meet your particular needs, each lodging property is classified by type according to the following characteristics:

- ⊙ **Motels/Motor Lodges.** These accommodations are in low-rise structures with rooms that are easily accessible to parking, which is usually free. Properties have small, functional lobbies, and guests enter their rooms from the outdoors. Service is often limited, and dining may not be offered in lower-rated motels. Shops and businesses are generally found only in higher-rated properties, as are bellstaff, room service, and restaurants serving three meals daily.

- ⊙ **Hotels.** A hotel is an establishment that provides lodging in a clean, comfortable environment. Guests can expect private bathrooms as well as some measure of guest services, such as luggage assistance, room service, and daily maid service.

⊛ **Resorts.** A resort is an establishment that provides lodging in a facility that is typically located on a larger piece of land. Recreational activities are emphasized and often include golf, spa, and tennis. Guests can expect more than one food and beverage establishment on the property, which aims to provide a variety of food choices at a variety of price points.

⊛ **All Suites.** In an All Suites property, guest accommodations consist of two rooms: a bedroom and a living room. Higher-rated properties offer facilities and services comparable to regular hotels.

⊛ **B&Bs/Small Inns.** The hotel alternative for those who prefer the comforts of home and a personal touch. It may be a structure of historic significance and often is located in an interesting setting. Breakfast is usually included and often is treated as a special occasion. Cocktails and refreshments may be served in the late afternoon or evening. Rooms are often individually decorated, but telephones, televisions, and private bathrooms may not be available in every room.

⊛ **Extended Stay.** These hotels specialize in stays of three days or more and usually offer weekly room rates. Service is often limited, and dining may not be offered at lower-rated properties.

Because most lodgings offer the following features and services, information about them does not appear in the listings unless exceptions exist:

⊙ Year-round operation with a single rate structure
⊙ Major credit cards accepted (note that Exxon or Mobil Corporation credit cards cannot be used to pay for room or other charges)
⊙ Air-conditioning and heat, often with individual room controls
⊙ Bathroom with tub and/or shower in each room
⊙ Cable television
⊙ Cots and cribs available
⊙ Daily maid service
⊙ Elevators
⊙ In-room telephones

Each lodging listing gives the name, address/location (when no street address is available), phone number(s), fax number, and total number of guest rooms. Also included are details on business, luxury, recreational, and dining facilities on the property or nearby. A key to the symbols at the end of each listing can be found on the inside front cover of this book.

For every property, we also provide pricing information. Because lodging rates change frequently, we opt to list a pricing category rather than specific prices. The pricing categories break down as follows:

- ☉ **$** = Up to $150
- ☉ **$$** = $151-$250
- ☉ **$$$** = $251-$350
- ☉ **$$$$** = $351 and up

All prices quoted by the Mobil Travel Guide are in effect at the time of publication; however, prices cannot be guaranteed. In some locations, short-term price variations may exist because of special events or holidays. Certain resorts have complicated rate structures that vary with the time of year; always confirm rates when making your plans.

RESTAURANTS

All dining establishments listed in our books have a full kitchen and offer table service and a complete menu. Parking on or near the premises, in a lot or garage, is assumed. If parking is not available, we note that fact in the listing.

Each listing also gives the cuisine type, address (or directions if no street address is available), phone and fax numbers, Web site (if available), meals served, days of operation (if not open daily year-round), reservation policy, and pricing category. We also indicate if a children's menu is offered. The price categories are defined as follows per diner and assume that you order an appetizer, an entrée, and one drink:

- ☉ **$** = $15 and under
- ☉ **$$** = $16-$35
- ☉ **$$$** = $36-$85
- ☉ **$$$$** = $86 and up

QUALITY RATINGS

The Mobil Travel Guide has been rating lodgings and restaurants in the United States since the first edition was published in 1958. For years, the guide was the only source of such ratings, and it remains among the few guidebooks to rate restaurants across the country and in Canada.

All listed establishments have been inspected by experienced field representatives and/or evaluated by a senior staff member. Our ratings are based on detailed inspection reports of the individual properties, on written evaluations of staff members who stay and dine anonymously, and on an extensive review of reader comments. Rating categories reflect both the features a property offers and its quality in relation to similar establishments.

Here are the definitions for the Mobil star ratings for lodgings:

⊙ ★ : A Mobil One-Star lodging is a limited-service hotel, motel, or inn that is considered a clean, comfortable, and reliable establishment.

⊙ ★ ★ : A Mobil Two-Star lodging is considered a clean, comfortable, and reliable establishment that has expanded amenities, such as a full-service restaurant on the premises.

⊙ ★ ★ ★ : A Mobil Three-Star lodging is well appointed, with a full-service restaurant and expanded amenities, such as a fitness center, golf course, tennis courts, 24-hour room service, and optional turn-down service.

⊙ ★ ★ ★ ★ : A Mobil Four-Star lodging provides a luxury experience with expanded amenities in a distinctive environment. Services may include, but are not limited to, automatic turndown service, 24-hour room service, and valet parking.

⊙ ★ ★ ★ ★ ★ : A Mobil Five-Star lodging provides consistently superlative service in an exceptionally distinctive luxury environment, with expanded services. Attention to detail is evident throughout the hotel, resort, or inn, from bed linens to staff uniforms.

The Mobil star ratings for restaurants are defined as follows:

⊙ ★ : A Mobil One-Star restaurant provides a distinctive experience through culinary specialty, local flair, or individual atmosphere.

⊙ ★ ★ : A Mobil Two-Star restaurant serves fresh food in a clean setting with efficient service. Value is considered in this category, as is family friendliness.

⊙ ★ ★ ★ : A Mobil Three-Star restaurant has good food, warm and skillful service, and enjoyable décor.

⊙ ★ ★ ★ ★ : A Mobil Four-Star restaurant provides professional service, distinctive presentations, and wonderful food.

⊙ ★ ★ ★ ★ ★ : A Mobil Five-Star restaurant offers one of few flawless dining experiences in the country. These establishments consistently provide their guests with exceptional food, superlative service, elegant décor, and exquisite presentations of each detail surrounding a meal.

TERMS AND ABBREVIATIONS IN LISTINGS

The following terms and abbreviations are used throughout the Mobil Travel Guide lodging and restaurant listings to indicate which amenities and services are available at each establishment. We've done our best to provide accurate and up-to-date information, but things do change, so if a particular feature is essential to you, please contact the establishment directly to make sure that it is available.

Complete meal Soup and/or salad, entrée, and dessert, plus a non-alcoholic beverage.

Continental breakfast Usually coffee and a roll or doughnut.

D Followed by a price, indicates the room rate for a double room—two people in one room in one or two beds (the charge may be higher for two double beds).

Each additional The extra charge for each additional person beyond the stated number of persons.

In-room modem link Every guest room has a connection for a modem that's separate from the main phone line.

Kitchen(s) A kitchen or kitchenette that contains a stove or microwave, sink, and refrigerator and is either part of the room or a separate, adjoining room. If the kitchen is not fully equipped, the listing will indicate "no equipment" or "some equipment."

Laundry service Either coin-operated laundry facilities or overnight valet service is available.

Luxury level A special section of a lodging, spanning at least an entire floor, that offers increased luxury accommodations. Management must provide no less than three of these four services: separate check-in and check-out, concierge, private lounge, and private elevator service (with key access). Complimentary breakfast and snacks are commonly offered.

Movies Prerecorded videos are available for rental or check-out.

Prix fixe A full, multicourse meal for a stated price; usually available at finer restaurants.

Valet parking An attendant is available to park and retrieve your car.

VCR VCRs are present in all guest rooms.

VCR available VCRs are available for hookup in guest rooms.

Special Information for Travelers with Disabilities

The Mobil Travel Guide **D** symbol indicates establishments that are at least partially accessible to people with mobility problems. Our criteria for accessibility are unique to our publications. Please do not confuse them with the universal symbol for wheelchair accessibility.

When the **D** symbol follows a listing, the establishment is equipped with facilities to accommodate people using wheelchairs or crutches or otherwise needing easy access to doorways and rest rooms. Travelers with severe mobility problems or with hearing or visual impairments may or may not find the facilities they need. Always phone ahead to make sure that an establishment can meet your needs.

All lodgings bearing our D symbol have the following facilities:
- ISA-designated parking near access ramps
- Level or ramped entryways to buildings
- Swinging building entryway doors a minimum of 39 inches wide
- Public rest rooms on the main level with space to operate a wheelchair and handrails at commode areas
- Elevator(s) equipped with grab bars and lowered control buttons
- Restaurant(s) with accessible doorway(s), rest rooms with space to operate a wheelchair, and handrails at commode areas
- Guest room entryways that are at least 39 inches wide
- Low-pile carpet in rooms
- Telephones at bedside and in the bathroom
- Beds placed at wheelchair height
- Bathrooms with a minimum doorway width of 3 feet
- Bath with an open sink (no cabinet) and room to operate a wheelchair
- Handrails at commode areas and in the tub
- Wheelchair-accessible peepholes in room entry door
- Wheelchair-accessible closet rods and shelves

All restaurants bearing our D symbol offer the following facilities:
- ISA-designated parking beside access ramps
- Level or ramped front entryways to the building
- Tables that accommodate wheelchairs
- Main-floor rest rooms with an entryway that's at least 3 feet wide
- Rest rooms with space to operate a wheelchair and handrails at commode areas

Making the Most of Your Trip

A few hardy souls might look back with fondness on a trip during which the car broke down, leaving them stranded for three days, or a vacation that cost twice what it was supposed to. For most travelers, though, the best trips are those that are safe, smooth, and within budget. To help you make your trip the best it can be, we've assembled a few tips and resources.

Saving Money

ON LODGING

Many hotels and motels offer discounts—for senior citizens, business travelers, families, you name it. It never hurts to ask—politely, that is. Sometimes, especially in the late afternoon, desk clerks are instructed to fill beds, and you might be offered a lower rate or a nicer room to entice you to stay. Simply ask the reservation agent for the best rate available. Also, make sure to try both the toll-free number and the local number. You may be able to get a lower rate from one than the other.

Becoming a member of MobilCompanion will entitle you to discounted rates at many well-known hotels around the country. For more information, call 877/785-6788 or visit www.mobilcompanion.com.

Timing your trip right can cut your lodging costs as well. Look for bargains on stays over multiple nights, in the off-season, and on weekdays or weekends, depending on the location. Many hotels in major metropolitan areas, for example, have special weekend packages that offer considerable savings on rooms; they may include breakfast, cocktails, and dinner discounts.

Another way to save money is to choose accommodations that give you more than just a standard room. Rooms with kitchen facilities enable you to cook some meals yourself, reducing your restaurant costs. A suite might save money for two couples traveling together. Even hotel luxury levels can provide good value, as many include breakfast or cocktails in the price of a room.

State and city taxes, as well as special room taxes, can increase your room rate by as much as 25 percent per day. We are unable to include information about taxes in our listings, but we strongly urge you to ask about taxes when making reservations so that you understand the total cost of your lodgings before you book.

Watch out for telephone-usage charges that hotels frequently impose on long-distance, credit-card, and other calls. Before phoning from your room, read the information given to you at check-in, and then be sure to review your bill carefully when checking out. You won't be expected to pay for charges that the hotel didn't spell out. Consider using your cell phone if you have one; or, if public telephones are available in the hotel lobby, your cost savings may outweigh the inconvenience of using them.

Here are some additional ways to save on lodgings:

- Stay in B&B accommodations; they're generally less expensive than standard hotel rooms, and the complimentary breakfasts cut down on food costs.
- If you're traveling with children, find lodgings at which kids stay free.
- When visiting a major city, stay just outside the city limits; these rooms are usually less expensive than those in downtown locations.
- Consider visiting national parks during the low season, when prices of lodgings near the parks drop 25 percent or more.
- When calling a hotel, ask whether it is running any special promotions or if any discounts are available; many times reservationists are told not to volunteer deals unless specifically asked about them.
- Check for hotel packages; some offer nightly rates that include a rental car or discounts on major attractions.

ON DINING

There are several ways to get a less expensive meal at a more expensive restaurant. Early-bird dinners are popular in many parts of the country and offer considerable savings. If you're interested in sampling a Mobil Four- or Five-Star establishment, consider going at lunchtime. Although the prices are probably still relatively high at midday, they may be half of those at dinner, and you'll experience the same ambience, service, and cuisine.

As a member of MobilCompanion, you can enroll in iDine. This program earns you up to 20 percent cash back at more than 1,900 restaurants on meals purchased with the credit card you register; the rebate appears on your credit card bill. For more information about MobilCompanion and iDine, call 877/785-6788 or go to www.mobilcompanion.com.

ON ENTERTAINMENT

Although some national parks, monuments, seashores, historic sites, and recreation areas may be used free of charge, others charge an entrance fee (ranging from $1 to $6 per person or $5 to $20 per carload) and/or a usage fee for special services and facilities. If you plan to make several visits to national recreation areas, consider one of the following money-saving programs offered by the National Park Service:

○ **National Parks Pass.** This annual pass is good for entrance to any national park that charges an entrance fee. If the park charges a per-vehicle fee, the pass holder and any accompanying passengers in a private noncommercial vehicle may enter. If the park charges a per-person fee, the pass applies to the holder's spouse, children, and parents as well as the holder. It is valid for entrance fees only; it does not cover parking, camping, or other fees. You can purchase a National Parks Pass in person at any national park where an entrance fee is charged; by mail from the National Park Foundation, PO Box 34108, Washington, DC 20043-4108; by calling 888/GO-PARKS; or at www.nationalparks.org. The cost is $50.

○ **Golden Eagle.** When affixed to a National Parks Pass, this sticker, available to people who are between 17 and 61 years of age, extends coverage to sites managed by the US Fish and Wildlife Service, the US Forest Service, and the Bureau of Land Management. It is good until the National Parks Pass to which it is affixed expires and does not cover usage fees. You can purchase one at National Park Service, Fish and Wildlife Service, and Bureau of Land Management fee stations. The cost is $15.

○ **Golden Age Passport.** Available to citizens and permanent US residents 62 and older, this passport is a lifetime entrance permit to fee-charging national recreation areas. The fee exemption extends to those accompanying the permit holder in a private noncommercial vehicle or, in the case of walk-in facilities, to the holder's spouse and children. The passport also entitles the holder to a 50 percent discount on federal usage fees charged in park areas, but not on concessions. Golden Age Passports must be obtained in person and are available at most National Park Service units that charge an entrance fee. The applicant must show proof of age, such as a driver's license or birth certificate (Medicare cards are not acceptable proof). The cost is $10.

○ **Golden Access Passport.** Issued to citizens and permanent US residents who are physically disabled or visually impaired, this passport is a free lifetime entrance permit to fee-charging national recreation areas. The fee exemption extends to those accompanying the permit holder in a private noncommercial vehicle or, in the case of walk-in facilities, to the holder's spouse and children. The passport also entitles the holder to a 50 percent discount on usage fees charged in park areas, but not on concessions. Golden Access Passports must be obtained in person and are available at most National Park Service units that charge an entrance fee. Proof of eligibility to receive federal benefits (under programs such as Disability Retirement, Compensation for Military Service-Connected Disability, and the Coal Mine Safety and Health Act) is required, or an affidavit must be signed attesting to eligibility.

A money-saving move in several large cities is to purchase a CityPass. If you plan to visit several museums and other major attractions, CityPass is a terrific option because it gets you into several sites for one substantially reduced price. Currently, CityPass is available in Boston, Chicago, Hollywood, New York, Philadelphia, San Francisco, Seattle, and southern California (which includes Disneyland, SeaWorld, and the San Diego Zoo). For more information or to buy one, call 888/330-5008 or visit www.citypass.net. You can also buy a CityPass from any participating CityPass attraction.

Here are some additional ways to save on entertainment and shopping:

- Check with your hotel's concierge for various coupons and special offers; they often have two-for-one tickets for area attractions and coupons for discounts at area stores and restaurants.
- Purchase same-day concert or theater tickets for half-price through the local cheap-tickets outlet, such as TKTS in New York City or Hot Tix in Chicago.
- Visit museums on their free or "by donation" days, when you can pay what you wish rather than a specific admission fee.

ON TRANSPORTATION

Transportation is a big part of any vacation budget. Here are some ways to reduce your costs:

- If you're renting a car, shop early over the Internet; you can book a car during the low season for less, even if you'll be using it in the high season.
- Rental car discounts are often available if you rent for one week or longer and reserve in advance.
- Get the best gas mileage out of your vehicle by making sure that it's properly tuned up and keeping your tires properly inflated. If your tires need to be replaced, you can save money on a new set of Michelins by becoming a member of MobilCompanion.
- Travel at moderate speeds on the open road; higher speeds require more gasoline.
- Fill the tank before you return your rental car; rental companies charge to refill the tank and do so at prices of up to 50 percent more than at local gas stations.
- Make a checklist of travel essentials and purchase them before you leave; don't get stuck buying expensive sunscreen at your hotel or overpriced film at the airport.

FOR SENIOR CITIZENS

Look for the senior-citizen discount symbol **SC** in this book's lodging and restaurant listings. Always call ahead to confirm that a discount is being offered, and be sure to carry proof of age. At places not listed in this book, it never hurts to ask if a senior-citizen discount is offered. Additional information for mature travelers is available from the American Association of Retired Persons (AARP), 601 E St NW, Washington, DC 20049; phone 202/434-2277; www.aarp.org.

Tipping

Tips are expressions of appreciation for good service. However, you are never obligated to tip if you receive poor service.

IN HOTELS

- Door attendants usually get $1 for hailing a cab.
- Bellstaff expect $2 per bag.
- Concierges are tipped according to the service they perform. Tipping is not mandatory when you've asked for suggestions on sightseeing or restaurants or for help in making dining reservations. However, a tip of $5 is appropriate when a concierge books you a table at a restaurant known to be difficult to get into. For obtaining theater or sporting event tickets, $5 to $10 is expected.
- Maids should be tipped $1 to $2 per day. Hand your tip directly to the maid, or leave it with a note saying that the money has been left expressly for the maid.

IN RESTAURANTS

Before tipping, carefully review your check for any gratuity or service charge that is already included in your bill. If you're in doubt, ask your server.

- Coffee shop and counter service waitstaff usually receive 15 percent of the bill, before sales tax.
- In full-service restaurants, tip 18 percent of the bill, before sales tax.
- In fine restaurants, where gratuities are shared among a larger staff, 18 to 20 percent is appropriate.
- In most cases, the maitre d' is tipped only if the service has been extraordinary, and only on the way out. At upscale properties in major metropolitan areas, $20 is the minimum.
- If there is a wine steward, tip $20 for exemplary service and beyond, or more if the wine was decanted or the bottle was very expensive.
- Tip $1 to $2 per coat at the coat check.

AT AIRPORTS

Curbside luggage handlers expect $1 per bag. Car-rental shuttle drivers who help with your luggage appreciate a $1 or $2 tip.

Staying Safe

The best way to deal with emergencies is to avoid them in the first place. However, unforeseen situations do happen, so you should be prepared for them.

IN YOUR CAR

Before you head out on a road trip, make sure that your car has been serviced and is in good working order. Change the oil, check the battery and belts, make sure that your windshield washer fluid is full and your tires are properly inflated (which can also improve your gas mileage). Other inspections recommended by the vehicle's manufacturer should also be made.

Next, be sure you have the tools and equipment needed to deal with a routine breakdown:

- Jack
- Spare tire
- Lug wrench
- Repair kit
- Emergency tools
- Jumper cables
- Spare fan belt
- Fuses
- Flares and/or reflectors
- Flashlight
- First-aid kit
- In winter, a windshield scraper and snow shovel

Many emergency supplies are sold in special packages that include the essentials you need to stay safe in the event of a breakdown.

Also bring all appropriate and up-to-date documentation—licenses, registration, and insurance cards—and know what your insurance covers. Bring an extra set of keys, too, just in case.

En route, always buckle up! In most states, wearing a seatbelt is required by law.

If your car does break down, do the following:

- Get out of traffic as soon as possible—pull well off the road.
- Raise the hood and turn on your emergency flashers or tie a white cloth to the roadside door handle or antenna.
- Stay in your car.
- Use flares or reflectors to keep your vehicle from being hit.

If you are a member of MobilCompanion, remember that En Route Support is always ready to help when you need it. Just give us a call and we'll locate and dispatch an emergency roadside service to assist you, as well as provide you with significant savings on the service.

IN YOUR HOTEL OR MOTEL

Chances are slim that you will encounter a hotel or motel fire, but you can protect yourself by doing the following:

- Once you've checked in, make sure that the smoke detector in your room is working properly.
- Find the property's fire safety instructions, usually posted on the inside of the room door.
- Locate the fire extinguishers and at least two fire exits.
- Never use an elevator in a fire.

For personal security, use the peephole in your room door and make sure that anyone claiming to be a hotel employee can show proper identification. Call the front desk if you feel threatened at any time.

PROTECTING AGAINST THEFT

To guard against theft wherever you go:

- Don't bring anything of more value than you need.
- If you do bring valuables, leave them at your hotel rather than in your car.
- If you bring something very expensive, lock it in a safe. Many hotels put one in each room; others will store your valuables in the hotel's safe.
- Don't carry more money than you need. Use traveler's checks and credit cards or visit cash machines to withdraw more cash when you run out.

For Travelers with Disabilities

To get the kind of service you need and have a right to expect, don't hesitate when making a reservation to question the management about the availability of accessible rooms, parking, entrances, restaurants, lounges, or any other facilities that are important to you, and confirm what is meant by "accessible."

The Mobil Travel Guide 🄳 symbol indicates establishments that are at least partially accessible to people with special mobility needs (people using wheelchairs or crutches or otherwise needing easy access to buildings and rooms). Keep in mind that our criteria for accessibility are unique to our publication and should not be confused with the universal symbol for wheelchair accessibility. Further information about these criteria can be found in the earlier section "How to Use This Book."

A thorough listing of published material for travelers with disabilities is available from the Disability Bookshop, Twin Peaks Press, Box 129, Vancouver, WA 98666; phone 360/694-2462; disabilitybookshop.virtual ave.net. Another reliable organization is the Society for Accessible Travel & Hospitality (SATH), 347 Fifth Ave, Suite 610, New York, NY 10016; phone 212/447-7284; www.sath.org.

Important Toll-Free Numbers and Online Information

Hotels and Motels

Adams Mark 800/444-2326
www.adamsmark.com

AmericInn 800/634-3444
www.americinn.com

AmeriHost Inn Hotels 800/434-5800
www.amerihostinn.com

Amerisuites 800/833-1516
www.amerisuites.com

Baymont Inns 877/BAYMONT
www.baymontinns.com

Best Inns & Suites 800/237-8466
www.bestinn.com

Best Value Inns 888/315-BEST
www.bestvalueinn.com

Best Western International 800/WESTERN
www.bestwestern.com

Budget Host Inn 800/BUDHOST
www.budgethost.com

Candlewood Suites 888/CANDLEWOOD
www.candlewoodsuites.com

Clarion Hotels 800/252-7466
www.choicehotels.com

Comfort Inns and Suites 800/252-7466
www.choicehotels.com

Country Hearth Inns 800/848-5767
www.countryhearth.com

Country Inns & Suites 800/456-4000
www.countryinns.com

Courtyard by Marriott 888/236-2427
www.courtyard.com

Cross Country Inn 800/621-1429
www.crosscountryinns.com

Crowne Plaza Hotels and Resorts 800/227-6963
www.crowneplaza.com

Days Inn 800/544-8313
www.daysinn.com

Delta Hotels 800/268-1133
www.deltahotels.com
Destination Hotels & Resorts 800/434-7347
www.destinationhotels.com
Doubletree Hotels 800/222-8733
www.doubletree.com
Drury Inns 800/378-7946
www.druryinn.com
Econolodge 800/553-2666
www.econolodge.com
Economy Inns of America 800/826-0778
www.innsofamerica.com
Embassy Suites 800/362-2779
www.embassysuites.com
ExelInns of America 800/FOREXEL
www.exelinns.com
Extended StayAmerica 800/EXTSTAY
www.extstay.com
Fairfield Inn by Marriott 888/236-2427
www.fairfieldinn.com
Fairmont Hotels 800/441-1414
www.fairmont.com
Four Points by Sheraton 888/625-5144
www.starwood.com
Four Seasons 800/545-4000
www.fourseasons.com
Hampton Inn/Hampton Inn and Suites 800/426-7866
www.hamptoninn.com
Hard Rock Hotels, Resorts and Casinos 800/HRDROCK
www.hardrock.com
Harrah's Entertainment 800/HARRAHS
www.harrahs.com
Harvey Hotels 800/922-9222
www.bristolhotels.com
Hawthorn Suites 800/527-1133
www.hawthorn.com
Hilton Hotels and Resorts (US) 800/774-1500
www.hilton.com
Holiday Inn Express 800/HOLIDAY
www.sixcontinentshotel.com
Holiday Inn Hotels and Resorts 800/HOLIDAY
www.holiday-inn.com

Homestead Studio Suites 888/782-9473
www.stayhsd.com

Homewood Suites 800/225-5466
www.homewoodsuites.com

Howard Johnson 800/406-1411
www.hojo.com

Hyatt 800/633-7313
www.hyatt.com

Ian Schrager .... Contact individual hotel
www.ianschragerhotels.com

Inter-Continental 888/567-8725
www.intercontinental.com

Joie de Vivre 800/738-7477
www.jdvhospitality.com

Kimpton Hotels 888/546-7866
www.kimptongroup.com

Knights Inn 800/843-5644
www.knightsinn.com

La Quinta 800/531-5900
www.laquinta.com

Le Meridien 800/543-4300
www.lemeridien.com

Leading Hotels of the World 800/223-6800
www.lhw.com

Loews Hotels 800/235-6397
www.loewshotels.com

MainStay Suites 800/660-6246
www.choicehotels.com

Mandarin Oriental 800/526-6566
www.mandarin-oriental.com

Marriott Conference Centers 888/236-2427
www.conferencecenters.com

Marriott Hotels, Resorts, and Suites 888/236-2427
www.marriott.com

Marriott Vacation Club International 800/845-5279
www.marriott.com/vacationclub

Microtel Inns & Suites 800/771-7171
www.microtelinn.com

Millennium & Copthorne Hotels 866/866-8086
www.mill-cop.com

Motel 6 .... 800/4MOTEL6
www.motel6.com

Omni Hotels 800/843-6664
www.omnihotels.com
Pan Pacific Hotels and Resorts 800/327-8585
www.panpac.com
Park Inn & Park Plaza 888/201-1801
www.parkhtls.com
The Peninsula Group .... Contact individual hotel
www.peninsula.com
Preferred Hotels & Resorts Worldwide 800/323-7500
www.preferredhotels.com
Quality Inn 800/228-5151
www.qualityinn.com
Radisson Hotels 800/333-3333
www.radisson.com
Raffles International Hotels and Resorts 800/637-9477
www.raffles.com
Ramada International 888/298-2054
www.ramada.com
Ramada Plazas, Limiteds, and Inns 800/2RAMADA
www.ramadahotels.com
Red Lion Inns 800/733-5466
www.redlion.com
Red Roof Inns 800/733-7663
www.redroof.com
Regal Hotels 800/222-8888
www.regal-hotels.com
Regent International 800/545-4000
www.regenthotels.com
Relais & Chateaux 800/735-2478
www.relaischateaux.com
Renaissance Hotels 888/236-2427
www.renaissancehotels.com
Residence Inns 888/236-2427
www.residenceinn.com
Ritz-Carlton 800/241-3333
www.ritzcarlton.com
Rockresorts 888/FORROCKS
www.rockresorts.com
Rodeway Inns 800/228-2000
www.rodeway.com
Rosewood Hotels & Resorts 888/767-3966
www.rosewood-hotels.com

Scottish Inn 800/251-1962
www.bookroomsnow.com

Select Inn 800/641-1000
www.selectinn.com

Sheraton 888/625-5144
www.sheraton.com

Shilo Inns 800/222-2244
www.shiloinns.com

Shoney's Inns 800/552-4667
www.shoneysinn.com

Signature/Jameson Inns 800/822-5252
www.jamesoninns.com

Sleep Inns 800/453-3746
www.sleepinn.com

Small Luxury Hotels of the World 800/525-4800
www.slh.com

Sofitel 800/763-4835
www.sofitel.com

SpringHill Suites 888/236-2427
www.springhillsuites.com

SRS Worldhotels 800/223-5652
www.srs-worldhotels.com

St. Regis Luxury Collection 888/625-5144
www.stregis.com

Staybridge Suites by Holiday Inn 800/238-8000
www.staybridge.com

Summerfield Suites by Wyndham 800/833-4353
www.summerfieldsuites.com

Summit International 800/457-4000
www.summithotels.com

Super 8 Motels 800/800-8000
www.super8.com

The Sutton Place Hotels 866/378-8866
www.suttonplace.com

Swissotel 800/637-9477
www.swissotel.com

TownePlace Suites 888/236-2427
www.towneplace.com

Travelodge 800/578-7878
www.travelodge.com

Universal 800/23LOEWS
www.loewshotel.com

Vagabond Inns 800/522-1555
www.vagabondinns.com
W Hotels 888/625-5144
www.whotels.com
Wellesley Inn and Suites 800/444-8888
www.wellesleyinnandsuites.com
WestCoast Hotels 800/325-4000
www.westcoasthotels.com
Westin Hotels & Resorts 800/937-8461
www.westin.com
Wingate Inns 800/228-1000
www.wingateinns.com
Woodfin Suite Hotels 800/966-3346
www.woodfinsuitehotels.com
Wyndham Hotels & Resorts 800/996-3426
www.wyndham.com

Airlines

Air Canada 888/247-2262
www.aircanada.ca
Alaska 800/252-7522
www.alaskaair.com
American 800/433-7300
www.aa.com
America West 800/235-9292
www.americawest.com
ATA 800/435-9282
www.ata.com
British Airways 800/247-9297
www.british-airways.com
Continental 800/523-3273
www.flycontinental.com
Delta 800/221-1212
www.delta-air.com
Island Air 800/323-3345
www.islandair.com
Mesa 800/637-2247
www.mesa-air.com
Northwest 800/225-2525
www.nwa.com
Southwest 800/435-9792
www.southwest.com

United 800/241-6522
www.ual.com
US Airways 800/428-4322
www.usairways.com

Car Rentals

Advantage 800/777-5500
www.arac.com
Alamo 800/327-9633
www.goalamo.com
Allstate 800/634-6186
www.bnm.com/as.htm
Avis 800/831-2847
www.avis.com
Budget 800/527-0700
www.budgetrentacar.com
Dollar 800/800-4000
www.dollarcar.com
Enterprise 800/325-8007
www.pickenterprise.com
Hertz 800/654-3131
www.hertz.com
National 800/227-7368
www.nationalcar.com
Payless 800/729-5377
www.800-payless.com
Rent-A-Wreck.com 800/535-1391
www.rent-a-wreck.com
Sears 800/527-0770
www.budget.com
Thrifty 800/847-4389
www.thrifty.com

Four-Star and Five-Star Establishments in Boston

★★★★★ Lodgings
Four Seasons Hotel Boston

★★★★ Lodgings
Boston Harbor Hotel
XV Beacon
The Ritz-Carlton, Boston
The Ritz-Carlton, Boston Commons

★★★★ Restaurants
Aujourd'hui
Grill 23 & Bar
Hamersley's Bistro
L'Espalier
No. 9 Park

Massachusetts

L eif Ericson—or even a French or Spanish fisherman—may have originally discovered the Cape Cod coast. However, the first recorded visit of a European to Massachusetts was that of John Cabot in 1497. Not until the Pilgrims landed at Provincetown and settled at Plymouth was there a permanent settlement north of Virginia. Ten years later, Boston was founded with the arrival of John Winthrop and his group of Puritans.

Population: 6,349,097
Area: 7,826 square miles
Elevation: 0-3,491 feet
Peak: Mount Greylock (Berkshire County)
Entered Union: Sixth of original 13 states (February 6, 1788)
Capital: Boston
Motto: By the sword we seek peace, but peace only under liberty
Nickname: Bay State
Flower: Mayflower
Bird: Chickadee
Tree: American Elm
Time Zone: Eastern
Website: www.mass-vacation.com

Native American wars plagued Massachusetts until the 1680s, after which the people experienced a relatively peaceful period combined with a fast-growing, mostly agricultural economy. In the 1760s, opposition to British taxation without representation exploded into the American Revolution. It began in Massachusetts, and from here, the American tradition of freedom and justice spread around the world. The Constitution of Massachusetts is the oldest written constitution still in effect. The New England town meeting, a basic democratic institution, still governs most of its towns. The state had a child labor law in 1836, a law legalizing trade unions in 1842, and the first minimum wage law for women and children.

Massachusetts proved to be fertile ground for intellectual ideas and activities. In the early 19th century, Emerson, Thoreau, and their followers expounded the Transcendentalist theory of the innate nobilty of man and the doctrine of individual expression, which exerted a major influence on American thought, then and now. Social improvement was sought through colonies of idealists, many of which hoped to prove that sharing labor and the fruits of labor were the means to a just society. Dorothea Dix crusaded on behalf of the mentally disturbed, and Horace Mann promoted universal education. In 1831, William Lloyd Garrison, an ardent abolitionist, founded his weekly, *The Liberator*. Massachusetts was the heartland of the Abolitionist movement, and her soldiers fought in the Civil War because they were convinced it was a war against slavery.

Massachusetts was also an important center during the Industrial Revolution. After the Civil War, the earlier success of the textile mills, like those in Lowell, generated scores of drab, hastily built, industrial towns. Now these mills are being replaced by modern plants with landscaped grounds. Modern industry is as much a part of Massachusetts as the quiet sandy beaches of Cape Cod with their bayberry and beach plum bushes.

Massachusetts has also been home to several generations of the politically prominent Kennedy family. John F. Kennedy, 35th president of the United States, was born in the Boston suburb of Brookline, as were his younger brothers, Senators Robert and Edward.

The Bay State offers mountains, ocean swimming, camping, summer resorts, freshwater and saltwater fishing, and a variety of metropolitan cultural advantages. No other state in the Union can claim so much history in so small an area, for in Massachusetts each town or city has a part in the American story.

When to Go/Climate

Massachusetts enjoys a moderate climate with four distinct seasons. Cape Cod and the Islands offer milder temperatures than other parts of the state and rarely have snow, while windchill in Boston (the windiest city in the United States) can make temperatures feel well below zero, and snow is not uncommon.

AVERAGE HIGH/LOW TEMPERATURES (°F)

Boston

Jan 36/22	**May** 67/50	**Sept** 73/57
Feb 38/23	**June** 76/60	**Oct** 63/47
Mar 46/31	**July** 82/65	**Nov** 52/38
Apr 56/40	**Aug** 80/64	**Dec** 40/27

Parks and Recreation

Water-related activities, hiking, riding, various other sports, picnicking and visitor centers, as well as camping, are available in many state parks. Day-use areas (approximately Memorial Day-Labor Day, some areas all year): $5/car. Camping (approximately mid-Apr-Oct, schedule may vary, phone ahead; two-week maximum, last Sat in May-Sat before Labor Day at many parks): campsites $10-$15/day; electricity $5/day. Pets on leash only; no pets in bathing areas. Information available from the Department of Environmental Management, Division of Forests & Parks, phone 617/727-3180.

FISHING AND HUNTING

Deep-sea and surf fishing are good; boats are available in most coastal towns. For information on saltwater fishing, contact the Division of Marine Fisheries, phone 617/727-3193. Inland fishing is excellent in more than 500 streams and 3,000 ponds. Nonresident fishing license $40.50; three-consecutive-day nonresident license $25.50. Nonresident hunting license: small game $75.50; big game $110.50. Inquire for trapping licenses. Fees subject to change. Licenses issued by town clerks, selected sporting good stores, or from the Division of Fisheries and Wildlife, phone 617/727-3151 or toll-free 800/ASK-FISH. Information on freshwater fishing, regulations, and a guide to stocked trout waters and best bass ponds are also available from the Division of Fisheries and Wildlife.

Driving Information

Safety belts are mandatory for all persons. Children under 13 years must be in a federally approved child safety seat or safety belt anywhere in a vehicle: it is recommended that children 40 pounds and under use a federally approved child safety seat and be placed in the back seat. For more information, phone 617/624-5070 or toll-free 800/CAR-SAFE (MA).

INTERSTATE HIGHWAY SYSTEM

The following list shows that these cities are within 10 miles of the indicated interstate highways. Check a highway map for the nearest exit.

Highway Number	Cities/Towns within 10 Miles
Interstate 90	Boston, Cambridge, Framingham, Great Barrington, Holyoke, Lee, Lenox, Natick, Newton, Pittsfield, Springfield, Stockbridge and West Stockbridge, Sturbridge, Sudbury Center, Waltham, Wellesley, Worcester.
Interstate 91	Amherst, Deerfield, Greenfield, Holyoke, Northampton, Springfield.
Interstate 93	Andover and North Andover, Boston, Lawrence, Lowell.
Interstate 95	Bedford, Boston, Burlington, Concord, Danvers, Dedham, Foxboro, Framingham, Lexington, Lynn, Lynnfield, Natick, Newton, Saugus, Sudbury Center, Waltham, Wellesley.

Additional Visitor Information

The Massachusetts Office of Travel and Tourism, phone 617/727-3201, has travel information. For a free *Massachusetts Getaway Guide,* phone toll-free 800/447-MASS.

Many properties of the Society for the Preservation of New England Antiquities (SPNEA) are located in Massachusetts and neighboring states. For complete information on these properties, contact SPNEA Headquarters, 141 Cambridge St, Boston 02114; phone 617/227-3956. For information regarding the 71 properties owned and managed by the Trustees of Reservations, contact 527 Essex St, Beverly, MA 01905, phone 508/921-1944.

Massachusetts has many statewide fairs, though none is considered the official state fair; contact the Massachusetts Department of Agriculture, Division of Fairs, phone 617/727-3037.

Several visitor centers are located in Massachusetts; they are located on the MA Turnpike (daily, 9 am-6 pm) at Charlton (eastbound and westbound), Lee (eastbound), and Natick (eastbound); also I-95 at Mansfield, between exits 5 and 6 (northbound); and on MA 3 at Plymouth (southbound).

Calendar Highlights

APRIL

Boston Marathon *(Boston)*. *Phone 617/236-1652.* Famous 26-mile footrace from Hopkinton to Boston.

Reenactment of Battle of Lexington and Concord *(Lexington)*. *Phone Lexington Historical Society, Massachusetts Ave. Phone 781/862-1703.* Reenactment of the opening battle of the American Revolution; parade.

Daffodil Festival *(Nantucket Island)*. *Phone Chamber of Commerce, 508/228-1700.* Festival is marked by more than a million blooming daffodils. Parade of antique cars, prize for best tailgate picnic.

JUNE

La Festa *(North Adams)*. *Phone 413/66-FESTA.* Ethnic festival, food, entertainment, events.

JULY

Harborfest *(Boston)*. *Hatch Shell on the Esplanade. Phone 617/227-1528.* Concerts, chowder fest, children's activities, Boston Pops Orchestra, fireworks.

Green River Music and Balloon Festival *(Greenfield)*. *Phone 413/733-5463.* Hot air balloon launches, craft show, musical entertainment, food.

September

The "Big E" (*Springfield*). *Phone 413/737-2443*. Largest fair in the Northeast; entertainment, exhibits, historic Avenue of States, Storrowton Village; horse show, agricultural events, "Better Living Center" exhibit.

October

Haunted Happenings (*Salem*). *Phone Salem Halloween Office, 978/744-0013. Various sites.* Psychic festival, historical exhibits, haunted house, costume parade, contests, dances.

November

Thanksgiving Week (*Plymouth*). *Phone 508/747-7525; toll-free 800/USA-1620.* Programs for various events may be obtained by contacting Destination Plymouth.

December

Stockbridge Main Street at Christmas (*Stockbridge and West Stockbridge*). *Phone 413/298-5200.* Events include a re-creation of Norman Rockwell's painting. Holiday marketplace, concerts, house tour, silent auction, sleigh/hay rides, caroling.

To the Berkshires!

Two major limited-access highways link Boston with the Berkshires, traversing the width of Massachusetts. The older, slower, more scenic Route 2 runs across the state's hilly northern tier; the Massachusetts Turnpike (I-90) is the quick way home. Begin on Route 2 in Cambridge. To explore Revolutionary War battle sights, take exit 56 (Waltham Street) into the center of Lexington and turn left on Route 2A for Battle Green. Continue west on Route 2A, stopping at the Battle Road Visitors Center and moving on to Concord's Minute Man National Historical Park sights. Pick up Route 2 west again in Concord. In Harvard, take exit 38A to the hilltop Fruitlands Museum with its paintings, Shaker furnishings, and local Indian artifacts. This is the Nashoba Valley, known for its orchards, served by the Johnny Appleseed information center just west of exit 35. Wachusett Mountain in Princeton (exit 25) is a popular ski area; there is also a state reservation with a road to its summit. Templeton (exit 21), just off the highway, is a classic old village with interesting shops and a local historical museum.

For a sense of central Massachusetts' countryside, detour south on Route 32 (exit 17) to the handsome old ridge town of Petersham. South of the village, turn west on Route 122, skirting the Quabbin Fervor, said to be one of the largest reservoirs in the world. Rejoin the highway in the town of Orange. Here Route 2 officially becomes "The Mohawk Trail" because it's said to shadow an old Indian trail through the hills. (Note the information center at the junction of Reservoir 2, I-91, and Route 5.) Take a detour to Old Deerfield and its many historic house museums, located 12 miles south on Route 5. Or continue on Route 2 as it climbs steeply from Greenfield out of the Connecticut River valley and into the Berkshire Hills. The vintage 1930s lookout towers and Indian trading posts along this stretch are relics from when this was the state's first scenic "auto touring" route.

The village of Shelburne Falls, just off Route 2, is known for its Bridge of Flowers, shops, and restaurants. The "trail" continues through the Deerfield River valley, threads the heavily wooded Mohawk Trail Forest (camping, swimming), and finally plunges down a series of hairpin turns into the Hoosac Valley and through the town of North Adams, site of MASS MoCA, the country's largest center for contemporary art. The Western Gateway Heritage State Park here tells the story of Hoosac Railroad Tunnel construction beneath the mountains you have just crossed.

Williamstown, 126 miles from Boston, marks the state's northwest corner. It's home to Williams College and two outstanding art museums, the Clark Art Institute and the Williams College Museum of Art. This is an obvious stop for food and lodging.

If you have more than one day, continue south on Route 7 from Williamstown. In Lanesborough, note the main access road to Mount Greylock, the highest mountain in the state. Pittsfield, site of the Berkshire Museum, is also the turnoff point for the Hancock Shaker Village (5 miles west on Route 20). Continue down Route 7 to Lenox, site of Tanglewood summer music festival, summer Shakespeare productions, several museums, and ample lodging. Take Route 7A south to Stockbridge and through the village to the Norman Rockwell Museum. Return on Route 102 to the entrance to the Massachusetts Turnpike (Route 90) at Lee, the quick way back to Boston. Stop at Sturbridge (exit 9) to tour Old Sturbridge Village. **(Approximately 290 miles)**

Boston

Founded 1630 **Pop** 589,141 **Elev** 0-330 ft **Area code** 617

Information Greater Boston Convention & Visitors Bureau, 2 Copley Pl, Suite 105, 02116; 617/536-4100 or toll-free 888/733-2678

Web www.bostonusa.com

Suburbs Braintree, Burlington, Cambridge, Dedham, Framingham, Lexington, Lynn, Newton, Quincy, Saugus, Waltham, Wellesley.

Greater Boston is a fascinating combination of the old and the new. It consists of 83 cities and towns in an area of 1,057 square miles with a total population of more than 3 million people. Boston proper is the hub of this busy complex, which many Bostonians still believe is the hub of the universe.

Boston is a haven for walkers; in fact, strolling along its streets is advised to get a true sense of this most European of all American cities. If you drive, a map is invaluable. Traffic is heavy. The streets (many of them narrow and one-way) run at odd angles and expressway traffic speeds.

Boston's wealth of historic sights makes it a must for all who are interested in America's past. John Winthrop and 800 colonists first settled in Charlestown, just north of the Charles River, and moved to Boston in 1630. Arriving too late to plant crops, 200 colonists died during the first winter, mostly of starvation. In the spring, a ship arrived with provisions, and the new Puritan commonwealth began to thrive and grow. Fisheries, fur trapping, lumbering, and trading with Native Americans were the foundation of Boston's commerce. The port is still viable, with 250 wharves along 30 miles of berthing space.

City Fun Facts

1. James Naismith invented basketball in Springfield in 1891. He taught physical education and wanted an indoor sport for his students during the winter months.

2. Harvard University, the nation's oldest college, was chartered in Cambridge in 1636.

3. Boston boasts the nation's first subway, built in 1897.

4. The Boston University Bridge (on Commonwealth Avenue) is the only place in the world where a boat can sail under a train driving under a car driving under an airplane.

5. Boston Common became the first public park in 1634.

6. The first post office, free public school, and public library were all founded in Boston.

The Revolutionary War began here in 1770. British troops fired on an angry mob, killing five in what has since been called the "Boston Massacre." In 1773, the Boston Tea Party dumped East Indian tea into the bay in a dramatic protest against restriction of colonial trade by British governors. Great Britain closed the port in retaliation. The course of history was set.

In April 1775, British General Thomas Gage decided to march on Concord to capture military supplies and overwhelm the countryside. During the night of April 18-19, Paul Revere, William Dawes, and Samuel Prescott spread the news to Lexington and Concord in a ride immortalized, somewhat inaccurately, by Henry Wadsworth Longfellow. The Revolutionary War had begun in earnest; the Battle of Bunker Hill followed the battles of Lexington and Concord. On March 17, 1776, General William Howe, commander of the British forces, evacuated the city.

Boston's list of distinguished native sons includes John Hancock, Samuel Adams, Paul Revere, Henry Ward Beecher, Edward Everett Hale, Ralph Waldo Emerson, William Lloyd Garrison, Oliver Wendell Holmes (father and son), and hundreds of others.

Mention Boston, and many people will automatically think of the gentry of Beacon Hill, with their elegant homes and rigid social code. However, the Irish have long had a powerful influence in Boston's politics and personality, while a stroll through an Italian neighborhood in the North End will be like stepping back to the old country.

Boston today has managed to retain its heritage and charm while thriving in the modern age. Urban renewal and increased construction have reversed an almost 40-year slump that plagued Boston earlier in the 20th century. With more than 100 universities, colleges, and trade and vocational schools in the area, Boston is a city as full of vigor and promise for the future as it is rich with the past.

Additional Visitor Information

Literature and information are available at the Greater Boston Convention & Visitors Bureau, Prudential Tower, PO Box 990468, 02199; phone 617/536-4100; the Prudential Visitor Center, and at the visitor information center on Tremont Street, Boston Common (daily; closed Jan 1, Thanksgiving, Dec 25). The National Park Visitor Center (daily) at 15 State Street also has helpful information. All have informative brochures with maps of the Freedom Trail and the Black History Trail.

Bostix, located in Faneuil Hall Marketplace, offers half-price tickets for music, theater, and dance performances on the day of performance; it also provides cultural information and a calendar of events. (Tues-Sun; closed Thanksgiving, Dec 25) Phone 617/723-5181 (recording).

Transportation

AIRPORT

Logan International Airport. Information 617/561-1800 or toll-free 800/235-6426; lost and found 617/561-1714; weather 617/936-1234; cash machines in Terminals A, B, C.

CAR RENTAL AGENCIES
See IMPORTANT TOLL-FREE NUMBERS.

PUBLIC TRANSPORTATION
Buses, subway, and elevated trains (Massachusetts Bay Transportation Authority), visitor pass available, phone 617/722-3200.

RAIL PASSENGER SERVICE
Amtrak 800/872-7245.

What to See and Do

Blue Hills Trailside Museum. *1904 Canton Ave, Milton (02186). Phone 617/333-0690.* Visitor center for the 7,000-acre Blue Hills Reservation. Deer, turkeys, otters, snakes, owls, and honeybees. Exhibit hall with natural science/history displays, including a Native American wigwam; viewing tower. Activities include hikes, films, and animal programs. Special events include maple sugaring (Mar), Hawks Weekend (Sept), and Honey Harvest (Oct). Visitor center and buildings (Wed-Sun; schedule may vary) **$**

Boston College. *140 Commonwealth Ave (02467).* (1863) 14,500 students.

  Bapst Library. *Phone 617/552-3200.* English Collegiate Gothic building with fine stained glass. Rare books display; changing exhibits. (Summer, Mon-Fri; rest of year, daily)

  Boston College Football. *Alumni Stadium. Phone 617/552-3000.* Although Boston College hasn't won a national championship since 1940, as the only Division I-A football team in the area, BC football remains a fall tradition in Boston. Tickets can be difficult to obtain as game day nears, so plan to buy your tickets online ahead of time. Keep yourself entertained before the game by spotting the BC superfans—students and alums who paint their bodies, wear multicolored wigs, and carry in-your-face signs meant for TV cameras. (Weekends in fall) **$$$$**

Boston Harbor Islands National Park Area. *349 Lincoln St (02043). 45 minutes from downtown Boston via ferry. Phone 781/740-1605. www.state.ma.us/dem/parks/bhis.htm.* The Boston Harbor Islands State Park encompasses several islands in Boston Harbor. Take the ferry to Georges Island (617/227-4321); from there, a free water taxi sails you to Lovells, Peddocks, Gallops, Grape, and Bumpkin islands. The islands boast sand dunes, a freshwater pond, and unique wildlife habitats. Camp on Lovells (the only island that allows swimming) and Peddocks islands (the largest at 134 acres) by petitioning in writing for a permit from the Metropolitan District Commission; write to MDC Reservations and Historic Sites, 98 Taylor St, Dorchester, MA 02122. Note that sites don't have electricity, you must carry in your own fresh water, and you're responsible for carrying out your trash when you leave. (May-mid-Oct) **FREE**

Boston Tours from Suburban Hotels. *56 Williams St, Waltham (02453). For reservations, schedule, and fee information, phone 781/899-1454.* Escorted bus tours departing from suburban hotels and motels along I-95/Hwy 128. Also departures from metro west suburban hotels in Natick/Framingham area. Tours follow Freedom Trail and include stops at Old North Church, "Old Ironsides," Faneuil Hall Marketplace, and Cambridge. Six-hour tour (daily). **$$$$**

BostonWalks. *Phone 617/489-5020. bostonwalks.tripod.com.* Although several groups offer guided tours of Boston, those arranged by BostonWalks are among the most unique. Nearly every guided-tour company, including BostonWalks, offers historical tours, but where else can you find walking and biking tours of churches and synagogues, unique ethnic areas, universities, medical areas, high-tech areas, and Boston's delightful neighborhoods? Groups must include 15 to 55 participants, and tours last two to three hours. **$$$$**

The Charles River Pathway (the Esplanade). *Take the Red Line ("T") to the Charles/MGHT stop. Phone 617/727-9547.* The Charles River Pathway, a flat, smooth asphalt surface, extends 18 miles along the Charles River, connecting Boston and Cambridge and ending in Watertown. The view of the Charles River is stunning, and at certain times of the year you may see university crew teams training. Use the trail to run or walk, joining the hundreds of Bostonians who train there daily. To bike the path, rent a bike at Back Bay Bikes & Boards (Boston), 336 Commonwealth Ave, phone 617/247-2336, www.backbaybicycles.com; Community Bicycle Supply (Boston), 496 Tremont St, phone 617/542-8623, www.communitybicycle.com; Cambridge Bicycle (Cambridge), 259 Massachusetts Ave, phone 617/876-6555; or Ata Cycle (Cambridge), 1773 Massachusetts Ave, phone 617/354-0907, www.atabike.com. The trail is also perfect for in-line skating, even if you're a novice. Rent blades at Beacon Hill Skate Shop (Boston), 135 Charles St, phone 617/482-7400; or Blades Board & Skate, with locations in Boston and Cambridge, phone 617/437-6300, www.blades.com. (Always open) **FREE**

Franklin Park Zoo. *1 Franklin Park Rd, Dorchester (02121). S on Jamaicaway, E on Hwy 203. Phone 617/541-LION. www.zoonewengland.org.* "Bird's World" indoor/outdoor aviary complex with natural habitats; African tropical forest; hilltop range with camels, antelopes, zebras, mouflon; children's zoo. (Daily; closed Jan 1, Thanksgiving, Dec 25) **$$**

Frederick Law Olmsted National Historic Site. *99 Warren St, Brookline (02445). Phone 617/566-1689. www.nps.gov/frla.* Former home and office of the founder of landscape architecture in America. Site archives contain documentation of firm's work. Site also includes landscaped grounds designed by Olmsted. Guided tours of historic offices. (Fri-Sun)

⭐ **The Freedom Trail.** *Phone 617/242-5642. www.thefreedomtrail.org.* This two- or three-hour walking tour takes you past Boston's most famous historical sites while also meandering through the city's vibrant neighborhoods. The Freedom Trail begins at Boston Common (see Beacon Hill) and ends at the Bunker Hill Monument, with more than a dozen sites in between. Red bricks or red paint mark the trail, which you can follow on your own (free brochures are available) or with guided assistance. Purchase the official *Freedom Trail Guidebook* (**$$**) as your step-by-step guide, travel with earphones and take an audio tour (**$$$**), or take a guided tour that's led by historic characters in costume (**$$$**). Dress appropriately—the weather in Boston can change rapidly. **FREE**

State House. *Beacon St at head of Park St (02108). Phone 617/727-3676.* (1795) Designed by Charles Bulfinch, the nation's first professional architect, it has since had wings added to both sides. Inside are statues, paintings, and other interesting materials. Hall of Flags on second floor; House and Senate Chambers, State Library on third floor. Tours (Mon-Fri; closed holidays).

Park Street Church. *1 Park St (02108). Phone 617/523-3383.* (1809) Often called "Brimstone Corner" because brimstone for gunpowder was stored here during the War of 1812. William Lloyd Garrison delivered his first antislavery address here in 1829. Tours. (July and Aug, limited hours; Sun services all year)

Granary Burying Ground. *Tremont and Bromfield sts (02108). Take the "T" to Park St, walk 1 block on Tremont St. Phone 617/635-4505.* Although Granary is Boston's third-oldest cemetery, it is, perhaps, its most famous. Revolutionary War patriots Paul Revere, John Hancock, Samuel Adams, and Peter Faneuil (whose headstone is marked "Peter Funal") all lie here. The name stems from a grain storage building (called a granary) that used to sit nearby. (Daily) **FREE**

King's Chapel and Burying Ground. *58 Tremont St (02108). Phone 617/227-2155.* King's Chapel, started by the Massachusetts Royal Governor who had no desire to worship in a Puritan church, has held church services at its location longer than any other church in the United States. When the congregation outgrew the church in 1754, a new building was erected around the old, which was then dismantled. The Burying Ground next door is the oldest cemetery in Boston. Stop in for concerts on Tuesdays at 12:15 pm and Sundays at 5 pm. (Daily; closed Sun-Fri in winter) **FREE**

Site of the first free public school in the US. *School St at City Hall Ave (02108). Take the Blue or Orange Line ("T") to State St. A mosaic in the sidewalk marks the site of the first free US public school.* The original building was demolished to make room for the expansion of King's Chapel. The school, now known as the Boston Latin School, was moved across the street.

Statue of Benjamin Franklin. *School St at City Hall Ave (02108).* This, Boston's first portrait statue, was created by Richard S. Greenough in 1856.

Old South Meeting House. *310 Washington St (02108), at the corner of Washington and Milk sts. Phone 617/482-6439.* Built as a Puritan meeting house (or church), colonists congregated at the Old South Meeting House each year from 1771 to 1775 to mark the death of those killed in the Boston Massacre and listen to speeches by prominent colonists. The most important date in Old South's history, however, is December 16, 1773, when 5,000 colonists gathered at the church to protest the British tax on tea and decide on a course of action. From there, men dressed as Native Americans snuck onto three ships laden with tea on Griffin's

Wharf and dumped all the tea overboard. Restored in 1997, the church no longer has an active congregation but is still a gathering place for political debate. An interactive exhibit called Voices of Protest recalls the Old South Meeting House's historic legacy. (Daily; closed Jan 1, Thanksgiving, Dec 24-25) **$**

Old State House/Site of the Boston Massacre. *206 Washington St (02109). Phone 617/720-1713.* Marked by a circle of cobblestones in the pavement. The Old State House (not to be confused with the golden-dome new State House) was originally built as the headquarters of the British government in Boston and is Boston's oldest surviving public building. Inside, the Bostonian Society operates a museum that reflects the prominent role the Old State House played in the American Revolution. The Massachusetts Assembly met there and debated political issues in front of all citizens who wanted to observe. After these issues were decided, politicians read summaries—including the Declaration of Independence on July 18, 1776—from the House's balcony. The balcony hovers above the spot where the Boston Massacre occurred in 1770, when British troops shot into a crowd that had gathered to hear a proclamation. There, in a small triangle surrounded by dense city traffic, the site of the massacre is marked with a circle of paving stones. Plan on one hour for a tour. (Mon-Sat; closed Jan 1, Thanksgiving, Dec 25) **$**

Faneuil Hall Marketplace. *4 S Market Bldg (02109). Take the Blue or Green Line ("T") to Government Center, then walk across the plaza, down the long set of stairs, and across busy Congress St. Phone 617/242-5675.* Faneuil Hall Marketplace offers the best variety of shops and kiosks in Boston, housed in five buildings and several plazas. The central building, Quincy Market, is filled with dining options, from coffee to seafood and everything in between; many are open earlier and later than the shops. Look for delightful street performers even in winter months, and especially the rest of the year. Faneuil Hall (pronounced "FAN-yal" or "FAN-yoo-ul") is more than just a shopping center: it has operated as a local marketplace since 1742, when wealthy merchant Peter Faneuil built and donated the marketplace to the city. The Hall is remembered as the site of town meetings that produced the policy of "no taxation without representation." Listen to a historical talk every half hour from 9:30 am to 4:30 pm in the second-floor auditorium. (Daily; closed holidays)

Paul Revere House. *19 North Sq (02113). Phone 617/523-2338.* Built in 1680 and well preserved today, the Paul Revere House is Boston's oldest building and includes authentic furnishings from the Revere family. This historical landmark offers a rare glimpse at colonial life, because few other houses from the period survived remodeling, fire damage, and demolition. At his house, Paul Revere plied his silversmith trade and sold his wares, often in exchange for food or livestock when case-strapped colonists couldn't pay. Although a staunch patriot, Revere was largely undistinguished among Sam Adams, John Hancock, and Ben Franklin. However, Revere's successful ride to Lexington and Concord on April 18, 1775, to warn of the approaching British army—a feat immortalized in Henry Wadsworth Longfellow's poem, *The Midnight Ride of Paul*

Revere—made him one of the best-known American historic figures. (Mid-Apr-late Oct, daily 9:30 am-5:15 pm; early Nov-mid-Apr, daily 9:30 am-4:15 pm; closed Mon in Jan, Feb, Mar; also Jan 1, Thanksgiving, Dec 25) **$$**

Old North Church. *193 Salem St (02113). Phone 617/523-6676.* Old North Church is the oldest church in Boston and continues today as Christ Church, with an Episcopal congregation of 150 members. On April 18, 1775, in the steeple of Old North Church, church sexton Robert Newman hung two lanterns to signal that the British Army was heading up the Charles River to Cambridge in order to march to Lexington and take possession of weapons stored there. When Paul Revere saw the signal, he jumped on his horse and rode to Lexington to warn the militia. The next day, the "shot heard 'round the world" was fired on Lexington Green, officially beginning the Revolutionary War. Sit in one of the box pews and listen to the ten-minute talk about the history of the church; it's free, although donations are gladly accepted. Behind-the-scenes tours and other presentations are available by appointment for a fee. (Daily; closed holidays)

Copp's Hill Burying Ground. *Hull and Snow Hill sts (02113). Take Causeway St to North Washington St. When North Washington becomes Commercial St, walk 2 more blocks, turn right, and climb the hill. Phone 617/635-4505.* Copp's Hill Burying Ground, named after William Copp, who owned the land, is the second-oldest burying ground in Boston. Robert Newman, who hung the lanterns in the steeple of Old North Church, is buried at Copp's Hill, as are the Mather family of Puritan ministers and a host of African Americans from the nearby New Guinea Community, who lie in unmarked graves. (Daily)

USS *Constitution*. *Located in Charlestown Navy Yard, Boston National Historical Park (02129). I-93: northbound, exit 25 and follow signs across Charlestown bridge; southbound, exit 28 to Sullivan Sq and follow signs. Phone 617/426-1812.* "Old Ironsides," launched in 1797, was engaged in more than 40 battles without defeat. It is the oldest commissioned Navy ship afloat in the world. Twenty-minute tours. Museum with ship artifacts is adjacent. (Daily)

Bunker Hill Monument. *Monument Square (02129). Phone 617/242-5641.* Standing 221 feet high (that's 294 steps, with no elevator), the Bunker Hill Monument marks the site of the first major battle of the Revolutionary War on June 17, 1775. It was here that American Colonel William Prescott ordered his troops not to "fire until you see the whites of their eyes," so that no bullets would be wasted. The British won the battle but suffered heavy casualties, and that limited success encouraged the colonists to continue the fight. (Daily 9 am-4:30 pm) **FREE**

Harborwalk. A blue line guides visitors from Old State House to New England Aquarium, ending at the Boston Tea Party Ship and Museum, forming a walking tour with many stops in between.

Isaac Royall House. *15 George St, Medford (02155). 3/4 mile S off I-93. Phone 781/396-9032.* (1637) Originally built as a four-room farmhouse by John

Winthrop, first governor of the Bay State Colony; enlarged in 1732 by Isaac Royall. Example of early Georgian architecture; examples of Queen Anne, Chippendale, and Hepplewhite furnishings. (May-Sept, Wed-Sun) **$$**

The Minuteman Commuter Bikeway. *Begins near Alewife ("T") station, goes through Lexington and Arlington, and ends at Bedford (note that you can't bring a bike on the "T" during rush hour). www.minutemanbikeway.org.* This 11-mile bike path looks like a miniature highway (but without the cars, of course), complete with on- and off-ramps, a center line, and traffic signs. The trail mimics portions of Paul Revere's famous ride, so you can stop off for a break from riding at the battleground at Battle Green and the historic park at Lexington Center. The path mingles with the Great Meadows Wildlife Refuge for a time. In winter, the bikeway opens for cross-country skiing. (Daily 5 am-9 pm) **FREE**

Shirley-Eustis House. *33 Shirley St (02119). Phone 617/442-2275.* (1747) Built for royal governor William Shirley, restored to Federal style of the period when Governor William Eustis lived here (1818-1825). (June-Sept, Thurs-Sun afternoons)

Suffolk Downs. *Take the Blue Line (the "T" or subway) to Suffolk Downs station, and then take a shuttle bus or walk for ten minutes. Phone 617/567-3900. www.suffolkdowns.com.* Suffolk Downs, which opened its doors in 1935, is steeped in horse racing history; in fact, Seabiscuit once won at Suffolk. The track offers pari-mutuel betting, which, unlike casino gambling, doesn't involve betting against the house, only against other spectators. The minimum wager per race is $2, and you can place as many bets as you'd like. Even if your horse doesn't come in first, you can still win: simply bet to win (first), place (second), show (third), and so on. Check out the Suffolk Downs Web site to perfect your horse betting jargon before you go. (Daily noon-2 am; closed Dec 25) **$**

"Whites of Their Eyes." *Bunker Hill Pavilion, 55 Constitution Rd (02129), just W of the USS Constitution, in Charlestown. Phone 617/241-7575.* This specially designed pavilion houses multimedia reenactment of the Battle of Bunker Hill using life-size figures and eyewitness narratives. Audience "viewpoint" from atop Breed's Hill. Continuous 30-minute shows. (Apr-Nov, daily; closed Thanksgiving)

Special Events

Boston Kite Festival. *Franklin Park, Bluehill Ave and Circuit Dr, Dorchester (02121). Phone 617/635-4505.* Bring your kite when you visit Boston in mid-May and visit the annual Boston Kite Festival. If you don't have a kite, don't let that stop you—festivities include kite-making clinics, face painting, live music, and kite-flying competitions. See thousands of kites, from beautiful and elaborate to simple, homemade varieties. Mid-May. **FREE**

Boston Marathon. *Starts in Hopkington, MA, and finishes at Copley Square, in front of the Boston Public Library, but the Copley Square "T" stop is closed on Marathon day. Take the Green Line C to any stop on Beacon St to see the finish. Phone 617/236-1652. www.bostonmarathon.org.* What separates the Boston Marathon from other marathons around the United States is that every person running the race has run another marathon in a fast enough time to qualify for this one. Qualifying standards, which are based on a combination of a previous marathon finish time, sex, and age, are tough—some people train for a lifetime to make the standard and run in this race. Because the course is notoriously hilly and difficult, few elite runners are able to run record times, and because the fast and flat London Marathon is held at about the same time of year as Boston, elite runners as a whole aren't as prevalent here as they once were. Still, Boston is one of the world's best marathons, so you won't find a single spot along the course where you're not in a crowd. Try to find a shady area in which to cheer on the runners. Third Mon in Apr at noon. **FREE**

Bunker Hill Day. *Charlestown. Phone 617/536-4100.* Mid-June.

First Night Boston. *Phone 617/542-1399. www.firstnight.org.* First Night is Boston's alternative to traditional New Year's Eve celebrations. This alcohol-free celebration begins with a Mardi Gras-style Grand Procession and features more than 250 performances in both indoor and outdoor venues. You'll be entertained with concerts, films (on seven screens), tango dancing, stand-up comedy, orchestral music, Boston Rock Opera, a magic show, puppets, and ice sculptures. The evening literally ends with a bang: a fireworks display at midnight. A badge gives you entrance to every event, and badges are for sale at retail outlets throughout the city. If you hang onto your badge after the event, it gets you discounts throughout the city later in the spring. After 8 pm on First Night, MTBA offers free transportation service. Keep in mind that Boylston Street and adjoining streets close in the afternoon for the Grand Procession; Atlantic Avenue and adjoining streets close later in the evening for the fireworks displays. Dec 31. **$$$**

Hotel

★ ★ ★ **MARRIOTT PEABODY.** *8A Centennial Dr, Peabody (01960). Phone 978/977-9700; toll-free 800/228-9290. www.marriott.com.* 260 rooms, 6 story. Check-out noon, check-in 3pm. TV; cable (premium). In-room modem link. Restaurant, bar. In-house fitness room. Indoor pool, whirlpool. Business center. Concierge. **$**

Restaurants

★ ★ **THE FIREPLACE.** *1634 Beacon St, Brookline (02446). Phone 617/975-1900; fax 617/975-1600. www.fireplacerest.com.* American menu. Lunch, dinner. Bar. Casual attire. **$$**

★ ★ ★ **OLIVES.** *10 City Sq, Charlestown (02129). Phone 617/242-1999.* This is where superstar chef Todd English's nationwide empire began. The dining room is casual and the portions of creative, hearty, flavorful Italian food are huge. Country Mediterranean menu. Closed major holidays. Dinner. Bar. Valet parking. **$$$**

★ **RUBIN'S KOSHER DELICATESSEN.** *500 Harvard St, Brookline (02446). Phone 617/731-8787; fax 617/566-3354. www.rubinskosher.com.*

Kosher deli menu. Closed Sat; Jewish holidays. Lunch, dinner. Totally non-smoking. **$**

D

Downtown

What to See and Do

Bay State Cruise Company. *Commonwealth Pier, World Trade Center. 184 High St (02110). Phone 617/748-1428.* All-day sail to Provincetown and Cape Cod from Commonwealth Pier. The 2 1/2- and 3 1/2-hour harbor and island cruises aboard *Spirit of Boston* highlight adventure and history. (Mid-June-Labor Day, daily; May-mid-June and after Labor Day-Columbus Day, Sat and Sun only) **$$$$**

Boston African American National Historic Site. *46 Joy St (02114). Smith Ct, off Joy St on Beacon Hill. Phone 617/725-0022.* Includes **African Meeting House.** Part of the Museum of Afro-American History. Built by free black Bostonians in 1806, building was an educational and religious center and site of the founding of the New England Anti-Slavery Society in 1832. (May-Sept, daily; rest of year, Mon-Sat) Thirty-minute tour (Memorial Day-Labor Day, daily; rest of year, by appointment) of Meeting House by museum staff. **FREE** The meeting House is the starting point for

> **Black Heritage Trail.** *46 Joy St (02114). Phone 617/742-5415.* Marked walking tour conducted by National Park Service, past sites in the Beacon Hill section that relate the history of 19th-century black Boston. Brochure and maps are at National Park Visitor Center. Two-hour guided tours by National Park Service (by appointment). **FREE**

Boston Bruins (NHL). *Fleet Center, One Fleet Center Pl (02114). Take the Green/Orange Line (the "T") to North Station. Phone 617/624-1000. www.bostonbruins.com.* The Bruins are one of the great hockey traditions in the NHL; in fact, the team was one of the original six teams in the league. In the early 1940s, the Bruins won back-to-back Stanley Cup championships, and the team won the Cup again 30 years later, when Bobby Orr scored a game-winning goal in overtime. Today, you can spend an exciting evening of Bruins hockey with family or friends; if you like to see a lot of body checking, try to get a seat as close to the ice as you can afford on one of the four corners of the rink. If you can manage the high price tag, pick up a Bobby Orr game sweater at the Bruins gift shop. **$$$$**

Boston by Little Feet. *77 N Washington St (02114). Phone 617/367-2345. www.bostonbyfoot.com.* Designed especially for 6- to 12-year-olds (accompanied by an adult), Boston by Little Feet is a 60-minute walking tour that follows the Freedom Trail and explores local architecture and history. You can take the tour regardless of the weather, but be sure to bring rain boots and an umbrella during inclement weather. Every young walker gets a free Explorer's Map and Guide. (May-Oct: Sat 10 am, Sun 2 pm, Mon 10 am; closed Nov-Apr) **$$**

Boston Celtics (NBA). *Fleet Center, One Fleet Center Pl (02114). Take the Green/Orange Line (the "T") to North Station. Phone 617/624-1000. www.nba.com/celtics.* The Celtics were more of a must-see tourist attraction when they played in Boston Garden. Today, playing at the as-yet soulless Fleet Center, the Celtics seem less impressive. Still, with 16 NBA championships notched in its belt, the team boasts more NBA titles than any other franchise, and 26 Celtics have gone on to become NBA Hall-of-Famers. **$$$$**

Boston Tea Party Ship and Museum. *300 Congress St (02210). Between Congress St Bridge and Northern Ave Bridge, opposite Fan Pier. Phone 617/ 338-1773. www.bostonteapartyship.com.* The Boston Tea Party Ship is a replica of one of the three tea ships docked in the harbor the night of the Boston Tea Party; dumping the tea overboard from these ships was one of the triggers of the Revolutionary War. Note that the Boston Tea Party Ship and Museum suffered serious fire damage in 2001 and, as of this writing, had not yet reopened. Continue checking the museum's Web site for updates. (Summer: daily 9 am-6 pm; spring and fall: daily 9 am-5 pm; closed Thanksgiving, Dec 1-Feb 28) **$$**

Children's Museum of Boston. *200 Congress St (02210). Phone 617/426-8855. www.bostonkids.org.* Advertised as "Boston's best place for kids 0-10," the Children's Museum lives up to its billing with interactive exhibits that highlight science, technology, art, and culture. Exhibitions range from re-creations of favorite kids' stories, a kid-size construction site, and a messy artist studio to performances on KidStage, a Latin American supermarket, a real loom and weaving area, a full-size wigwam, and a rock climbing area. Offerings change periodically, and three or four are always housed outdoors in the Science Playground. Each Friday from 3-5 pm and Saturday and Sunday from 2-4 pm, take the ZOOMSci challenge at the ZOOM Zone within the museum: you solve puzzles and work through a variety of math challenges. Note that admission is just $1 on Fridays from 5-9 pm. Plan on at least half a day. (Sat-Thurs 10 am-5 pm, Fri to 9 pm; closed Thanksgiving, Dec 25) **$$**

Community Boating, Inc. *21 David Mugar Way (02114). Embankment Rd on the Charles River Esplanade between the Hatch Shell and the Longfellow Bridge. Phone 617/523-7406. www.community-boating.org.* Whether you're an experienced sailor or you always wanted to learn, you can spend a day or two sailing while in Boston. Community Boating runs the largest and oldest public sailing program in the country. Purchasing a two-day membership allows you unlimited use of boats and sailing instruction, along with windsurfing and kayaking. Also check out Boston Sailing Center, Lewis Wharf, 617/227-4198, www.bostonsailingcenter.com, which is more expensive but is open year-round, even in the chilliest weather. (Apr-Nov: Mon-Fri 1 pm-sunset, Sat-Sun 9 am-sunset; closed Dec-Mar) **$$$$**

Copp's Hill Burying Ground. *Hull and Snow Hill sts (02113). Take Causeway St to North Washington St. When North Washington becomes Commercial St, walk 2 more blocks, turn right, and climb the hill; on the Freedom Trail. Phone 617/635-4505.* Copp's Hill Burying Ground, named after William Copp, who owned the land, is the second-oldest burying ground in Boston.

Robert Newman, who hung the lanterns in the steeple of Old North Church, is buried at Copp's Hill, as are the Mather family of Puritan ministers and a host of African Americans from the nearby New Guinea Community, who lie in unmarked graves. (Summer: daily 9 am-5 pm; winter: daily 9 am-3 pm) **FREE**

Guided Walking Tours. Boston by Foot. *Hull and Snow Hill sts (02113). Phone 617/367-2345 or 617/367-3766 (recording).* Ninety-minute architectural walking tours include the heart of the Freedom Trail (daily); Beacon Hill (daily, departures vary); Victorian Back Bay Tour (Fri-Sun); North End (Fri and Sat); children's tour (daily); downtown Boston (Sun). All tours (May-Oct). Tour of the month each fourth Sun; custom tours. **$$$**

Harrison Gray Otis House. *141 Cambridge St (02114), enter from Lynde St. Phone 617/227-3956.* (1796) Otis, a lawyer and statesman, built this first of three houses designed for him by Charles Bulfinch. A later move to Beacon Hill left this house as a rooming house for 100 years. Restored to reflect Boston taste and decoration of 1796-1820. Some family furnishings are present. The house reflects the proportion and delicate detail Bulfinch introduced to Boston, strongly influencing the Federal style in New England. Museum. The headquarters for the Society for the Preservation of New England Antiquities is located here. Tours (Wed-Sun). **$$**

L'Arte Di Cucinare. *6 Charter St (02113). Take the Green Line ("T") to Haymarket Station and walk beneath the Expressway to Salem St. Phone 617/523-6032. www.cucinare.com.* Michele Topor, a 30-year resident of the North End and a passionate gourmet chef herself, takes you on a 3 1/2-hour tour of the North End markets, where you taste a delicious variety of local foods in a historic setting (the North End is Boston's oldest neighborhood). You're introduced to shopkeepers and chefs throughout your tour and hear fascinating recipes and ideas for food selection. You can also arrange for special tours: 2 hours instead of 3 1/2, a morning tour with cappuccino and pastries, an olive-oil and balsamic-vinegar-tasting tour, an Italian regional dinner tour at North End restaurants, or anything else you can dream up. Reservations are required, and each tour is limited to 13 people. (Wed-Sat 10 am-1:30 pm, 2-5:30 pm, Fri 3-6:30 pm; closed Sun-Tues, Thurs) **$$$$**

Massachusetts State House. *24 Beacon St (02114). Phone 617/727-3676. www.state.ma.us/sec/trs.* The Massachusetts State House (which replaced the Old State House, next to the site of the Boston Massacre) is an architectural marvel. As you travel around Boston, you can't miss the golden dome (sheathed in 23-carat gold leaf) of the state house that replaced the original copper. Designed by Charles Bulfinch and built on land owned by John Hancock, patriot Paul Revere, and Governor Samuel Adams laid the cornerstone on July 4, 1795. (Mon-Sat; closed state holidays) **FREE**

MDC Memorial Hatch Shell. *Charles River Esplanade (02114). On the Charles River, between Storrow Dr and the water. Phone 617/727-9547, ext 450.* Packing as much as possible into the three months of the summer tourist season, the MDC Memorial Hatch Shell offers free entertainment nearly every night of the week. Offerings range from dance performances to rock concerts by big-name bands to a Boston Pops concerts sometime around the Fourth of July. Enjoy Free Friday Flicks throughout the summer. Although the offerings are those that you'd find on DVD (either recent releases or classics), the movies somehow look better on the big screen. Bring a blanket to sit on, a picnic dinner to munch on, and a sweater to ward off cool river breezes. (Early June-early Sept) **FREE**

Museum of Science. *Science Park, Charles River Dam and Storrow Dr (02114). Take the Lechmere Green Line to the Science Park stop. Phone 617/723-2500. www.mos.org.* The Museum of Science blends science with entertainment that the whole family can enjoy. Exhibitions range from a T. Rex model (complete with 58 teeth), presentations with live animals at the Wright Theater, a chick hatchery, and a beautiful lighthouse that explains light, optics, and color. One exhibit, called "Where in the world are you?" allows visitors to enter clue-filled geographic areas and make educated guesses about where they are. Another exhibit, Cahner's ComputerPlace, features a gallery of the most effective software for kids. While visiting Boston, the city of Ben Franklin's youth, visit the museum's Theater of Electricity for presentations about lightning and electrical currents. The museum also sponsors a Community Solar System, a scale-model solar system that includes a model of Mercury in the museum and one of Pluto all the way across Boston at the Riverside T stop. You can easily spend half a day at this museum. (Early July-early Sept: Sat-Thurs 9 am-7 pm; Fri to 9 pm; early Sept-early July: Sat-Thurs 9 am-5 pm, Fri to 9 pm; closed Thanksgiving, Dec 25) **$$$** Also here is

Charles Hayden Planetarium. *Science Park, Charles River Dam and Storrow Dr (02114). Phone 617/523-6664.* Shows approximately 50 min-utes. (Same hours as museum) Children under 4 years not admitted. **$$$**

New England Aquarium. *Central Wharf (02110). Near Faneuil Hall Marketplace. Phone 617/973-5200. www.neaq.org.* Boston's Central Wharf houses the New England Aquarium, which boasts a colorful array of dolphins, sea lions, penguins, turtles, sharks, eels, harbor seals, and fish from around the world. You can't miss the bright-red Echo of the Waves sculpture that rotates high above the expansive Aquarium plaza, or the 187,000-gallon Giant Ocean Tank inside. The Aquarium has an educational and research bent, so ecological and medical exhibits abound, but all the aquatic sights will captivate your entire family. Every 90 minutes, sea lions perform. Kids and adults alike will marvel at aquatic films offered at the Simons IMAX Theater (**$$**). To get a hands-on look at marine life in Boston Harbor—including taking water samples and hauling in lobster traps—take the Science at Sea harbor tour (**$$$**), which operates daily except in winter. Plan to spend from a few hours to a full day. (July-Labor Day: Mon-Tues, Fri 9 am-6 pm, Wed-Thurs to 8 pm, Sat-Sun to 7 pm; Sept-June: Mon-Fri 9 am-5 pm, Sat-Sun, holidays to 6 pm; closed Thanksgiving, Dec 25) **$$$**

New England Aquarium Whale Watches. *Phone 617/973-5206. www.neaq.org/ visit/ww.tickets.html.* Stellwagen Bank, 25 miles from Boston, is a terrific area for whale-watching. From Boston, the New England Aquarium's tour takes you out to see the feeding grounds of a variety of whales, many of which are endangered, and you may see dolphins as well. The tour emphasizes education—it puts naturalists on board to teach about whale behavior, allows kids and adults to experiment with hands-on exhibits, and shows films about whale history. Allow four to five hours round-trip. Purchase tickets in advance. Boston Harbor Cruises (www.bostonharborcruises.com, phone 617/227-4321) and Beantown Whale Watch also operate whale cruises in Boston (www.beantownwhalewatch.com, phone 617/542-8000). (Early May-late Oct; closed Thanksgiving, Dec 25) **$$$$**

Old North Church. *193 Salem St (02113). On the Freedom Trail. Phone 617/523-6676. www.oldnorth.com.* Old North Church is the oldest church in Boston and continues today as Christ Church, with an Episcopal congregation of 150 members. On April 18, 1775, in the steeple of Old North Church, church sexton Robert Newman hung two lanterns to signal that the British Army was heading up the Charles River to Cambridge in order to march to Lexington and take possession of weapons stored there. When Paul Revere saw the signal, he jumped on his horse and rode to Lexington to warn the militia. The next day, the "shot heard 'round the world" was fired on Lexington Green, officially beginning the Revolutionary War. Sit in one of the box pews and listen to the ten-minute talk about the history of the church; it's free, although donations are gladly accepted. Behind-the-scenes tours and other presentations are available by appointment for a fee. (Daily; closed holidays) **FREE**

Paul Revere House. *19 North Sq (02113). On the Freedom Trail. Phone 617/523-2338. www.paulreverehouse.org.* Built in 1680 and well preserved today, the Paul Revere House is Boston's oldest building and includes authentic furnishings from the Revere family. This historical landmark offers a rare glimpse at colonial life, because few other houses from the period survived remodeling, fire damage, and demolition. At his house, Paul Revere plied his silversmith trade and sold his wares, often in exchange for food or livestock when case-strapped colonists couldn't pay. Although a staunch patriot, Revere was largely undistinguished among Sam Adams, John Hancock, and Ben Franklin. However, Revere's successful ride to Lexington and Concord on April 18, 1775, to warn of the approaching British army—a feat immortalized in Henry Wadsworth Longfellow's poem, *The Midnight Ride of Paul Revere*—made him one of the best-known American historic figures. (Mid-Apr-late Oct, daily 9:30 am-5:15 pm; early Nov-mid-Apr, daily 9:30 am-4:15 pm; closed Mon in Jan, Feb, Mar; also Jan 1, Thanksgiving, Dec 25) **$$**

Special Events

Chowderfest. *1 City Hall Plz (02201). Phone 617/227-1528. www.boston harborfest.com/chowderfest.* During Harborfest, an event that begins a few days before July 4 and ends a few days after, Boston's finest restaurants compete to have their chowda called "Boston's Best Chowder." More than 2,000 gallons of New England clam chowder (you won't find that Manhattan tomatoey variety here) are yours to sample and judge in this enjoyable annual event. Early July. **$$**

Esplanade Concerts. *Hatch Shell, Charles River Esplanade (02114). Phone toll-free 888/733-2678.* Musical programs by the Boston Pops in the Hatch Shell on the Esplanade. Two weeks in July.

Harborfest. *Hatch Shell, Charles River Esplanade (02114). Phone 617/227-1528.* Boston Pops Orchestra, fireworks. Six days over July 4.

Motel/Motor Lodge

★ ★ **HOLIDAY INN.** *5 Blossom St (02114). Phone 617/742-7630; toll-free 800/465-4329; fax 617/742-4192. www.holiday-inn.com.* 303 rooms, 15 story. Check-out noon, check-in 4 pm. TV; cable (premium). In-room modem link. Laundry services. Restaurant, bar. In-house fitness room. Health club privileges. Pool. Overlooks Charles River. **$$**

D ⇌ 🏂 🔌

Hotels

★ ★ ★ ★ **BOSTON HARBOR HOTEL.** *70 Rowes Wharf (02110). Phone 617/439-7000; toll-free 800/752-7077; fax 617/345-6799. www.bhh.com.* Privileged guests rest their weary heads at the Boston Harbor Hotel. Boston's rich heritage comes alive here at Rowes Wharf, once a home to revolutionaries and traders. Occupying an idyllic waterfront location, the hotel is across the street from the financial district and three blocks from the Freedom Trail and Faneuil Hall Market. The Boston Harbor Hotel shares an especially civilized lifestyle with its guests. Here, they need not worry about the snarls of traffic, thanks to the hotel's fantastic airport ferry service. This full-service hotel takes care of every possible amenity, ensuring satisfaction and comfort. Rooms and suites are beautifully appointed in rich colors; to pay a few dollars more for one with a view is well worth it. The views of the harbor are sensational, whether enjoyed in the privacy of a guest room or in one of the public spaces. Meritage presents diners with an inventive menu and an extensive wine list in striking contemporary surroundings. 230 rooms, 8 story. Pets accepted, some restrictions. Check-out 1 pm. TV; cable (premium), VCR available. In-room modem link. Restaurant, bar. Room service 24 hours. In-house fitness room, spa, sauna, steam room. Indoor pool, whirlpool, poolside service. Valet parking. Business center. Concierge. **$$$**

D 🐾 ⇌ 🏂 🔌 🏃

★ ★ ★ **LE MERIDIEN BOSTON.** *250 Franklin St (02110). Phone 617/451-1900; toll-free 800/543-4300; fax 617/423-2844. www.lemeridienboston.com.* Le Meridien is an elegant choice while visiting Boston. Just a stone's throw from Faneuil Hall, the Freedom Trail, and other historic sites, this hotel is a perfect base for retracing the steps of famous patriots. A sense of old-world Europe is felt throughout Le Meridien, from the discreet façade with its signature red awnings to the magnificent lobby done in jewel tones. The guest rooms are equally delightful, and many offer wonderful views of the gardens of Post Office Square. Extra touches are provided to ensure exceedingly comfortable visits. The remarkable French cuisine at Julien is only the beginning, where sparkling chandeliers and glittering gold leaf details will make any guest feel like royalty. Once the Governor's Reception Room of Boston's Federal Reserve Bank, the Julien Bar is a sensational place, while the Mediterranean dishes of Café Fleuri have universal appeal. 343

rooms, 9 story. Pets accepted, some restrictions; fee. Check-out 1 pm. TV; cable (premium), VCR available. In-room modem link. Restaurant, bar. Room service 24 hours. In-house fitness room, massage, sauna. Indoor pool. Valet parking. Business center. Concierge. **$$$**

★ ★ ★ **SEAPORT HOTEL.** *1 Seaport Ln (02210). Phone 617/385-4500; toll-free 877/732-7678; fax 617/385-4001.* Located on Boston's scenic waterfront and within minutes of Logan International Airport, this hotel features spacious guest rooms, each with a picturesque view of the Boston Harbor or skyline. 426 rooms, 18 story. Pets accepted, some restrictions. Check-out 1 pm. TV; cable (premium), VCR available. In-room modem link. Restaurant, bar. In-house fitness room, massage, sauna. Indoor pool. Valet parking. Business center. Concierge. On harbor. Totally nonsmoking. **$**

Restaurants

★ ★ **ANTHONY'S PIER 4.** *140 Northern Ave (02210). Phone 617/482-6262; fax 617/426-2324. www.pier4.com.* Closed Dec 25. Lunch, dinner. Bar. Jacket required. Outdoor seating. **$$$**

★ ★ **FILIPPO.** *283 Causeway St (02114). Phone 617/742-4143; fax 617/742-4145.* Italian menu. Closed Thanksgiving, Dec 25. Lunch, dinner. Bar. Children's menu. Valet parking (dinner). **$$$**

★ ★ **THE HUNGRY I.** *71 1/2 Charles St (02114). Phone 617/227-3524; fax 617/227-0237.* French country menu. Closed July 4, Thanksgiving, Dec 25. Dinner, Sun brunch. Bar. 1840s house in historic district. Casual attire. Outdoor seating (Sun brunch only). **$$$**

★ ★ **IL BOCCONCINO.** *272 Cambridge St (02114). Phone 617/720-0692.* Italian menu. Closed. Lunch, dinner. Casual attire. **$$**

★ ★ **JIMMY'S HARBORSIDE.** *242 Northern Ave (02210). Phone 617/423-1000; fax 617/451-0669. www.jimmysharborside.com.* American, seafood menu. Closed Dec 25. Lunch, dinner. Bar. Children's menu. Casual attire. Valet parking. **$$$**

★ ★ **LUCIA.** *415 Hanover St (02113). Phone 617/523-9148; fax 617/367-8952.* In these days of avant garde Italian, it's nice to still find simple yet creative Italian dining in Boston. Look for the Sistine Chapel frescos while you sip your cappuccino. There's also a second location in Winchester. Regional Italian menu. Closed Thanksgiving, Dec 25. Lunch, dinner. Bar. Children's menu. Valet parking (dinner). **$$**

★ ★ ★ **MAMMA MARIA.** *3 North Sq (02113). Phone 617/523-0077; fax 617/523-4348. www.mammamaria.com.* Romantics flock to the porch at this classic Northern Italian restaurant, but the food's incredibly well-executed no matter where you sit. Diners also have a good view of North Square, and there's also valet parking. Northern Italian menu. Menu changes seasonally. Closed most major holidays. Dinner. Bar. Overlooks historic area; Paul Revere house across square. Casual attire. Valet parking. Private dining rooms. **$$$**

D

★ ★ **NORTH STREET GRILL.** *229 North St (02113). Phone 617/720-2010.* American menu. Breakfast, lunch, dinner, late night. Bar. Casual attire. **$$**

★ ★ **PICCOLO NIDO.** *257 North St (02113). Phone 617/742-4272; fax 617/227-5154. www.piccolonido.com.* Italian menu. Closed Sun; July 4, Dec 25. Dinner. Casual attire. **$$**

D

★ ★ **RISTORANTE TOSCANO.** *47 Charles St (02114). Phone 617/723-4090; fax 617/720-4280.* Northern Italian menu. Closed some major holidays. Lunch, dinner. Bar. Valet parking (dinner). **$$$**

D

★ ★ ★ **SAGE.** *69 Prince St (02113). Phone 617/248-8814; fax 617/248-1879. www.northendboston.com/sage.* This North End find is all about the food, although the service is more than adequate. Chef/owner Anthony Susi is a true workhorse, turning out inexpensive yet gourmet dishes by the dozen almost single-handedly. The menu changes with the seasons. New American menu. Closed Sun. Dinner. **$$$**

D

★ ★ **TARANTA.** *210 Hanover St (02113). Phone 617/720-0052.* Italian menu. Dinner. Casual attire. **$$$**

D

★ ★ **TERRAMIA.** *98 Salem St (02113). Phone 617/523-3112.* Italian menu. Closed some major holidays. Dinner. Children's menu. Totally non-smoking. **$$$**

D

Beacon Hill

What to See and Do

Boston Common. *Beacon and Tremont sts (02108). Take the Red or Green Line ("T") to Park St. Phone 617/525-4100.* As the oldest public park in the United States, Boston Common is steeped in history. Established in 1640, Bostonians used the Common as a pasture for grazing their cattle; later, the colonial militia used it to train soldiers, and it even served as a British military camp. Colonists gathered to hear speeches, witness public hangings, and watch spirited fencing duels. Today, the Common's 45 acres are still a vibrant center of the city—a perfect place to stroll, in-line skate, play

Frisbee, catch a free concert, or enjoy a picnic (watch out for dog droppings, however). The park is a perfect place to begin walking the Freedom Trail; the park itself is loaded with signs, plaques, and monuments, most notably that of Robert Gould Shaw, who led the Union Army's 54th Massachusetts Colored Regiment, the first all-black army unit in the United States. (Daily) **FREE** Also here are

Central Burying Ground. *Boylston and Tremont sts (02116).* The grave of Gilbert Stuart, the painter, is here; technically not a part of the Common, although in it.

Swan Boats/Boston Public Garden. *Arlington, Boylston, Charles, and Beacon sts (02108). Take the Green Line to Arlington Station. Phone 617/ 522-1966. www.swanboats.com.* The launching point for the swan boats is the Boston Public Garden (daily), the first botanical garden in the United States, with 24 acres featuring a splendid variety of flowers and ornamental shrubs that bloom from early April until mid-October. Entry to the Public Garden is free. Each swan boat, so named because it's decorated with a larger-than-life swan, operates by pedal power (the driver's, not yours) for a 15-minute ride around the Public Garden Lagoon. (Daily dawn-dusk; Swan Boats: Spring 10 am-4 pm, summer to 5 pm, fall Mon-Fri noon-4 pm, Sat-Sun 10 am-4 pm) **$**

Boston Common Frog Pond Rink. *Beacon and Tremont sts (02108). Take the Red or Green Line ("T") to Park St. Phone 617/635-2120.* Ice skating abounds each winter in Boston, with outdoor rinks spread throughout the city. Frog Pond, the largest of these rinks, is a natural mud pond on Boston Common during spring, summer, and fall. From November to March, however, the city transforms the wading pool into an enormous outdoor skating rink and maintains it all winter, regardless of the weather. At the rink, you can rent skates ($5), get the feeling back in your toes by standing in the warming room, and use the public rest room. Other skating rinks in the area—all of which are free—include Bajko Memorial Rink (Boston), Turtle Pond Parkway, 617/364-9188; Devine Memorial Rink (Boston), Morrissey Blvd, 617/436-4356; Porazzo Memorial Rink (Boston), Constitution Beach, 617/ 567-9571; and Simoni Memorial Rink (Cambridge), Gore St, 617/354-9523. (Mid-Nov-mid-Mar: Sun, Tues-Thurs 10 am-9 pm, Mon to 5 pm, Fri-Sat to 10 pm; closed in spring, summer, and fall) **$**

Faneuil Hall Marketplace. *4 S Market Bldg, 5th Fl (02109). Take the Blue or Green Line ("T") to Government Center, then walk across the plaza, down the long set of stairs, and across busy Congress St. On the Freedom Trail. Phone 617/242-5675 or 617/242-5642. www.faneuilhallmarketplace.com.* Faneuil Hall Marketplace offers the best variety of shops and kiosks in Boston, housed in five buildings and several plazas. The central building, Quincy Market, is filled with dining options, from coffee to seafood and everything in between; many are open earlier and later than the shops. Look for delightful street performers even in winter months, and especially the rest of the year. Faneuil Hall (pronounced FAN-yal or FAN-yoo-ul) is more than just a shopping center: it has operated as a local marketplace since 1742, when wealthy merchant Peter Faneuil built and donated the marketplace to the city. The Hall is remembered as the site of town meetings that produced the policy of "no taxation without representation." Listen to a historical talk every half hour from 9:30 am to 4:30 pm in the second-floor auditorium. (Mon-Sat 10 am-9 pm, Sun noon-6 pm; closed holidays)

Filene's Basement. *426 Washington St (02108). Take the Red or Orange Line ("T") to the Downtown Crossing stop. Phone 617/348-7974. www. filenesbasement.com.* Located directly beneath Filene's Department Store, the Basement is famous for its automatic markdowns: after two weeks at full price, merchandise falls by percentages until, five weeks later, it's 75 percent off. (Any unsold merchandise is then given to charity.) Filene's Basement is also the site of an annual wedding gown sale—brides-to-be race each other to racks in the hopes of finding the right dress for a fraction of its retail price. (Mon-Fri 9:30 am-7:30 pm, Sat from 9 am, Sun 11 am-7 pm; closed Easter, Thanksgiving, Dec 25)

Granary Burying Ground. *Tremont and Bromfield sts (02108). Take the "T" to Park St, walk 1 block on Tremont St. On the Freedom Trail. Phone 617/635-4505.* Although Granary is Boston's third-oldest cemetery, it is, perhaps, its most famous. Revolutionary War patriots Paul Revere, John Hancock, Samuel Adams, and Peter Faneuil (whose headstone is marked "Peter Funal") all lie here. The name stems from a grain storage building (called a granary) that used to sit nearby. (Daily 9 am-5 pm) **FREE**

Haymarket. *Blackstone St (02109), off I-93. Around the corner from Faneuil Hall Marketplace; take the Orange or Green line to the Haymarket stop.* Rain or shine, winter or summer, Bostonians flock to Haymarket for the freshest fruits, vegetables, and seafood you've ever seen. If you do your shopping in a grocery store back home, you won't believe the differences in price (far lower) and quality (much higher) here. The market is bustling with lively scents and sounds, including languages from around the world. Haggling is the norm and remains friendly—you'll want three yellow peppers for $1, and the vendor will want to sell you six for $2. Start your day at Haymarket, buying a few pieces of fruit to snack on, and then meander through the city or walk the Freedom Trail. (Fri-Sat) **FREE**

King's Chapel and Burying Ground. *58 Tremont St (02108). On the Freedom Trail. Phone 617/227-2155. www.kings-chapel.org.* King's Chapel, started by the Massachusetts Royal Governor who had no desire to worship in a Puritan church, has held church services at its location longer than any other church in the United States. When the congregation outgrew the church in 1754, a new building was erected around the old, which was then dismantled. The Burying Ground next door is the oldest cemetery in Boston. Stop in for concerts on Tuesdays at 12:15 pm and Sundays at 5 pm. (Daily; closed Sun-Fri in winter) **FREE**

Louisburg Square. This lovely little residential square with its central park is the ultimate in traditional Boston charm. Louisa May Alcott, William Dean Howells, and other famous Bostonians have lived here. It is one of the most treasured spots in Boston. Christmas caroling is a tradition here.

The Mother Church, the First Church of Christ, Scientist. *Christian Science Center, 175 Huntington Ave (02115). Phone 617/450-3790.* Tours. (Daily; closed holidays) Adjacent is

Christian Science Publishing Society. *Massachusetts Ave at Clearway St (02115). Phone 617/450-3793. (The Christian Science Monitor)* Inquire about tours. Mapparium, a walk-through stained-glass globe, is here. Call ahead.

Museum of Afro American History/Black Heritage Trail. *14 Beacon St, Suite 719 (02108). The self-guided trail begins at the Robert Gould Shaw/45th Massachusetts Regiment Memorial on Beacon Hill. Phone 617/725-0022. www.afroammuseum.org.* The Museum of Afro American History (MAAH) preserves and exhibits the contributions of African-American Bostonians and New Englanders during colonial settlement and the Revolutionary War. The museum also features workshops for kids and adults, a public lecture series, storytelling for children, and poet and author visits. The Black Heritage Trail explores stops on the Underground Railroad; Phillip's School, one of Boston's first integrated public schools; African-American churches, in which, unlike other churches in the area, members could sit on the main level during services and participate in church business; and historic homes of prominent African-American leaders. Guided walking tours are offered daily throughout the summer and at other times by request. (Memorial Day-Labor Day, daily 10 am-4 pm; Labor Day-Memorial Day, Mon-Sat 10 am-4 pm; closed Jan 1, Thanksgiving, Dec 25) **FREE**

Nichols House Museum. *55 Mt. Vernon St (02108). Phone 617/227-6993.* (1804) Typical domestic architecture of Beacon Hill from its era; one of two homes on Beacon Hill open to the public. Attributed to Charles Bulfinch; antique furnishings and art from America, Europe, and the Orient from the 17th to early 19th centuries. Collection of Rose Standish Nichols, landscape designer and writer. (Tues-Sat afternoons) **$$**

Old South Meeting House. *310 Washington St (02108). Corner of Washington and Milk sts, on the Freedom Trail. Phone 617/482-6439. www.oldsouthmeeting house.org.* Built as a Puritan meeting house (or church), colonists congregated at the Old South Meeting House each year from 1771 to 1775 to mark the death of those killed in the Boston Massacre and listen to speeches by prominent colonists. The most important date in Old South's history, however, is December 16, 1773, when 5,000 colonists gathered at the church to protest the British tax on tea and decide on a course of action. From there, men dressed as Native Americans snuck onto three ships laden with tea on Griffin's Wharf and dumped all the tea overboard. Restored in 1997, the church no longer has an active congregation but is still a gathering place for political debate. An interactive exhibit called Voices of Protest recalls the Old South Meeting House's historic legacy. (Apr-Oct, daily 9:30 am-5 pm; Nov-Mar, daily 10 am-4 pm; closed Jan 1, Thanksgiving, Dec 24-25) **$**

Old State House/Site of Boston Massacre. *206 Washington St (02109). On the Freedom Trail. Phone 617/720-1713. www.bostonhistory.org.* The Old State House (not to be confused with the golden-dome new State House) was originally built as the headquarters of the British government in Boston and is Boston's oldest surviving public building. Inside, the Bostonian Society operates a museum that reflects the prominent role the Old State House played in the American Revolution. The Massachusetts Assembly met there and debated political issues in front of all citizens who wanted to observe. After these issues were decided, politicians read summaries—including the Declaration of Independence on July 18, 1776—from the House's balcony. The balcony hovers above the spot where the Boston Massacre occurred in 1770, when British troops shot into a crowd that had gathered to hear a proclamation. There, in a small triangle surrounded by dense city traffic, the site of the massacre is marked with a circle of paving stones. Plan on one hour for a tour. (Mon-Sat 9 am-5 pm; closed Jan 1, Thanksgiving, Dec 25) **$**

Park Street Church. *1 Park St (02108). Phone 617/523-3383. www.parkstreet.org. On the Freedom Trail.* (1809) Often called "Brimstone Corner" because brimstone for gunpowder was stored here during the War of 1812. William Lloyd Garrison delivered his first antislavery address here in 1829. Tours. (July and Aug, limited hours; Sun services all year)

Site of the first US free public school. *School St at City Hall Ave (02108). Blue or Orange Line ("T") to State St. On the Freedom Trail.* A mosaic in the sidewalk marks the site of the first free US public school. The original building was demolished to make room for the expansion of King's Chapel. The school, now known as the Boston Latin School, was moved across the street.

Statue of Benjamin Franklin. *School St at City Hall Ave (02108). On the Freedom Trail.* This, Boston's first portrait statue, was created by Richard S. Greenough in 1856.

Special Events

First Night Celebration. *Boston Common. Beacon and Tremont sts (02108). Phone 617/536-4100.* Dec 31.

Patriot's Day Celebration. *City Center (02108). Phone 617/536-4100.* Third Mon in Apr.

Hotels

★ ★ ★ ★ ★ **FOUR SEASONS HOTEL BOSTON.** *200 Boylston St (02116). Phone 617/338-4400; toll-free 800/819-5053; fax 617/423-0154. www.fourseasons.com.* The Four Seasons Hotel would make any Boston Brahmin proud. Discriminating travelers are drawn to this refined hotel where the finer things in life may be enjoyed. The Four Seasons offers its guests a prime location overlooking Beacon Hill's Public Garden and the State Capitol. All of Boston is easily explored from here, and the hotel makes it carefree with courtesy town car service. Antiques, fine art, sumptuous fabrics, and period furniture create a magnificent setting in the rooms and suites, while impeccable and attentive service heightens the luxurious experience. Aquatic workouts with a view are available at the indoor pool with floor-to-ceiling windows overlooking the city, and the fitness center keeps guests in tiptop shape. Aujourd'Hui (see) is an epicurean's delight with its sensational New American cuisine and distinguished dining room. The Bristol presents diners with a casually elegant alternative. 274 rooms, 15 story. Pets accepted, some restrictions. Check-out 1 pm, check-in 3 pm. TV; cable (premium), VCR available (movies). In-room modem link. Laundry services. Restaurant, bar; entertainment. Room service. Babysitting services available. In-house fitness room, spa, massage, sauna. Indoor pool, whirlpool, poolside service. Valet, garage parking. Business center. Concierge. **$$$$**

D 🐾 ≈ 🕴 ⊠ 🏃

★ ★ **HARBORSIDE INN OF BOSTON.** *185 State St (02109). Phone 617/723-7500; fax 617/670-2010. www.harborsideinnboston.com.* 54 rooms, 8 story. Closed Christmas week. Check-out noon, check-in 3 pm. TV; cable (premium). Laundry services. Restaurant, bar. Concierge. **$$**

D ✗ ⊠

★ ★ **MARRIOTT BOSTON LONG WHARF.** *296 State St (02109). Phone 617/227-0800; toll-free 800/228-9290; fax 617/227-2867. www.marriott.com.* Set besides the picturesque Boston Harbor at the historic Long Wharf, this hotel offers guests elegance and comfort. 402 rooms, 7 story. Check-out noon, check-in 4 pm. TV; cable (premium), VCR available (movies). In-room modem link. Laundry services. Restaurant, bar. In-house fitness room, sauna. Indoor pool, whirlpool, poolside service. Valet parking. Business center. Luxury level. **$$**

D ≈ 🕴 🏃

★ ★ ★ **MILLENNIUM BOSTONIAN HOTEL BOSTON.** *26 North St, Faneuil Hall Marketplace (02109). Phone 617/523-3600; toll-free 800/343-0922; fax 617/523-2454. www.millenniumhotels.com.* Understated elegance, attentive service, as well as spacious and well-appointed guest rooms are the hallmarks of this European-style luxury hotel. 201 rooms, 7 story. Check-out 3 pm, check-in noon. TV; cable (premium), VCR available. In-room modem link. Fireplaces. Restaurant (see also SEASONS). Bar; entertainment Tues-Sat. Room service. In-house fitness room. Health club privileges. Valet parking. Business center. Concierge. One block to harbor. **$$**

D 🕴 ⊠ SC 🏃

★ ★ ★ **NINE ZERO.** *90 Tremont St (02108). Phone 617/772-5800; toll-free 800/434-7347; fax 617/772-5810. www.ninezerohotel.com.* 190 rooms, 19 story. Pets accepted, some restrictions. Check-out noon, check-in 3 pm. TV; cable (premium). Internet access. Restaurant, bar. Room service. In-house fitness room, massage. Valet parking. **$$$**

D 🐾 🕴 ⊠

★ ★ ★ **OMNI PARKER HOUSE.** *60 School St (02108). Phone 617/227-8600; toll-free 800/843-6664; fax 617/742-5729. www.omnihotels.com.* This hotel was founded in 1855 by Harvey D. Parker and has long been known as the longest continuously operating hotel in America. Offering guests modern amenities while maintaining its historic charm, this hotel offers refined elegance and superb service. 572 rooms, 15 story. Check-out noon, check-in 3 pm. TV; cable (premium), VCR available. In-room modem link. Restaurant (see also PARKER'S). Bar; entertainment Mon-Sat. Concierge. **$$**

⊠ ⊠ SC

★ ★ ★ ★ **THE RITZ-CARLTON, BOSTON COMMON.** *10 Avery St (02111). Phone 617/574-7100; toll-free 800/241-3333; fax 617/574-7200. www.ritzcarlton.com.* While only a short skip across the park from its sister property, The Ritz-Carlton, Boston Common is a world apart from its traditional counterpart with its modern sensibility of clean lines, neutral tones, and hip atmosphere. This contemporary construction attracts the fashionable set seeking the high levels of service synonymous with Ritz-Carlton properties. Flanked by the financial and theater districts, The Ritz-Carlton, Boston Common is convenient for business and leisure travelers alike. The rooms and suites have a distinctly serene feel with muted tones of taupe, cream, and celadon and polished woods. JER-NE restaurant (see) is a feast for the tongue and the eyes with its inventive creations and sensational décor. An open kitchen enables guests to watch the talented chefs in action, while the bar has a vibrant scene. After a night of indulgence, Ritz-Carlton guests often head to the massive Sports Club/LA, a veritable temple of fitness. *Secret Inspector's Notes:* Be sure to obtain a fitness menu from the Sports Club/LA prior to arriving, as the classes offered and the level of personal training available are far superior to those in many gyms around the country. 193 rooms, 4 story. Pets accepted, some restrictions; fee. Complimentary continental breakfast. Check-out noon, check-in 3 pm. TV; cable (premium). In-room modem link. Restaurant, bar. Room service. Babysitting services available. In-house fitness room, spa, massage. Health club privileges. Indoor pool. Valet parking. Business center. Concierge. Luxury level. **$$$$**

D ⊠ ⊠ ⊼ ⊠ ⊼

★ ★ ★ ★ **XV BEACON.** *15 Beacon St (02108). Phone 617/670-1500; fax 617/670-2525. www.xvbeacon.com.* Dazzling and daring, XV Beacon is the hipster's answer to the luxury hotel. This turn-of-the-century Beaux Arts building in Beacon Hill belies the sleek décor found within. This highly stylized, seductive hotel flaunts a refreshing change of pace in traditional Boston. Decidedly contemporary, XV Beacon employs whimsical touches, like the plaster busts found at reception, to wink at the city's past. Original artwork, commissioned specifically for the hotel by well-known artists, decorates the walls of both public and private spaces. The guest rooms and suites are furnished in an eclectic style in a palette of rich chocolate browns, blacks, and creams. Rooms feature canopy beds with luxurious Italian linens and gas fireplaces covered in cool stainless steel. Completed in crisp white with simple fixtures, the bathrooms are a modernist's dream. The nouvelle cuisine at The Fed (see also THE FEDERALIST) is delicious and fresh, thanks to the chef's rooftop garden and in-kitchen fish tanks. *Secret Inspector's Notes:* XV Beacon is a luxury lover's dream. The rooms are stocked with everything from private-label lip balms and Kiehl's shampoos to decadent minibars full of Stags Leap, Dominus, and Krug wines.

The rooftop sundeck is a hidden spot to enjoy the sunshine or sunset with room service gladly providing cool drinks or snacks. 61 rooms, 10 story. Pets accepted, some restrictions. Check-out noon, check-in 3 pm. TV; cable (premium), VCR available, CD available. Restaurant, bar. Room service 24 hours. Babysitting services available. In-house fitness room. Health club privileges. Whirlpool. Valet parking. Concierge. **$$$$**

B&B/Small Inn

★ ★ ★ **CHARLES STREET INN.** *94 Charles St (02114). Phone 617/314-8900; toll-free 877/772-8900; fax 617/371-0009. www.charlesstreetinn.com.* This property is situated amidst the boutiques and antique shops of Beacon Hill. Guest rooms, named after New England luminaries such as Frederick Law Olmstead and Louisa May Alcott, are elegantly furnished with lovely antiques. 9 rooms, 5 story. Complimentary continental breakfast. Check-out 11 am, check-in 3 pm. TV; VCR available, CD available. Laundry services. Golf on premise. Outdoor tennis. Concierge. **$$**

Restaurants

★ ★ **AQUA.** *120 Water St (02109). Phone 617/720-4900; fax 617/227-3611. www.aquaboston.com.* American menu. Closed Sun; major holidays. Lunch, dinner. Bar. Casual attire. **$$$**

★ ★ ★ ★ **AUJOURD'HUI.** *200 Boylston St (02116). Phone 617/338-4400; fax 617/423-0154. www.fourseasons.com.* With floor-to-ceiling windows overlooking Boston's famed Public Garden, Aujourd'hui is a beautiful spot for a business lunch or an intimate dinner. Brimming with old-world charm, this spacious and elegant dining room, located in the Four Seasons, is lined with rich oak paneling and decorated with tall potted palms and oil paintings. The tables are set with Italian damask linens and decorated with antique plates and lovely fresh flowers. The kitchen aims to please here, and it succeeds with an innovative selection of seasonal New American fare prepared with regional ingredients and global flavors. The predominantly American wine list complements the kitchen's talent. A lighter menu of more, shall we say, nutritionally responsible dishes (read: low salt, low fat, low cholesterol) is also available. The service at Aujourd'hui enhances the dining experience. Like the restaurant, it is formal yet charming. *Secret Inspector's Notes:* There's clearly a new toque in the kitchen at Aujourd'hui. Food that was once delicate and reserved has become bold and exciting, with flavors that jump off the plate and dance on the palate. American, French, international menu. Menu changes seasonally. Breakfast, lunch, dinner, Sun brunch. Bar. Children's menu. Jacket required. Reservations required. Valet parking. **$$$$**

★ ★ ★ **BAY TOWER.** *60 State St (02109). Phone 617/723-1666; fax 617/723-7887. www.baytower.com.* Although the restaurant was once known primarily for its stunning 33rd-floor view of the city, this Financial District contemporary American has undergone somewhat of a rebirth in the last few years. Entrées include rack of lamb, cornish hen, and carrot-ginger risotto. Closed Sun; Dec 25. Dinner. Bar; entertainment. Valet parking Fri, Sat. **$$$**

D

★ ★ **CAFE MARLIAVE.** *10 Bosworth St (02108). Phone 617/423-6340; fax 617/542-1133.* Italian menu. Closed some major holidays. Lunch, dinner. Bar. **$$**

★ ★ **DAVIDE.** *326 Commercial St (02109). Phone 617/227-5745; fax 617/227-8976. www.davideristorante.com.* This old-world spot would make anyone feel like an Italian, considering the ease of the dining experience: The wine list is accessible and (mostly) inexpensive; the service is relaxed and friendly; and, of course, the food sparkles. Don't miss the wild boar sausage. Italian menu. Dinner. Bar. Valet parking. **$$$**

★ **DURGIN PARK.** *340 Faneuil Hall Marketplace (02109). Phone 617/227-2038; fax 617/720-1542.* American menu. Closed Dec 25. Lunch, dinner. Bar; entertainment. Children's menu. Near Faneuil Hall. Established in 1826. Casual attire. Outdoor seating. **$$**

D

★ ★ ★ **THE FEDERALIST.** *15 Beacon St (02108). Phone 617/670-2515; toll-free 800/982-3226; fax 617/670-2525. www.xvbeacon.com.* This much-acclaimed-before-it-opened restaurant is becoming one of Boston's "to be seen" places. Its clubby, tongue-in-cheek salute to old Boston, with faux crumbling columns and plaster busts of colonial luminaries, continues on to the menu, where you can find updated versions of Yankee classics. Seafood menu. Breakfast, lunch, dinner. **$$$**

D

★ ★ ★ **JER-NE.** *10 Avery St (02114). Phone 617/574-7176. www.ritzcarlton.com.* American menu. Breakfast, lunch, dinner. Bar. Casual attire. **$$$**

D

★ ★ **LALA ROKH.** *97 Mt. Vernon St (02108). Phone 617/720-5511. www.lalarokh.com.* Mediterranean/Persian menu. Closed some major holidays. Dinner. Casual attire. Valet parking. **$$**

D

★ ★ ★ **LOCKE OBER.** *3 Winter Pl (02108). Phone 617/542-1340; fax 617/542-6452. www.lockeober.com.* Established in 1875, Boston's famed Locke Ober restaurant is a classic's classic. This glitzy, turn-of-the-(previous)-century dining landmark buzzes with electricity as the room fills to the seams with assorted foodies, superstars, financiers, and celebrity political types. Under the skilled leadership of co-owner and chef Lydia Shire, traditional American fare feels fresh and exciting and makes a persuasive case for eating nothing that flirts with fusion ever again. The menu speaks in simple yet spectacular terms, featuring classic plates from America's past, like beef Stroganoff with hand-cut egg noodles, as well as old French standards like duck l'orange and onion soup gratinée. The Indian pudding is a signature dessert, as is the fresh strawberry shortcake, when in season. Continental menu. Closed Sun; major holidays. Lunch, dinner. Bar. Built in 1875. Jacket required. **$$$**

★ ★ ★ **MAISON ROBERT.** *45 School St (02108). Phone 617/227-3370; fax 617/227-5977. www.maisonrobert.com.* Dine in the Bonhomme Richard Room, which is located on the first floor of the Treasurer's Office of the Old City Hall, and enjoy the view of Boston. High ceilings, grand chandeliers, and arched windows set the stage for an impressive meal. French menu. Closed some major holidays. Lunch, dinner. Bar. Jacket required. Valet parking. Outdoor seating. **$$$$**

D

★ ★ ★ ★ **NO. 9 PARK.** *9 Park St (02108). Phone 617/742-9991; fax 617/742-9993.* In the shadow of the Massachusetts State House in historic Beacon Hill, you will find No. 9 Park, a 19th-century mansion turned elegant dining salon. Inside, you'll find a kitchen that serves some of the most wonderful European country-style cuisine in the region. Many of the ingredients on the seasonal menu are identified by farm; chef-owner Barbara Lynch makes an effort to support top-of-the-line small producers of sustainable agriculture. Perfectly prepared with a healthy dose of flavor and style, Lynch's sophisticated, tempting menu of modern European fare runs the gamut from beef to fish to venison and pheasant, depending on the season. After dinner, stop at the beautifully appointed bar for a cognac or port, and give yourself some more time to relax before you go back to the real world. No. 9 Park is a magical sort of place that you just won't want to leave. French, Italian menu. Closed Sun; holidays. Lunch, dinner. Bar. Children's menu. Casual attire. Valet parking. **$$$$**

D

★ ★ **PARKER'S.** *60 School St (02108). Phone 617/227-8600; fax 617/742-5729. www.omnihotels.com.* They say that Boston cream pie was invented here (as well as Parker House rolls). Whether you believe that old saw is up to you, but don't miss the seafood selections, especially clam chowder and lobster. American menu. Breakfast, lunch, dinner. Bar. Piano (night). Children's menu. Valet parking. **$$$**

D

★ ★ ★ **RADIUS.** *8 High St (02108). Phone 617/426-1234; fax 617/426-2526.* Chef and partner Michael Schlow is a man who understands what people are looking for in a dining experience. First, there's atmosphere.

Radius is a stunningly chic, slick, modern space decked out in sliver and garnet red. Crowded with some of Boston's most stylish residents, you will step inside and instantly feel like you're on the set of *Sex and the City*. Second, there's the food. Schlow offers diners a chance to taste some truly inspired modern French cooking. There is an emphasis on the seasons here, so the menu changes often, but what doesn't change is the quality of the ingredients and the care with which the kitchen assembles each magnificent dish. Schlow doesn't like to overload the plate (or the belly) with heavy sauces. This is refined, light-handed cooking using infused oils, emulsions, juices, vegetable purées, and reductions to heighten flavors and add texture and balance to every dish. Dining here is a wonderful feast for all the senses. Lunch, dinner. Bar. Valet parking (dinner). **$$$$**

D

★ ★ ★ **SEASONS.** *26 North St, Faneuil Hall Marketplace (02109). Phone 617/523-3600; fax 617/523-2593. www.millenniumhotels.com.* Contemporary American menu. Closed major holidays. Breakfast, lunch, dinner. Bar. Children's menu. Valet parking. **$$$$**

D

★ ★ **SPIRE.** *90 Tremont St (02108). Phone 617/772-0202. www.ninezerohotel.com.* American menu. Breakfast, lunch, dinner. Bar. Children's menu. Casual attire. **$$**

D

★ ★ ★ **TORCH.** *26 Charles St (02114). Phone 617/723-5939. www.boston torch.com.* Owned by husband-and-wife team Evan and Candace Deluty, this intimate, unpretentious Beacon Hill spot does its best to make diners feel right at home. Evan Deluty describes his cooking as "modern French cuisine with Asian and Italian influences." French, Italian menu. Closed Mon. Dinner. Casual attire. **$$$**

D

★ ★ **THE VAULT.** *105 Water St (02109). Phone 617/292-9966; fax 617/ 292-7571.* American menu. Closed Sun; major holidays. Lunch, dinner. Bar. Totally nonsmoking. **$$$**

★ ★ **YE OLDE UNION OYSTER HOUSE.** *41 Union St (02108). Phone 617/227-2750; fax 617/227-6401. www.unionoysterhouse.com.* Seafood menu. Closed Thanksgiving, Dec 25. Lunch, dinner. Bar. Children's menu. Historic oyster bar established 1826; originally a silk and dry goods shop (1742). Valet parking (dinner). **$$**

D

★ **ZUMA'S TEX-MEX CAFE.** *7 N Market St (02109). Phone 617/367-9114; fax 617/523-0304.* Tex-Mex menu. Closed Dec 25. Lunch, dinner. Bar. **$$**

D

The South End & Chinatown

What to See and Do

Bernard Toale Gallery. *450 Harrison Ave (02118). Phone 617/482-2477. www.bernardtoalegallery.com.* The Bernard Toale Gallery offers you an opportunity to view (and buy, if you're so inclined) paintings, drawings, photographs, and sculptures from some of today's hottest artists. Both established artists and select up-and-comers display works at the gallery, so you get a chance to take in cutting-edge works that have not yet made their way into contemporary art museums. Look for occasional readings, videos, and fashion shows, too. Allow one or two hours. (Tues-Sat 10:30 am-5:30 pm; Aug by appointment only; closed Sat in July) **FREE**

Duck Tours. *790 Boylston St (02199). Phone 800/226-7442. www.boston ducktours.com.* Boston Duck Tours take you from land to sea in a World War II half-boat, half-truck vehicle known as a Duck. Your conDUCKtor starts the 80-minute tour on land, leading you past Boston Common, the golden-domed State House, Public Gardens, the Big Dig, Faneuil Hall Marketplace, Boston's North End, Government Center, Copley Square, Prudential Tower, Newbury Street, Bunker Hill, and the Fleet Center. The Duck then transforms into an amphibious vehicle and dives into the Charles River for more sightseeing. (Apr-Nov: tours every 30 minutes from 9 am to one hour before sunset; closed Dec-Mar) **$$$$**

John F. Kennedy National Historic Site. *83 Beals St, Brookline (02446). Phone 617/566-7937.* The birthplace and early childhood home of the nation's 35th president is restored in appearance to 1917, the year of his birth. Ranger-guided tours. (Apr-Nov, Wed-Sun; closed Jan 1, Thanksgiving, Dec 25) Golden Eagle Passport accepted (see MAKING THE MOST OF YOUR TRIP). **$$**

Make Way for Ducklings Tour. *99 Bedford St (02111). Phone 617/426-1885. www.historic-neighborhoods.org.* When Robert McCloskey wrote *Make Way for Ducklings* in 1940, he described two duck parents, Mr. and Mrs. Mallard, trying to find the perfect spot in which to raise their family. After the fictional duck family toured Boston's well-known sites, they settled in Boston's Public Garden, and Bostonians have been in love with this Caldecott-winning children's book ever since. Now you can re-create the duck's route via the Make Way for Ducklings tour, although you must make reservations in advance. Take advantage of other duckling events, such as the fancy and expensive Ducklings Day Tea held in April (reservations required) and the Ducklings Day Parade that begins at 1 pm on Mother's Day at Boston Common—children come to the parade dressed as their favorite characters from the story. **$$**

★ **Museum at the John Fitzgerald Kennedy Library.** *5 miles SE on I-93, off exit 15, at University of Massachusetts Columbia Point campus (02125).*

Phone 617/929-4500; toll-free 866/JFK-1960. www.cs.umb.edu/jfklibrary/ museum.htm. Designed by I. M. Pei, the library is considered one of the most beautiful contemporary works of architecture in the country. The library tower houses a collection of documents from the Kennedy administration as well as audiovisual programs designed to re-create the era. (Daily, closed Jan 1, Thanksgiving, Dec 25) Picnic facilities on oceanfront. **$$$**

Peter L. Stern. *55 Temple Pl (02111). Phone 617/421-1880.* Peter L. Stern stocks rare and antique books, including many first editions of 19th- and 20th-century literature, and a full offering of mystery books. If you've never stepped foot inside a rare bookstore before, Stern is a great place to start. Seeing books that have remained intact for nearly 200 years makes a terrific connection with the past, especially in this historic city. (Mon-Sat 9 am-5 pm; closed Sun, holidays)

The Shops at the Pru. *800 Boylston St (02199). Take the Green Line E ("T") to the Prudential stop. Phone 617/267-1002. www.prudentialcenter.com.* The presence of Saks Fifth Avenue as the mall's anchor may lead you to believe that The Shops at the Pru are expensive, but they're actually midpriced and very much like those in your local mall at home. The mall connects to Copley Place (see also COPLEY PLACE), which is far more upscale. The Prudential Center also boasts the Skywalk (**$$**), which offers you a panoramic view of the city from the 50th floor. (Mon-Sat 10 am-8 pm, Sun 11 am-6 pm; closed Jan 1, Easter, Thanksgiving, Dec 25)

Motel/Motor Lodge

★ **RAMADA INN.** *800 Morrissey Blvd (02122). Phone 617/287-9100; toll-free 800/886-0056; fax 617/265-9287. www.ramada.com.* 177 rooms, 2-5 story. Check-out 11 am. TV; cable (premium). In-room modem link. Laundry services. Health club privileges. Game room. Outdoor pool. **$**

D ⛵ ⛷

Hotel

★ ★ ★ **TREMONT BOSTON.** *275 Tremont St (02116). Phone 617/426-1400; toll-free 877/999-3223; fax 617/482-6730. www.wyndham.com.* This small, sophisticated hotel is located in the Western Promenade historic neighborhood. There are antiques and art throughout the inn, and a lovely urban garden awaits you. It is a short walk to the midtown Arts District and there are museums, art galleries, boat rides, fine restaurants, and recreational activities nearby. 377 rooms, 15 story. Check-out noon. TV; cable (premium), VCR. In-room modem link. Restaurant, bar; entertainment Thurs-Sun. In-house fitness room. Valet parking. Business center. Concierge. Luxury level. **$**

D ⅄ ⛷ SC ⋀

Restaurants

★ ★ ★ **AQUITAINE.** *569 Tremont St (02118). Phone 617/424-8577; fax 617/424-0281. www.aquitaineboston.com.* An offshoot of fellow South End restaurant Metropolis (both are owned by Seth and Shari Woods), this French bistro wavers between classical and nouveau. Regulars rave about the steak frites; there's also an intriguing wine list as well as a helpful staff. Closed major holidays. Dinner, brunch. **$$$**

D

★ ★ ★ **BLU.** 4 Avery St (02111). Phone 617/375-8550. American menu. Lunch, dinner. Bar. Children's menu. Casual attire. Outdoor seating. **$$**

D

★ ★ **BOB THE CHEF'S.** 604 Columbus Ave (02118). Phone 617/536-6204; fax 617/536-0907. www.bobthechefs.com. Creole/Cajun menu. Closed Mon; some major holidays. Lunch, dinner, Sun brunch. Bar. Jazz Thurs, Fri evening, Sun brunch. Totally nonsmoking. **$$**

★ **CLAREMONT CAFE.** 535 Columbus Ave (02118). Phone 617/247-9001; fax 617/437-0062. www.claremontcafe.com. Continental menu. Closed Mon; major holidays. Breakfast, lunch, dinner, Sun brunch. Valet parking. Totally nonsmoking. **$$**

D

★ ★ **GINZA.** 16 Hudson St (02111). Phone 617/338-2261; fax 617/426-3563. www.bostondine.com. Waitresses in kimonos and Japanese pop music set the scene for this bustling sushi restaurant that is a favorite among many. The sushi chefs work quickly and efficiently preparing delicious bites. Japanese menu. Lunch, dinner. **$$$**

D

★ **GRAND CHAU-CHOW.** 45 Beach St (02111). Phone 617/292-5166; fax 617/292-4646. Chinese, seafood menu. Lunch, dinner. **$$**

★ ★ ★ **ICARUS.** 3 Appleton St (02116). Phone 617/426-1790; fax 617/426-2150. www.icarusrestaurant.com. This formal contemporary American restaurant in the South End features chef Chris Douglass' seasonal creations, such as seared foie gras, porcini-crusted sea scallops, or the "pasta whim" of the day. There's also valet parking, as well as live jazz on weekends. Closed most major holidays. Dinner, Sun brunch. Bar. Jazz Fri evening. Converted 1860s building. Valet parking. **$$**

Back Bay

What to See and Do

Bean Pot Hockey. Phone 617/552-3000. www.bu.edu/athletics/icehockey. The Bean Pot refers to games between four Boston-based teams: Boston College, Boston University, Harvard University, and Northeastern University. Attending a hockey game between any two of the four is sure to be an intense experience, because all four teams compete vigorously for the Bean Pot each year. If you like to see body checking up close, get the lowest seats you can afford at any of the four corners of the rink. (Oct-Apr) **$$$$**

Berklee Performing Center at Berklee College of Music. *136 Massachusetts Ave (02115). Take the Green Line ("T") to the Hynes Convention Center/ICA stop. Exit left onto Massachusetts Ave and cross Boylston St. The Berklee Performance Center is about 30 yards from the corner. Phone 617/747-2261. www.berkleebpc.com.* The Berklee Performance Center is the performing arm of the Berklee College of Music, a prestigious Boston institution. Housed in a 1,200-seat renovated theater, this state-of-the-art venue hosts both student performances and national concerts, most notably featuring jazz and pop musicians. Ticket prices for nationally known performers are higher than admission fees for student performances. **$$**

The Bible Exhibit. *Belvidere St (02115), opposite the Prudential Center. Phone 617/450-3732.* Nondenominational exhibit; audiovisual activities; rare Biblical treasures; historical timeline; large Plexiglas wall-map with lighted journeys of six Biblical figures; historic editions; children's story corner; exploring center for reference; film and slide program on the hour. (Wed-Sun; closed Jan 1, Thanksgiving, Dec 25)

Blue Man Group. *74 Warrenton St (02116). Phone 617/931-2787. www. blueman.com.* Blue Man Group is a percussion (drums) band and performance group that's literally blue—all three members cover themselves in blue body paint. The group performs by thumping on drums, banging on barrels, and pounding on pipes. The heart-pounding, entertaining, dramatic performance includes audience members (although no one is forced to participate against his will); if you so choose, you may even get painted, too! Performances last just over two hours. (Closed Mon-Tues) **$$$$**

Boston Ballet. *270 Tremont St (02116). Phone 617/695-6955. www. bostonballet.com.* A delight for children and adults, the Boston Ballet offers classic and more contemporary performances by a company of some of the finest dancers in the world. If you're visiting Boston in late November or December, don't miss *The Nutcracker,* performed annually before more than 140,000 people, the largest audience for a ballet production in the world. (Performances held Oct-May) **$$$$**

Boston Breakers. *Harry Agganis Way at Commonwealth Ave (02215). Take the Massachusetts Turnpike (I-90) east to exit 18 (Cambridge-Allston). Bear right after the toll toward Cambridge. Turn right on Storrow Dr. Take the first exit (Boston University) just past the overpass. Right at stop sign on to Commonwealth Ave. Nickerson Field is located on the right-hand side at the fifth traffic light on Harry Agganis Way. Take the Green Line B to the Pleasant St stop. Phone 671/931-2000 or 781/292-1016. www.bostonbreakers.com.* The professional women's soccer team in the Boston area plays at Nickerson Field at Boston University. Unlike some professional sports that pay extraordinary base salaries that can lead to isolation among players, Breakers players are extremely accessible, offering autographs, appearing at youth soccer clinics and camps, and spending time in the community to promote the sport. (Closed Oct-Mar) **$$$$**

Boston Public Library. *700 Boylston St (02116). Phone 617/536-5400. www.btl.org.* (1895) This Italian Renaissance building by Charles McKim includes a central courtyard and fountain. Mural decorations, bronze doors, sculpture. Contemporary addition (1972), by Philip Johnson, houses large circulating library, recordings, and films. Film and author programs; exhibits. Central Library. (Daily; schedule may vary)

Boston Red Sox (MLB). *Fenway Park, 4 Yawkey Way (02215). Near Brookline Ave; take the Green Line (the "T" or subway) to Kenmore or Fenway. Phone 617/482-4SOX. www.redsox.mlb.com.* Going to Fenway isn't just about watching men play baseball; it's about steeping yourself in the tradition of one of the finest ball clubs in history. Fenway, built in 1901, is home of the Green Monster, the 37-foot, left-field wall where balls disappear in blazing green reflections. Cy Young pitched a perfect game at Fenway in 1904, and in 1914, young Babe Ruth came to play for the Sox. Since the Red Sox first began wearing numbers on their uniforms in 1931, the team has retired the uniforms of five players: Joe Cronin, Ted Williams, Bobby Doerr, Carl Yastremski, and Carlton Fisk. If you're unable to catch a Red Sox game, consider visiting the Pawtucket Red Sox (AAA Minors) in Pawtucket, RI (401/724-7300) or the Lowell Spinners (A Minors) in Lowell, MA (978/459-2255). (Mar-Oct) **$$$$**

Fenway Park Tours. *Fenway Park, 4 Yawkey Way (02215). Phone 617/236-6666. boston.redsox.mlb.com.* Take a tour of Fenway Park, not only the oldest park in Major League Baseball, but also the most charming. Soak in over 100 years of Red Sox history and tradition as you stroll next to the famous Green Monster (Fenway's 37-foot left-field wall that obscures even the easiest pop-ups), take a tour of the press box, and stand on the warning track. The brick stadium is aging by today's standards—views are obstructed, seats are small, and plush boxes are rare—so it, too, will likely be torn down to make way for a new one. Take a tour while you still can. (May-Sept, Mon-Fri) **$$**

Boston Symphony Orchestra/Boston Pops. *301 Massachusetts Ave (02115). Phone 617/266-1492. www.bso.org.* Symphony Hall, with its perfect acoustics, is home to both the Boston Symphony Orchestra (BSO) and the Boston Pops (a livelier version of the symphony), both of which are world-class orchestras. If the pricey tickets (up to $90) are an obstacle, stop by the box office at 9 am Friday or 5 pm Tuesday or Thursday—you may be able to pick up a special ticket for just $8, although it certainly won't be the best seat in the house. The Boston Pops also give free outdoor concerts in the Hatch Shell Amphitheater on the Esplanade during Harborfest in early July. If you're not in town while either orchestra is playing, find out which musical act is playing at Symphony Hall so that you can appreciate its terrific design. (BSO performances Oct-Apr; Pops performances May-early July, mid- to late Dec) **$$$$**

Boston University. *595 Commonwealth Ave (02115). Phone 617/353-2300 (tours); 617/353-2169 (information center).* (1839) 28,000 students. The information center is located at 771 Commonwealth Avenue in the George Sherman Union. Also located here is the George Sherman Union Gallery. Mugar Memorial Library houses papers of Dr. Martin Luther King, Jr., as well as those of Robert Frost, Isaac Asimov, and other writers and artists. Boston University Art Gallery exhibits at the School for the Arts, 855

Commonwealth Avenue. Campus tours from the Admissions Office, 121 Bay State Road.

Boston Women's Heritage Trail. *22 Holbrook St (02130). Phone 617/522-2872. www.bwht.org.* Women played an essential role in Boston's rich history, yet their contributions were often overlooked. The Boston Women's Heritage Trail (BWHT) leads you through Boston's historical, cultural, religious, and scientific sites, highlighting the critical part that women played in each. To walk the entire trail may take several days, but you can walk a portion of the trail and visit only the sites that interest you in just an hour or two. **FREE**

Brush Hill Tours. *14 Charles St S (02116). Phone 781/986-6100.* Fully lectured three-hour bus tours of Boston/Cambridge (Late Mar-mid-Nov); 1/2-day tours of Lexington/Concord, Salem/Marblehead (mid-June-Oct), and Plymouth (May-Oct); full-day tours of Cape Cod (includes Provincetown) and Newport, Rhode Island (June-Sept). Also 1 1/2-hour tours along Freedom Trail aboard the Beantown Trolleys. Departures from major downtown hotels, Copley Square, and Boston Common (Daily). **$$$$**

Copley Place. *100 Huntington Ave (02116). Phone 617/369-5000. www.shopcopleyplace.com.* With more than 100 stores and a glass atrium in a beautiful setting, Copley Place is all about upscale, including names like Neiman Marcus, Louis Vuitton, Christian Dior, and Gucci. If you're looking for dinner and a movie, Copley Place fills that bill, too, with ten restaurants and an 11-screen theater. (Mon-Sat 10 am-8 pm, Sun noon-6 pm)

Gibson House Museum. *137 Beacon St (02116). Phone 617/267-6338.* Victorian town house with period furnishings. Tours (May-Oct, Wed-Sun afternoons; Nov-Apr, Sat and Sun; closed holidays).

Guild of Boston Artists. *162 Newbury St (02116). Phone 617/536-7660.* Changing exhibits of paintings, graphics, and sculpture by New England artists. (Sept-July, Tues-Sat; closed Jan 1, Thanksgiving, Dec 25) **FREE**

Institute of Contemporary Art. *955 Boylston St (02115). Opposite Prudential Center. Phone 617/266-5152. www.icaboston.org.* The Institute of Contemporary Art offers some of the world's finest modern art exhibits. Because no collection is permanent, every trip to the Institute is likely to be different from the last. Note that museum admission is free every Thursday after 5 pm, as is the *Viewpoints* series, held at 6:30 pm on certain Thursdays, in which artists, staff members, and others speak to visitors about particular works of art. Allow two to four hours for a visit. (Wed, Sat-Sun noon-5 pm, Thurs to 9 pm, Fri to 7 pm; closed Mon-Tues, holidays) **$$**

Isabella Stewart Gardner Museum. *280 The Fenway (02115). Take the Green Line E ("T") to the Museum stop; walk 2 blocks straight ahead. Phone 617/566-1401. www.gardnermuseum.com.* The Gardner Museum is housed in the 19th-century home of Isabella Stewart Gardner that itself is a work of art. The collections include masterpieces from around the world—both paintings and sculptures—that are displayed year-round, and special exhibits are installed from time to time. You can spend from two hours to half a day at the museum. On weekends in fall, winter, and spring, look for free afternoon concerts. (Tues-Sun 11 am-5 pm; concerts late Sept-May; closed Jan 1, Thanksgiving, Dec 25) **$$$**

John Hancock Observatory. *Trinity Pl and St. James Ave (02116). At Copley Sq. Phone 617/572-6429.* The observatory, considered the best place to see Boston, is located on the 60th floor of the John Hancock Tower. It offers a panoramic view of Boston and eastern Massachusetts and exciting multi-media exhibits of Boston, past and present. They include "Boston 1775," a sound and light show about Boston since revolutionary days; a taped narration by the late Walter Muir Whitehill, architectural historian; and a lighted display of New England scenes. In addition, "Aviation Radio" allows visitors to tune in on the cross-talk between planes at Logan International's tower while viewing the action at the airport. (Daily; closed Thanksgiving, Dec 25) **$$$**

Kitchen Arts. *161 Newbury St (02116). Phone 617/266-8701.* Dubbed "a hardware store for cooks," Kitchen Arts isn't just any cooking store: it's the best-stocked cooking store you'll likely ever find—an absolute foodie's paradise. You'll find everything you see in ordinary culinary stores—pots and pans, mixing bowls, appliances, kitchen tools, knives, measuring cups, cutting boards, spatulas—but a greater variety and a much wider selection than anywhere else. (Mon-Sat 10 am-6 pm, Sun noon-5 pm; closed holidays) **FREE**

Louis Boston. *234 Berkeley St (02116). Phone 617/262-6100. www.louisboston.com.* Louis Boston is about as upscale as upscale gets; in fact, this men's and women's clothing store is considered among the finest in the world. The 140-year-old building is an architectural delight: it once housed the New England Museum of Natural History. Although Louis Boston has been at the location only since 1989, the company dates back to the late 1800s. The building also houses a café and a salon. (Mon-Tues 10 am-6 pm, Wed-Thurs to 7 pm, Fri-Sat to 6 pm; closed Sun, Easter, Thanksgiving, Dec 25)

Museum of Fine Arts. *465 Huntington Ave (02115). Take the Green Line E Phone 617/267-9300. www.mfa.org.* The Museum of Fine Arts (MFA) is a rare treasure, even if art museums have never been your favorite tourist spots. The vast number of collections are unique, combining classic and contemporary art with ancient artifacts. To see everything the museum has to offer takes from a half to a full day. If the museum seems intimidating, try taking a free guided tour before heading off to see what interests you. If you're hoping to see a particular exhibit, check the Web site before leaving on your trip. Note that from 4 pm-closing on Wednesdays, admission is free, although a $14 contribution is suggested. Also on Wednesday evenings throughout the summer, the MFA hosts courtyard concerts. (Mon-Tues 10 am-4:45 pm, Wed to 9:45 pm, Thurs-Fri to 5 pm, Sat-Sun to 5:45 pm) **$$$**

Newbury Street. *1-361 Newbury St (02116). www.newbury-st.com.* If you're a shop-a-holic, Newbury Street's eight blocks between Arlington Street and Massachusetts Avenue are a must-stop during your Boston vacation. Shops and galleries—from clothing to antiques to art galleries—tend to be pricey, so you may want to plan to window-shop only. Special finds include the

Society of Arts and Crafts (glassware, jewelry), Simeon Pearce (glassware), Kitchen Arts (gourmet kitchen supplies), and the Avenue Victor Hugo Bookshop. In fair weather, get a bite to eat at a café with outdoor seating and people-watch for an afternoon. Also consider visiting at Christmas, when the street lights up with decorations, music, and food.

Old South Church. *645 Boylston St (02116). Phone 617/536-1970. www.oldsouth.org.* Operating continuously as a church community since 1669, Old South Church began when colonists objected to Massachusetts' requirement that religious dissenters join the First Church of Boston and formed the Third Church of Boston (later Old South Church) in protest. The current building—sometimes referred to as New Old South Church—was completed in 1875 in a medieval architectural style that boasts impressive mosaics, stained glass, and cherry woodwork. (Worship held Sun 11 am)

Ryan Family Amusements. *Lansdowne St (02215). Underneath Fenway Park. Phone 617/267-8495. www.ryanfamily.com.* With 20 lanes, nearly a dozen pool tables, and an array of video games, Ryan's offers fun for the entire family. Fridays and Saturdays at 9:30 pm, enjoy cosmic bowling with laser lights and eardrum-bursting music. Other bowling alleys in the area include Boston Bowl (Boston), 820 William T Morrissey Blvd, 617/825-3800, and Lane & Games (Cambridge), 195 Concord Turnpike, 617/876-5533. (Mon, Wed-Thurs noon-11 pm; Tues from 9 am; Fri-Sat noon-midnight; Sun noon-9 pm) **$$$**

Shreve, Crump & Low. *330 Boylston St (02116). Phone 617/421-1880.* Any store that's over 200 years old is worth a visit, and Shreve's is no exception. For two centuries, this jewelry store has been selling engagement rings, watches, silver gifts, and estate jewelry. Now the oldest jeweler in the United States, the store also includes the country's oldest antique shop and oldest bridal registry. (Mon-Sat 10 am-5:30 pm; closed Sun, holidays)

Symphony Hall. *301 Massachusetts Ave (02115). Phone 617/266-1492.* Home of Boston Symphony (late Sept-early May) and Boston Pops (May-mid-July, Tues-Sun).

Tealuxe. *108 Newbury St (02116). Phone 617/927-0400. www.tealuxe.com.* Tealuxe, a tea lovers' utopia, offers more than 100 varieties of tea in its café. The interior architecture is reminiscent of a British estate, and jazz music plays in the background. You can also purchase teas to take home, along with teapots, teacups and mugs, and other tea paraphernalia. Don't let the historical significance of a tea shop in Boston escape you. Also check out a second location at Zero Brattle Street in Cambridge. (Mon-Thurs 8 am-8 pm, Fri to 10 pm, Sat 9 am-10 pm, Sun 9 am-8 pm; closed Thanksgiving, Dec 25) **FREE**

Trinity Church. *206 Clarendon St (02116). Phone 617/536-0944. www.trinity churchboston.org.* This Henry Hobson Richardson building is the noblest work of the architect. It was inspired by Phillips Brooks, the ninth rector of Trinity Church, and author of the Christmas carol, "O Little Town of Bethlehem." The church combines Romanesque design with beautiful frescos, Craftsman-style stained glass, and ornate carvings. Trinity still serves as an Episcopal church today, with services at 8 am, 9 am, 11 am, and 6 pm.

On Fridays at 12:15 pm, stop in for a free organ recital and take a guided or unguided tour. (Daily 8 am-6 pm) **$**

The Wang Theater/The Shubert Theater. *265 and 270 Tremont St (02116). Phone 617/482-9393. www.wangcenter.org.* Broadway shows, theater productions, dance and opera companies, and musical performers appear at the 3,600-seat Wang Theater, which is a world-class venue for the performing arts. Formerly called the Metropolitan Theater, The Wang Theater was designed to look like a French palace and has been completely restored to its original grandeur and beauty. The Shubert Theater next door hosts an impressive array of quality local theater, dance, and opera productions, many of which appeal to children. **$$$$**

Special Events

Charles River Regatta. *Harvard and Mass Ave bridges (02115). Phone toll-free 888/733-2678.* Third Sun in Oct.

Motel/Motor Lodge

★ ★ **BEST WESTERN BOSTON – THE INN AT LONGWOOD MEDICAL.** *342 Longwood Ave (02115). Phone 617/731-4700; toll-free 800/780-7234; fax 617/731-6273. www.bestwestern.com.* 155 rooms, 8 story. Check-out noon, check-in 3 pm. TV; cable (premium). In-room modem link. Restaurant. **$$**

Ⓓ ⬕

Hotels

★ ★ **BOSTON PARK PLAZA HOTEL AND TOWERS.** *64 Arlington St (02116). Phone 617/426-2000; toll-free 800/225-2008; fax 617/426-5545. www.bostonparkplaza.com.* 1,020 rooms, 15 story. Check-out noon, check-in 3 pm. TV; cable (premium). In-room modem link. Laundry services. Restaurant, bar. In-house fitness room. Health club privileges. Business center. Concierge. **$$**

🏋 🏃

★ ★ ★ **THE COLONNADE HOTEL.** *120 Huntington Ave (02116). Phone 617/424-7000; toll-free 800/962-3030; fax 617/424-1717. www. colonnadehotel.com.* Located in the historic area of Boston's Back Bay, this luxury hotel offers guests attentive service and spacious rooms. With the Hynes Convention Center conveniently located next door and Back Bay's elite shopping street just blocks away, this hotel makes for a truly comfortable stay. 292 rooms, 1 story. Pets accepted. Check-out noon. TV; cable (premium), VCR available. In-room modem link. Restaurant, bar. Room service. Supervised children's activities (May-Sept), ages 8-13. In-house fitness room. Outdoor pool, poolside service. Parking. Business center. Concierge. **$$**

Ⓓ 🛎 🛏 🏋 ⬕ 🏃

★ ★ **COPLEY SQUARE HOTEL.** *47 Huntington Ave (02116). Phone 617/536-9000; toll-free 800/225-7062; fax 617/267-3547. www.copleysquare*

hotel.com. 149 rooms, 7 story. Check-out noon, check-in 3 pm. TV; cable (premium). In-room modem link. Restaurant, bar. Concierge. Family-owned hotel; established in 1891. **$$**

D ⊠

★ ★ ★ **THE ELIOT SUITE HOTEL.** *370 Commonwealth Ave (02215). Phone 617/267-1607; fax 617/536-9114. www.eliothotel.com.* This hotel is located in the prestigious Back Bay area of Boston and is convenient to the Hynes Convention Center and various shopping, entertainment, and cultural sites. All suites feature French doors to the bedrooms, Italian marble baths, and down comforters. The hotel, surrounded by lush greenery, is also home to the critically acclaimed Clio restaurant (see) serving contemporary French-American cuisine. 174 rooms, 9 story. Pets accepted, some restrictions. Check-out noon, check-in 3 pm. TV; cable (premium), VCR available (movies). In-room modem link. Restaurant. Health club privileges. Valet parking. Business center. Concierge. **$$$$**

D ⊲ ⊠ 沃

★ ★ ★ **THE FAIRMONT COPLEY PLAZA BOSTON.** *138 St. James Ave (02116). Phone 617/267-5300; toll-free 800/527-4727; fax 617/247-6681. www.fairmont.com.* Ideally situated in the heart of the theater district, this landmark hotel was built in 1925 and is considered by many as the grande dame of Boston. Named after the great American painter John Singleton Copley, this traditional hotel still provides guests with elegant surroundings and superb service. The lobby flaunts an exquisitely high-domed ceiling with beautiful ornate furnishings, as well as dramatic marble pillars and some remarkable imported rugs. 379 rooms, 7 story. Pets accepted; fee. Check-out noon, check-in 3 pm. TV; cable (premium), VCR available. In-room modem link. Restaurant, bar. Room service. In-house fitness room. Valet parking. Business center. Concierge. **$$$**

D ⊲ 沃 ⊠ 沃

★ ★ ★ **HILTON BOSTON BACK BAY.** *40 Dalton St (02115). Phone 617/236-1100; toll-free 800/874-0663; fax 617/867-6104. www.hilton.com.* This hotel is ideally situated in the heart of Boston's historic Back Bay and adjacent to the Hynes Convention Center. From the meeting facilities with the state-of-the-art audio and visual equipment to the fitness room and indoor sky-lit swimming pool, this hotel charms both business and leisure travelers. 385 rooms, 26 story. Pets accepted, some restrictions; fee. Check-out noon, check-in 3 pm. TV; cable (premium). In-room modem link. Restaurant, bar. In-house fitness room. Indoor pool. Business center. Concierge. **$**

D ⊲ ⊷ 沃 ⊠ SC 沃

★ ★ ★ **LENOX HOTEL.** *61 Exeter St (02116). Phone 617/536-5300; toll-free 800/225-7676; fax 617/267-1237. www.lenoxhotel.com.* Experience the charm of this replica of a classic European hotel located in the heart of Boston. Considered by many as the "baby grande dame," this Boston landmark welcomes guests with personalized service, charmingly appointed guest rooms, and a level of elegance and style that exceeds even the most discriminating travelers' expectations. 214 rooms, 11 story. Check-out noon. TV; VCR available. In-room modem link. Many decorative and wood-burning fireplaces. Laundry services. Restaurant, bar. In-house fitness room. Airport transportation. Concierge. **$$$**

D 👤 ⊠

★ ★ ★ **MARRIOTT BOSTON COPLEY PLACE.** *110 Huntington Ave (02116). Phone 617/236-5800; toll-free 800/228-9290; fax 617/236-5885. www.marriott.com.* Ideally situated 4 miles from Logan Airport and just minutes from attractions such as the Museum of Fine Arts, Newbury Street shops, and Boston's Italian North End, this hotel boasts one of the largest ballrooms in New England and offers guests recreational activities as well a variety of dining options. 1,194 rooms, 38 story. Check-out noon. TV; cable (premium), VCR available (movies). In-room modem link. Restaurant, bar; entertainment. Room service. In-house fitness room, massage therapy, sauna. Game room. Indoor pool, whirlpool. Valet parking. Business center. Concierge. Luxury level. **$$**

D 🏊 👤 ⊠ SC 👤

★ ★ **RADISSON HOTEL BOSTON.** *200 Stuart St (02116). Phone 617/482-1800; toll-free 800/333-3333; fax 617/451-2750. www.radisson.com/ bostonma.* Centrally located in the heart of Boston and the theater district, this hotel caters to the business traveler but provides the comforts of home for the leisure traveler as well. Guests will enjoy the attentive service, spacious guest rooms, and exquisitely enclosed lap pool and well-maintained health club. 356 rooms, 24 story. Check-out noon, check-in 3 pm. TV; cable (premium). In-room modem link. Restaurant. In-house fitness room. Indoor pool. Golf on premise. Valet parking. **$$**

D 🐾 🏊 👤 ⊠

★ ★ ★ ★ **THE RITZ-CARLTON, BOSTON.** *15 Arlington St (02117). Phone 617/536-5700; toll-free 800/241-3333; fax 617/536-9340. www.ritzcarlton.com.* Distinguished and refined, The Ritz-Carlton is unquestionably the grande dame of Boston. This lovely hotel, faithfully restored to its 1920s splendor, has been a cherished city landmark for many years. Located across from Boston Common, this aristocratic hotel opens its doors to a rarefied world of genteel manners and distinguished surroundings. The guest rooms are a celebration of traditional style; luxurious marble bathrooms encourage soothing soaks. The suites include wood-burning fireplaces, and the hotel even offers a considerate fireplace butler service. The sun-filled Café is an ideal place for shoppers to take a break from the boutiques of Newbury Street, while a proper afternoon tea can be enjoyed in the Lounge. The Bar has a fascinating history, having survived Prohibition, and its wood-paneled walls and roaring fireplace exude a clubby feel. Long considered a local institution, The Dining Room (see) continues to delight guests with its polished service and sophisticated cuisine. 275 rooms, 17 story. Pets accepted, some restrictions. TV, cable. Restaurant. Room service. In-house fitness room, sauna. Airport transportation available. Concierge. **$$$$**

D 🐾 👤 ⊠

★ ★ ★ **SHERATON BOSTON HOTEL.** *39 Dalton St (02199). Phone 617/236-2000; toll-free 800/325-3535; fax 617/236-1702. www.sheraton.com.* Ideally located in the historic Back Bay and adjacent to the Hynes Convention Center, this hotel offers guests attentive service along with an elegant atmosphere. Offering a level of style that guests have come to appreciate, this hotel has been recently renovated and attractively furnished. For leisure excursions be sure to enjoy the indoor swimming pool, sundeck, sauna, and fitness center where a personal trainer is available to ensure a fabulous workout. 1,215 rooms, 29 story. Pets accepted, some restrictions. Check-out noon, check-in 3 pm. TV; cable (premium). In-room modem link. Laundry services. Room service 24 hours. Restaurant, bar; entertainment. In-house fitness room. Indoor pool, outdoor pool, whirlpool. Business center. Luxury level. **$$**

★ ★ ★ **THE WESTIN COPLEY PLACE.** *10 Huntington Ave (02116). Phone 617/262-9600; toll-free 800/937-8461; fax 617/424-7483. www.westin.com.* This grand hotel is located in the heart of the historic Back Bay and boasts some of the largest guest rooms in Boston along with panaromic views of the city. Conveniently connected by skybridge to the Hynes Convention Center and elite shopping at Copley Place, guests will find delight in the spacious and well-appointed guest rooms, as well as the superb service. 808 rooms, 36 story. Check-out noon, check-in 3 pm. TV; cable (premium). In-room modem link. Restaurant (see also PALM); entertainment. Room service. In-house fitness room, sauna. Health club privileges. Indoor pool, whirlpool. Valet parking. Airport transportation. Business center. Concierge. Luxury level. **$$**

★ ★ ★ **WYNDHAM CHELSEA HOTEL.** *201 Everett Ave (02150). Phone 617/884-2900; toll-free 877/999-3223; fax 617/884-7888. www.wyndham.com.* 195 rooms, 7 story. Check-out noon, check-in 4 pm. TV; cable (premium). In-room modem link. Restaurant, bar. In-house fitness room. Indoor pool, whirlpool. Business center. Concierge. **$**

All Suite

★ ★ ★ **DOUBLETREE HOTEL.** *400 Soldiers Field Rd (02134). Phone 617/783-0090; toll-free 800/222-TREE; fax 617/783-0897. www.doubletree .com.* From the spacious and luxurious guest rooms to the well-equipped business facility, this hotel offers a perfect oasis for both the business and leisure travelers. It is located on the beautifully scenic Charles River, and close to all of Boston's greater delights. 308 rooms, 15 story. Check-out noon. TV; cable (premium). In-room modem link. Laundry services. Restaurant, bar; entertainment Wed-Sat. In-house fitness room, sauna. Game room. Indoor pool, whirlpool. Business center. Concierge. On river. **$**

B&B/Small Inn

★ ★ **NEWBURY GUEST HOUSE.** *261 Newbury St (02116). Phone 617/437-7666; fax 617/262-4243. www.hagopianhotels.com.* 32 rooms, 4 story. Complimentary continental breakfast. Check-out noon, check-in 3 pm. TV. Restaurant. Parking. Built in 1882. **$**

D

Restaurants

★ ★ ★ **AMBROSIA ON HUNTINGTON.** *116 Huntington Ave (02116). Phone 617/247-2400; fax 617/247-4009. www.ambrosiaonhuntington.com.* Located next to Copley Place in the heart of Boston, Ambrosia on Huntington is an elegant, swanky spot to hunker down and dine on an exciting and eclectic array of sushi, sashimi, and contemporary seasonal dishes, many roasted to juicy perfection in the restaurant's rustic brick oven. The menu is the brainchild of chef-owner Anthony Ambrosia, who marries Asian and French flavors and techniques resulting in such signatures as an appetizer of a half lobster over Breton crêpes dressed with shiitake vinaigrette and a chive risotto with soy "peas." French menu with Asian influences. Closed some major holidays. Dinner. Bar. Casual attire. Valet parking (dinner). **$$$**

D

★ **BAR CODE.** *955 Boyleston St (02115). Phone 617/421-1818.* American menu. Dinner, late night. Bar. Casual attire. Outdoor seating. **$$**

D

★ ★ ★ **BRASSERIE JO.** *120 Huntington Ave (02116). Phone 617/425-3240. www.colonnadehotel.com.* Like its sister brasserie in Chicago, this restaurant serves authentic French, or more specifically Alsatian, cuisine with the usual flair of the Lettuce Entertain You group. Shoppers and theater attendees will delight in its location: the Colonnade Hotel next to Copley Place. French Bistro menu. Breakfast, lunch, dinner. Bar. Children's menu. Casual attire. Outdoor seating. **$$**

D

★ ★ **BROWN SUGAR CAFE.** *129 Jersey St (02215). Phone 617/266-2928. www.brownsugarcafe.com.* Thai menu. Closed Jan 1, July 4, Thanksgiving. Lunch, dinner. Bar. Casual attire. Outdoor seating. Totally nonsmoking. **$$**

D

★ ★ ★ **CAFE LOUIS.** *234 Berkley St (02116). Phone 617/266-4680; fax 617/375-9427. www.louisboston.com.* The waitstaff is quite friendly at this Back Bay offshoot that has roots in Providence's Al Forno restaurant. Traditionally influenced Italian menu. Closed Sun; most major holidays. Lunch, dinner. Jazz in summer. Casual attire. Free valet parking. Outdoor seating. Totally nonsmoking. **$$$**

D

★ ★ ★ **THE CAPITAL GRILLE.** *359 Newbury St (02115). Phone 617/262-8900; fax 617/262-9449. www.thecapitalgrille.com.* Steak menu. Closed July 4. Dinner. Bar. Valet parking. **$$$**

D

★ ★ **CASA ROMERO.** *30 Gloucester St (02115). Phone 617/536-4341; fax 617/536-6191. www.casaromero.com.* Mexican menu. Closed Jan 1, July 4, Dec 25. Dinner. Bar. Outdoor seating. Totally nonsmoking. **$$$**

D

★ **CHARLEY'S.** *284 Newbury St (02115). Phone 617/266-3000; fax 617/425-0261. www.great-food.com.* Seafood, steak menu. Lunch, dinner. Bar. Children's menu. Renovated Victorian school. Outdoor seating. **$$**

D

★ ★ **CIAO BELLA.** *240A Newbury St (02116). Phone 617/536-2626; fax 617/437-7585. www.ciaobella.com.* Italian menu. Closed Thanksgiving, Dec 25. Lunch, dinner. Bar. Casual attire. Reservations required. Valet parking. Outdoor seating. **$$$**

★ ★ ★ **CLIO.** *370 Commonwealth Ave (02215). Phone 617/536-7200; fax 617/578-0394. www.cliorestaurant.com.* Once you dine at Clio, you may want to write to chef-owner Ken Oringer and ask him to clone his modern American restaurant and open one in your neighborhood. Picture-perfect plates arrive and practically glisten with attention to detail. The presentations are so intricate that you may want to photograph rather than eat. Ingredients are treated like notes in a melody; each one complements the next, and the result is a culinary symphony. Fresh fish plays a big role on the menu, and for those who prefer their seafood raw, Clio has a separate sashimi bar that features a pricey selection of rare fish that Oringer has flown in from around the world. With food this global and attentive service to match, the room is jammed nightly with a who's who of Boston's media and financial elite. The energy of the room gives Clio a steady buzz of Bostonian social electricity, and the food coming out of the kitchen gives you reason to return. *Secret Inspector's Notes:* Be sure to inform the staff of your appetite level when dining at Clio, as the portions of some dishes are miniscule while others are generous. In addition, consult the serious waiters about your flavor preferences: some creations are more flavor-forward, while others are more appropriate for those interested in a milder dish. The wine selections are outstanding, and the staff will eagerly assist you in making a selection. Unfortunately, exotic sushi may not be enjoyed in the dining room, but only at the adjoining sushi bar. Breakfast, dinner, Sun brunch. Bar. Valet parking. **$$$**

★ ★ ★ **DAVIO'S.** *75 Arlington St (02116). Phone 617/357-4810.* Lunch, dinner. Bar. Children's menu. Casual attire. **$$**

D

★ ★ ★ **THE DINING ROOM.** *15 Arlington St (02117). Phone 617/536-5700; fax 617/536-9340. www.ritzcarlton.com.* Mentioning the "dining room" to an insider is like referring to Boston as "the city": One needs say no more.

Chef Mark Allen mixes and matches fresh ingredients with usually successful results. The view of the Public Gardens can't be beat. French menu. Closed Mon. Dinner, Sun brunch. Pianist. Children's menu. Jacket required. Valet parking. **$$$**

D

★ ★ ★ ★ **GRILL 23 & BAR.** *161 Berkeley St (02116). Phone 617/542-2255; fax 617/542-5114. www.grill23.com.* The restaurant market is filled with formulaic steakhouse concepts: lots of beef paired with lots of testosterone, served up in a dark wood-paneled boy's club of a room. Grill 23 may serve lots of beef (seven juicy cuts are available, and each is dry-aged USDA Prime sirloin) and indeed houses its share of testosterone (hoards of handsome men in suits line the buzzing bar), but this high-energy beefeater's heaven is formulaic in no other way. Set in the historic Salada Tea Building in Boston's Back Bay, Grill 23 & Bar is a vast and stunning space, with original sculptured ceilings, massive Corinthian columns, mahogany paneling, and hardwood and marble floors that give the space a sense of history and warmth. In addition to the terrific selection of USDA Prime sirloin prepared in the restaurant's grand exhibition kitchen, the menu offers exciting and decidedly non-steakhouse dishes as well, which explains why just as many women are in attendance as men. The "Fruits of the Sea" section includes tastings from the shimmering raw bar—lobster, shrimp, and clams—as well as caviar, sashimi, and assorted fish tartare, while entrées offer inventive American fare: roasted and grilled fish, poultry, lamb shanks, and the like. In colder months, the upstairs lounge is the place to be with its blazing fire and cozy seating. Seafood, steak menu. Menu changes weekly. Closed holidays. Dinner. Bar. Jacket required. Valet parking. **$$$**

D

★ **GYUHAMA.** *827 Boylston St (02116). Phone 617/437-0188.* Japanese menu. Lunch, dinner, late night. Bar. Casual attire. **$$**

★ ★ ★ ★ **HAMERSLEY'S BISTRO.** *553 Tremont St (02116). Phone 617/423-2700; fax 617/423-7710. www.hamersleysbistro.com.* Buttercup walls, mile-deep plush banquettes, authentic farmhouse wood-beamed ceilings, and a warm amber glow give Hamersley's Bistro the air of home. The food coming out of chef-owner Gordon Hamersley's lively open kitchen (Hamersley is usually on the line, cooking in a baseball hat) makes you realize that you are, in fact, not at home. If the food were this good at your home, it is doubtful that you would ever bother leaving. The house specialty, chicken roasted with garlic, lemon, and parsley, is the perfect example of how simple food can shine. The bird has a crisp, taut, golden skin, and its flesh is moist, succulent, and saturated with flavor. While the menu centers on hearty American bistro fare, do not take this to mean that the food here is boring, dull, or tired. Standards are expertly prepared with care and skill, and the kitchen is not afraid to bring in eclectic global flavors to create inventive dishes for guests who have been dining here for more than a decade. The kitchen also offers a weekly vegan special that could turn on the most ardent of carnivores. Hamersley's eclectic wine list changes with the seasons, as does the menu, and the restaurant's warm staff is more than happy (and very able) to help guide you to the right selection for your meal. *Secret Inspector's Notes:* Don't be confused by the casual décor and family-like treatment from the staff. The food at Hamersley's is as incredible as it gets. If it's a true flavor high you're seeking, this is the place. There are no stacked presentations, no ridiculous china, and no ingredients you've never heard of; just honest, breathtakingly perfect food like you wish you could make yourself. French, American menu. Closed holidays. Dinner. Bar. Valet parking. Outdoor seating. Totally nonsmoking. **$$$**

D

★ ★ **JAE'S CAFE AND GRILL.** *212 Stuart St (02116). Phone 617/451-7722; fax 617/451-7744.* Pan-Asian menu. Lunch, dinner. Bar. Casual attire. Totally nonsmoking. **$$**

D

★ ★ **KASHMIR.** *279 Newbury St (02116). Phone 617/536-1695; fax 617/536-1598. www.kashmirspices.com.* Indian menu. Lunch, dinner. Children's menu. Jacket (evenings). Valet parking. Outdoor seating. **$$$**

★ ★ ★ ★ **L'ESPALIER.** *30 Gloucester St (02115). Phone 617/262-3023; fax 617/375-9297. www.lespalier.com.* Housed in a charming 19th-century town house, L'Espalier makes it easy to slip into another era. The restaurant feels like a Merchant-Ivory film come to life. Luxuriously appointed with vintage drapes framing tall bay windows, fresh flowers, fine linens, and antique china adorning each table, L'Espalier is a decidedly sophisticated venue for a decadent and delicious dining experience. The menu is prepared with impeccable French technique and a nod to New England's regional ingredients and comfortable style. The chef prepares prix fixe and tasting menus as well as a Degustation of Caviar—each of five courses is prepared with caviar—for those feeling very indulgent. At L'Espalier, you'll find that your first bite tastes as good as your last. The kitchen consistently wows, sending out one extraordinary dish after another. A glorious monster of a wine list offers an amazing variety of wines and vintages, with a wide enough price range to allow for great choices under $50. Regional New England, French menu. Closed Sun; most major holidays. Dinner. Bar. Casual attire. Reservations required. **$$$**

D

★ ★ ★ **MASA.** *439 Tremont St (02116). Phone 617/338-8884.* Southwestern menu. Dinner, late night. Bar. Casual attire. Outdoor seating. **$$$**

D

★ ★ ★ **MISTRAL.** *223 Columbus Ave (02116). Phone 617/867-9300; fax 617/351-2601. www.mistralbistro.com.* Although the vaulted ceilings and sophisticated décor may scream glam central, chef Jamie Mammanno's creative cuisine departs from those kinds of expectations. Entrées such as veal carpaccio and tuna tartare are complemented by a superb wine list.

French, Mediterranean menu. Closed Thanksgiving, Dec 25. Dinner. Bar. Valet parking. **$$$**

D

★ ★ ★ **PALM.** *200 Dartmouth St (02116). Phone 617/867-9292; fax 617/867-0789. www.thepalm.com.* Italian, steak menu. Closed some major holidays. Lunch, dinner. Bar. Valet parking. **$$$**

D

★ ★ **TAPEO.** *266 Newbury St (02116). Phone 617/267-4799; fax 617/267-1602. www.tapeo.com.* Spanish menu. Closed major holidays. Dinner. Bar. Outdoor seating. **$$**

D

★ ★ ★ **VIA MATTA.** *79 Park Plz (02116). Phone 617/422-0008. www.viamattarestaurant.com.* Italian menu. Closed Sun. Lunch, dinner. Bar. Casual attire. **$$**

D

★ ★ **WHITE STAR TAVERN.** *565 Boylston St (02116). Phone 617/536-4477; fax 617/536-6022.* American menu. Closed Dec 25. Lunch, dinner, Sat-Sun brunch. Bar. Outdoor seating. **$$**

D

Boston Airport Area

Hotels

★ ★ ★ **HILTON BOSTON LOGAN AIRPORT.** *85 Terminal Rd (02128). Phone 617/569-9300; toll-free 800/774-1500; fax 617/568-6800. www.hilton.com.* Experience the quiet elegance and superb service of this state-of-the-art luxury hotel located inside Boston Logan Airport. 603 rooms, 10 story. Pets accepted, some restrictions. Check-out 11 am, check-in 3 pm. TV; cable (premium). In-room modem link. Restaurant, bar. In-house fitness room. Indoor pool, poolside service. Free airport transportation. Business center. Concierge. **$**

D 🐾 ➦ 👫 ✈ 🏊 🚶

★ ★ ★ **HYATT HARBORSIDE.** *101 Harborside Dr (02128). Phone 617/568-1234; toll-free 800/233-1234; fax 617/567-8856. www.hyatt.com.* Located adjacent to Logan Airport, this elegant hotel has a friendly staff, spacious guest rooms, and a meeting facility designed with the business traveler in mind. For leisure activities, guests can enjoy the indoor lap pool or premier health and fitness center—both with views of the scenic waterfront and Boston skyline. 277 rooms, 15 story. Check-out noon, check-in 3 pm. TV; cable; VCR available. In-room modem link. Restaurant, bar. In-house fitness room, sauna. Indoor pool, whirlpool. Free airport transportation. Business center. Adjacent to water shuttle. **$$**

D ➦ 👫 💆 ✈ 🏊 SC 🚶

Side Trips — Day Trips

History abounds in Boston and its outlying areas. You can take a tour of Harvard University in Cambridge. You can see where the "Father of the Beat Generation," Jack Kerouac, grew up in Lowell. You can also explore the site of the famed Salem Witch Trials. Take a day to travel to some of Boston's surrounding cities—it will greatly enhance your trip.

Cambridge

6 minutes; 3 miles from Boston

Settled 1630 **Pop** 101,355 **Elev** 40 ft **Area code** 617

Information Chamber of Commerce, 859 Massachusetts Ave, 02139; 617/876-4100

Web www.cambcc.org

The city of Cambridge—academically inclined, historically rich, internationally flavored—occupies an enviable geographic position alongside the northern banks of the Charles River. It is home to two of the nation's most prestigious institutions of higher learning, Harvard University and the Massachusetts Institute of Technology (MIT). The Radcliffe Institute for Advanced Study and Lesley University can also be found here. It should come as no surprise that one-fourth of Cambridge's 95,000 residents are students and that one-sixth of the city's jobs are in higher education.

A group of approximately 700 Puritans set sail from England in 1630, making their way across the Atlantic Ocean to the Massachusetts Bay Colony, where they settled in the area now known as Cambridge. The nation's oldest university, Harvard, was founded six years later. At the time of the American Revolution, Cambridge existed as a quiet farming village, its population comprised mainly of descendants of the original Puritans. Over the course of the 18th century, an increasing number of immigrants, mostly Irish, arrived. The immigration trend continued into the 20th century, with Italians, Portuguese, and Russians seeking a better life in this hamlet to the immediate northwest of Boston. Today, Cambridge is well known for its diversity and multiculturalism, a reputation underscored by the fact that 80 different nations are represented by the children attending the city's public schools.

Cambridge offers a vibrant nightlife, with numerous restaurants, theaters, and clubs surrounding the city's squares: Central Square, Harvard Square, and Inman Square. Some of the best entertainment can be enjoyed on the city's sidewalks, where street performers—ranging from illusionists to musicians to puppeteers—often draw large crowds. Like most college towns, Cambridge has plenty of bookshops. One of the most popular is Curious George Goes to WordsWorth, a two-story bookshop housing more than 20,000 children's titles.

What to See and Do

Cambridge Antique Mall. *201 Msgr O'Brien Hwy (02140). Take the Green Line ("T") to the Lechmere stop. Phone 617/868-9655. www.marketantique.com.* Stroll through five floors of antique furniture, books, artwork, toys, clothing, and more. More than 150 dealers offer up antiques here, which seems most appropriate in this historic town. Although no one's making any promises, you can't help but wonder whether a dresser or rocking chair once sat prominently in John Hancock's house or Paul Revere's workshop. (Tues-Sun 11 am-6 pm; closed holidays)

Christ Church. *Garden and Mason sts at the Common. Phone 617/876-0200. www.firstchurchcambridge.org.* (1759) Episcopal. The oldest church building in Cambridge. A fine Georgian colonial building designed by Peter Harrison that was used as a colonial barracks during the Revolution. (Daily) **FREE**

The Dance Complex. *536 Massachusetts Ave (02139). Take the Red Line to the Central Square MBTA station, exit toward Pearl St/Main St. Phone 617/547-9363.* Ready to dance the night away but need to first brush up on your skills? Sashay into The Dance Complex, a not-for-profit dance studio that offers drop-in classes in everything from salsa to hip-hop. With more than 60 teachers on staff, you're sure to find a class to fit your needs. After you're ready to rumba, check out www.havetodance.com for links to some of the best dancing venues in Boston. (Mon-Thurs 9 am-9:30 pm, Fri to 9 pm, Sat to 6 pm, Sun 10 am-5 pm) **$$$**

Formaggio Kitchen. *244 Huron Ave (02138). Phone 617/354-4750. www. formaggiokitchen.com.* Whether you consider yourself a *gourmet* or a *gourmand*, you'll easily lose yourself in this culinary playground. With a selection of 200 artisanal cheeses, the finest pastas, chocolates from Italy, France, and the US, as well as a variety of exotic spices, mouthwatering snacks, and Italian coffees, the famed Formaggio Kitchen is a food-lover's dream. While you're here, pick up some professional-quality cutlery or select one of the many gift baskets for a foodie friend back home. A second location has opened in South Boston at 268 Shawmut Avenue.

Grolier Poetry Book Shop. *6 Plympton St (02138). Take the Red Line ("T") to Harvard Square. Phone 617/547-4648. www.grolierpoetrybookshop.com.* With more than 15,000 volumes of poetry, Grolier's is a gathering place for poets and those who delight in poetry books and readings. The shop holds weekly readings on Tuesdays, Fridays, or Sundays. The oldest continuously operating poetry bookshop in the US, the store is now nearly 80 years old. (Mon-Sat noon-6:30 pm; closed Sun, holidays)

✪ **Harvard University.** *24 Quincy St (02138). Harvard Sq.* 18,179 students. This magnificent university, America's oldest, was founded in 1636. Two years later, when a minister named John Harvard died and left half his estate and his considerable personal library, it was named for him. Includes Harvard and Radcliffe colleges as well as ten graduate and professional schools. Harvard Yard, as the original campus is called, is tree-shaded and occupied by stately red-brick buildings. In and around the yard are

Harvard Medical Area. *Huntington and Longwood aves (02115). Phone 617/432-1000.* One of the world's great centers of medicine.

Harvard Museum of Natural History. *26 Oxford St (02138). Phone 617/495-3045. www.hmnh.harvard.edu.* The Harvard Museum of Natural History (HMNH) combines three museums in one: a botanical museum that examines the study of plants, the museum of zoology that examines the study of animals, and a geological museum that examines the study of rocks and minerals. All three explore the evolution of science and nature throughout time. A collection of glass models of plants—more than 3,000 plant lookalikes rendered carefully in glass—is the only exhibit of its kind in the world. (Daily; closed July 4, Thanksgiving, Dec 25, Jan 1) **$$**

Harvard University Art Museums. *32 Quincy St (02138). Phone 617/495-9400. www.artmuseums.harvard.edu.* Three museums make up the Harvard Art Museums: the Fogg Art Museum (including wide-ranging collections of paintings and sculpture), the Busch-Reisinger Museum (which features mostly German art), and the Arthur M. Sackler Museum (offering ancient art, plus Asian and Islamic collections). Admission to one museum covers all three; allow a half-day for all. Entry to the museums is free on Wednesdays and Saturdays until noon. (Mon-Sat 10 am-5 pm, Sun 1-5 pm; closed holidays) **$$**

The Houses of Harvard-Radcliffe. *Between Harvard Square and the Charles River, and NE of Harvard Yard between Shepard and Linnaean sts.*

Information Center. *1350 Massachusetts Ave (02138). Phone 617/495-1573.* Provides maps, brochures. (June-Aug, daily; rest of year, Mon-Sat) Student-guided tours begin here.

John F. Kennedy School of Government. *79 JFK St (02138), on the banks of the Charles River.* (1978) Contains a library, classrooms, and a public affairs forum for lectures.

Massachusetts Hall. *24 Quincy St (02138).* Oldest building (1720) and architectural inspiration for the campus. **FREE**

Peabody Museum of Archaeology and Ethnology. *11 Divinity Ave (02138). Phone 617/496-1027. www.peabody.harvard.edu.* Anthropology and ethnology are sciences that record how humans develop culturally. The Peabody Museum, one of the oldest anthropology museums in the world, traces human cultural history in the Western Hemisphere with four major exhibits. In addition, the museum sponsors interactive programs for kids, public lectures, and summer science camps. (Daily 9 am-5 pm; closed Jan 1, July 4, Thanksgiving, Dec 25) **$$**

University Hall. *Harvard Yard (02138). Phone 617/495-0450.* (1813-1815) Designed by Charles Bulfinch, made of Chelmsford granite in contrast to the surrounding brick, and one of the Yard's most handsome buildings. **FREE**

Widener Library. *1329 Massachusetts Ave (02138). South side of Harvard Yard. Phone 617/495-4166.* (1915) Has an enormous Corinthian portico; more than 3 million books. Near it are Houghton, with a fine collection of rare books, and Lamont, the first undergraduate library in America. **FREE**

House of Blues. *96 Winthrop St (02138). Take the Red line ("T") to Harvard. Phone 617/491-2583. www.hob.com.* This isn't any old chain version of House of Blues, but the original location that drips with hipness. Concerts include performers from Etta James and James Taylor to Norah Jones and John Mayer (**$$$$**). The food is southern and bluesy, too, so stop off for dinner on the way. On Sunday mornings, catch the roof-raising Gospel Sunday Brunch (**$$$$**) at 10 am, noon, or 2 pm. (Mon-Wed 11:30-1 am; Thurs-Sat to 2 am; Sun 4:30 pm-1 am) **$$$**

Longfellow National Historic Site. *105 Brattle St (02138), 1/2 mile from Harvard. Phone 617/876-4491.* This Georgian-style house, built in 1759, was Washington's headquarters during the 1775-1776 siege of Boston, and Henry Wadsworth Longfellow's home from 1837 until his death in 1882. Longfellow taught at Harvard, and his books are located here. (Daily; closed Jan 1, Thanksgiving, Dec 25) **$$**

Massachusetts Institute of Technology (MIT). *77 Massachusetts Ave (02139). Phone 617/253-4795. www.mit.edu.* (1861) 9,500 students. One of the greatest science and engineering schools in the world. On the Charles River, the campus includes 135 acres of impressive neoclassic and modern buildings. Information center in the lobby of the main building; guided tours, two departures (Mon-Fri). On campus are

Hart Nautical Galleries. *55 Massachusetts Ave (02139).* Shows ship and marine engineering development through displays of rigged merchant and naval ship models; changing exhibits. (Daily) **FREE**

List Visual Arts Center at MIT. *Wiesner Building, 20 Ames St (02139).* Changing exhibits of contemporary art. (Oct-June, daily; closed holidays; free) The MIT campus also has an outstanding permanent collection of outdoor sculpture, including works by Calder, Moore, and Picasso, and significant architecture, including buildings by Aalto, Pei, and Saarinen. Walking tour map at information center.

MIT Museum. *265 Massachusetts Ave (02139). Phone 617/253-4444.* Collections and exhibits that interpret the Institute's social and educational history, developments in science and technology, and the interplay of technology and art. (Tues-Sun; closed Mon, holidays) **$$**

Radcliffe College's Schlesinger Library Culinary Collection. *10 Garden St (02138). Take the Red Line ("T") to the Harvard Square station. Walk through Harvard Square, down Brattle St; Radcliffe Yard is 3 blocks away, at the corner of Brattle and James sts. Phone 617/495-8647. www.radcliffe.edu/schles.* Through Radcliffe's culinary collection, you'll have access to more than 9,000 cookbooks and other culinary texts. Although you can't borrow from the library, you can conduct culinary research by tapping into the books of some of the world's greatest chefs, including Samuel Narcisse Chamberlain, Julia Child, and Sophie Coe. (Mon-Tues, Thurs-Fri 9 am-5 pm, Wed 9 am-8 pm; closed holidays, Dec 25-Jan 1) **FREE**

The Radcliffe Institute for Advanced Study. *Admissions office at 8 Garden St (02138). Phone 617/495-8601.* (1879) 2,700 women. Coordinate institution with Harvard. Unique women's educational and scholarly resources, including the Arthur and Elizabeth Schlesinger Library on the History of Women in America (at 3 James St). More than 850 major collections of history of women from 1800 to present.

Special Event

Head of the Charles Regatta. *The race starts on the Charles, near Boston University. Take the Green Line B to Boston University and walk to the BU Bridge. Phone 617/868-6200. www.hocr.org.* The Head of the Charles Regatta is a 3-mile rowing race that involves 7,000 athletes, 1,470 rowing shells, and 300,000 spectators. Oarspeople, including Olympic and World champions, Olympic medalists, and national champions from around the world, race the Charles River, from Boston to Cambridge and under the Charles Eliot Bridge to the finish line. In addition, after the close of the Head of the Charles Regatta, you can watch the Charles Schwab Championship sprint at 5 pm Sunday, when the top three rowers from the preceding day's Championship Single take to their shells for a 550-meter dead sprint along the Charles, from River Street Bridge to the Weeks Footbridge. Late Oct. **FREE**

Motels/Motor Lodges

★ **BEST WESTERN HOMESTEAD INN.** *220 Alewife Brook Pkwy (02138). Phone 617/491-8000; toll-free 800/491-4914; fax 617/491-4932. www.bestwestern.com.* 69 rooms, 4 story. Complimentary continental breakfast. Check-out noon. TV; cable (premium). In-room modem link. Indoor pool, whirlpool. **$**
🏊 🖨 SC

★ ★ **DOUBLETREE HOTEL.** *110 Mount Auburn St (02138). Phone 617/864-5200; toll-free 800/458-5886; fax 617/864-2409. www.doubletree.com.* 73 rooms, 4 story. Pets accepted, some restrictions; fee. Check-out noon, check-in 3 pm. TV; cable (premium). In-room modem link. Babysitting services available. **$$**
D 🐾 🖨 SC

★ ★ ★ **DOUBLETREE HOTEL.** *1201 Massachusetts Ave (02138). Phone 617/491-2222; toll-free 800/458-5886; fax 617/520-3711. www. theinnatharvard.com.* Located in the heart of Harvard Square and just steps away from museums, shopping, and theaters, this hotel offers elegance and warmth. 113 rooms, 4 story. Check-out noon. TV. Laundry services. Restaurant, bar. Room service. Valet parking. In-room modem link. Concierge. **$$**

D ⇘ SC

Hotels

★ ★ ★ **THE CHARLES HOTEL.** *1 Bennett St (02138). Phone 617/864-1200; toll-free 800/882-1818; fax 617/864-5715. www.charleshotel.com.* This upscale hotel just off Harvard Square defines luxury lodging in Cambridge. For that reason, it attracts celebrities and other high-profile guests, as well as the wealthy parents of Harvard students. Its guest rooms mix Shaker-inspired design with a multitude of modern amenities—duvets, high-speed Internet access, three two-line phones, Bose Wave radios, color televisions in the bathrooms, and more. Dine in either of its two restaurants, and be sure to tune into the sweet sounds of jazz at the Regattabar, where swingin' national bands hit the stage. The hotel also has an onsite athletic center with indoor pool, a day spa, and indoor parking. 293 rooms, 10 story. Pets accepted, some restrictions; fee. Check-out noon, check-in 3 pm. TV; cable (premium), VCR available. In-room modem link. Restaurant, bar. Room service 24 hours. Babysitting services available. In-house fitness room, spa, massage, steam room. Indoor pool, whirlpool. Valet parking. Concierge. **$$**

D ⇗ ⇘ ⋔ ⇘ SC

★ ★ **HOLIDAY INN.** *30 Washington St (02143). Phone 617/628-1000; toll-free 800/465-4329; fax 617/628-0143. www.holiday-inn.com.* 184 rooms, 9 story. Check-out noon. TV; cable (premium). In-room modem link. Laundry services. Restaurant, bar. In-house fitness room, sauna. Indoor pool, whirlpool. Free parking. **$$**

D ⇘ ⋔ ⇘ SC

★ ★ ★ **HYATT REGENCY CAMBRIDGE.** *575 Memorial Dr (02139). Phone 617/492-1234; toll-free 800/233-1234; fax 617/441-6489. www.hyatt.com.* Ideally situated along the picturesque Charles River and with views of the alluring Boston skyline, guests are offered a level of style and comfort that one comes to expect from the Hyatt. From the lavishly appointed lobby and spacious guest rooms, as well as the charming gazebo nestled in the well-maintained courtyard, guests will immediately feel relaxed and welcomed. 479 rooms, 16 story. Check-out noon, check-in 4 pm. TV; cable (premium), VCR available. In-room modem link. Restaurant, bar. In-house fitness room, sauna, steam room. Indoor pool, whirlpool. Business center. Concierge. Luxury level. **$**

D ⇘ ⋔ ⇘ ⇗

★ ★ ★ **MARRIOTT BOSTON CAMBRIDGE.** *2 Cambridge Ctr (02142). Phone 617/494-6600; toll-free 800/228-9290; fax 617/494-0036. www.marriott.com.* Nestled in the heart of the Cambridge Business Community and just a couple miles from Logan International Airport, this hotel offers guests all the comforts of home. Rooms are spacious and have been equipped with guests' needs in mind. Guests can relax in the indoor pool or enjoy a invigorating workout in the well-maintained health club. Nearby attractions include downtown Boston, Harvard Square, and the Museum of Science. 444 rooms, 26 story. Check-out noon, check-in 4 pm. TV; cable (premium), VCR available. In-room modem link. Laundry services. Restaurant, bar; entertainment. In-house fitness room, massage, sauna. Health club privileges. Indoor pool, whirlpool, poolside service. Valet parking. Business center. Luxury level. **$**

D ⇌ 🏃 ⛖ 🏃

★ ★ ★ **ROYAL SONESTA HOTEL.** *5 Cambridge Pkwy (02142). Phone 617/806-4200; toll-free 800/766-3782; fax 617/806-4232. www.sonesta.com/boston.* Perched along the Charles River, this magnificent hotel offers guests panaromic Boston views, handsomely appointed and spacious guest rooms, as well as a state-of-the-art health spa featuring massage therapists, reflexology, and an indoor and outdoor pool with a retractable roof and sun deck. This luxury hotel is ideally situated across from the waterfront shopping area and next door to the Museum of Science. 421 rooms, 10 story. Check-out noon, check-in 3 pm. TV; cable (premium). In-room modem link. Restaurant, bar. Room service. In-house fitness room, massage. Health club privileges. Indoor/outdooor pool. Concierge. **$$**

D ⇌ 🏃 ⛖ SC

★ ★ ★ **SHERATON COMMANDER HOTEL.** *16 Garden St (02138). Phone 617/547-4800; toll-free 800/535-5007; fax 617/868-8322. www.sheraton.com.* 199 rooms, 7 story. Check-out noon, check-in 3 pm. TV; cable (premium). In-room modem link. Restaurant, bar. In-house fitness room. Concierge. **$**

D 🏃 ⛖ SC

B&B/Small Inn

★ ★ ★ **A CAMBRIDGE HOUSE BED AND BREAKFAST INN.** *2218 Massachusetts Ave (02140). Phone 617/491-6300; toll-free 800/232-9989; fax 617/868-2848. www.acambridgehouse.com.* Despite its location in metro Boston, about 1 1/2 miles from Harvard Square, this cozy inn offers couples the perfect setting for a romantic getaway. Many of the guest rooms in this turn-of-the-century, three-story frame house have heavenly four-poster beds lavishly dressed with fine linens and pillows, and most have gas-log fireplaces. In warm weather, the lovely backyard garden adds even more charm. The nightly rate includes a hearty breakfast buffet and hors d'oeuvres and pasta in the evening. 15 rooms. Complimentary full breakfast.

Check-out noon, check-in 2 pm. TV. In-room modem link. Free parking. Victorian house (1892) lavishly decorated in period style. **$$**

D 🖼

Restaurants

★ ★ **ARGANA.** *1287 Cambridge St (02139). Phone 617/868-1247.* Moroccan, Mediterranean menu. Breakfast, lunch, dinner, late night. Bar. Casual attire. **$$**

D

★ ★ **BLUE ROOM.** *1 Kendall Sq (02139). Phone 617/494-9034.* Closed July 4, Thanksgiving, Dec 24-25. Dinner, Sun brunch. Bar. Pianist Sun. Outdoor seating. **$$**

★ **BOMBAY CLUB.** *57 JFK St (02138). Phone 617/661-8100; fax 617/661-6956. www.bombayclub.com.* Indian menu. Closed Thanksgiving, Dec 25. Lunch, dinner, Sat-Sun brunch. Bar. Totally nonsmoking. **$$**

D

★ ★ **CHEZ HENRI.** *1 Shepard St (02138). Phone 617/354-8980; fax 617/441-8784.* Cuban, French menu. Closed Memorial Day, July 4. Dinner. **$$$**

D

★ ★ **DALI.** *415 Washington St, Somerville (02143). Phone 617/661-3254; fax 617/661-2813. www.dalirestaurant.com.* Spanish menu. Closed most major holidays; also Dec 31. Lunch, dinner. Bar. **$$$**

D

★ ★ **EAST COAST GRILL.** *1271 Cambridge St (02139). Phone 617/491-6568; fax 617/868-4278.* Guests should plan to wait during peak hours at this local favorite—strong margaritas, fresh dishes, and friendly staff keep guests coming back. Although the menu focuses on seafood, vegetarians will delight in the "All Vegetable Experience of the Day," which piles all the side dishes onto a huge plate with grilled vegetables. Barbecue, Caribbean, seafood menu. Closed Dec 25. Dinner. **$$$**

D

★ **GRENDEL'S DEN.** *89 Winthrop St (02138). Phone 617/491-1160; fax 617/491-1050.* International menu. Closed Thanksgiving, Dec 24-25. Lunch, dinner. Bar. Casual attire. Outdoor seating. **$$**

D

★ ★ ★ **HARVEST.** *44 Brattle St (02138). Phone 617/868-2255; fax 617/868-5422.* This restaurant has returned under new ownership, the same three partners who own Grill 23, and offers American dishes enhanced by classic techniques. Guests will enjoy the open kitchen, great bread, and large number of seafood choices, as well as the nightly risotto special. American menu. Lunch, dinner. Children's menu. Outdoor seating. **$$$**

D

★ ★ **HELMAND.** *143 1st St (02142). Phone 617/492-4646; fax 617/497-6507. www.helmand.com.* Afghan menu. Closed Jan 1, Thanksgiving, Dec 25. Dinner. Totally nonsmoking. **$$**

D

★ **LA GROCERIA.** *853 Main St (02139). Phone 617/876-4162; fax 617/864-9566.* Italian menu. Closed Jan 1, Thanksgiving, Dec 25. Lunch, dinner. Bar. Children's menu. Valet parking (weekends). **$$**

D

★ **MUQUECA.** *1093 Cambridge St (02139). Phone 617/354-3296; fax 617/492-0665.* Brazilian menu. Closed Mon; holidays. Lunch, dinner. Children's menu. Casual attire. **$$**

★ **REDBONES.** *55 Chester St (02144). Phone 617/628-2200; fax 617/625-5909. www.redbonesbbq.com.* Barbecue menu. Closed Thanksgiving, Dec 25. Lunch, dinner. Bar. **$$**

D

★ ★ ★ **RIALTO.** *1 Bennett St (02138). Phone 617/661-5050; fax 617/234-8093. www.rialto-restaurant.com.* Located in the Charles Hotel, Rialto is home to chef/owner Jodi Adams' distinctive brand of boldly flavored Mediterranean-inspired fare. Adams' approach to food is honest and straightforward, paying homage to the seasons and to fresh, locally grown fruits and vegetables. This approach allows her to create stellar up-to-the-minute dishes from the varying culinary regions of France, Italy, and Spain. If you'd like to actually enjoy your dinner, try not to fill up on the basket of incredible home-baked breads beforehand. A complementary wine list features more than 100 bottles from Spain, Italy, France, and the United States. The sunny room is filled with deep, dramatic, high-backed banquettes; flower-topped tables; and richly colored hardwood floors and is lined with soaring floor-to-ceiling windows equipped with vintage wooden shutters. The effect is a sophisticated yet immensely comfortable urban space—a room that seduces you into lingering over dessert, cheese, and after-dinner drinks. *Secret Inspector's Notes:* An unassuming room and incredibly friendly staff set the perfect tone for enjoying Jody Adams' creative Mediterranean cuisine. The staff is gracious in recommending specialty dishes, and no course, from creative cocktails to sinful desserts, will disappoint. Dining on the other side of the Charles River for a change from downtown Boston's formality is truly a joy. French, Mediterranean menu. Closed holidays. Dinner. Bar. Children's menu. Casual attire. **$$$**

D

★ ★ **ROKA.** *1001 Massachusetts Ave (02138). Phone 617/661-0344.* Japanese menu. Lunch, dinner. Casual attire. **$$**

D

★ ★ ★ **SALTS.** *798 Main St (02139). Phone 617/876-8444; fax 617/876-8569. www.salts.netrelief.com.* This newcomer to Central Square is a tiny neighborhood place with mustard-colored walls and purple wainscoting that has people all over town talking. The simple food has a slight Eastern

European accent, and the atmosphere is quiet and elegant. Closed Mon. Dinner. **$$**

★ ★ **SANDRINE'S.** *8 Holyoke St (02138). Phone 617/497-5300; fax 617/ 497-8504. www.sandrines.com.* The casual but attentive service and colorful, elegant décor add to this Alsatian restaurant's appeal. French menu. Closed Jan 1, Labor Day, Dec 25. Lunch, dinner. Bar. Children's menu. Casual attire. Totally nonsmoking. **$$$**

D

★ ★ **TEMPLE BAR.** *1688 Massachusetts Ave (02138). Phone 617/547-5055. www.templebarcambridge.com.* American menu. Dinner, Sat-Sun brunch. Bar. Casual attire. **$$**

D

Cape Cod

Barnstable

1 hour 40 minutes; 89 miles from Boston
See also Hyannis, South Yarmouth

Settled 1637 **Pop** 47,821 **Elev** 37 ft **Area code** 508 **Zip** 02630

Information Cape Cod Chamber of Commerce, Rtes 6 and 132, PO Box 790, Hyannis 02601-0790; 508/362-3225 or 888/33-CAPECOD

Web www.capecodchamber.org

Farmers first settled Barnstable because the marshes provided salt hay for cattle. Later, the town prospered as a whaling and trading center, and when these industries declined, land development made it the political hub of the Cape. It is the seat of Barnstable County, which includes the entire Cape. Like other Cape communities, it does a thriving resort business.

What to See and Do

Cape Cod Art Association Gallery. *3480 Rte 6A (02630). Phone 508/362-2909.* Changing exhibits, exhibitions by New England artists; demonstrations, lectures, classes. (Apr-Nov, daily, limited hours; rest of year, inquire for schedule) **FREE**

Cape Cod Pathways. *3225 Rte 6A (02630). Phone 508/362-3828. www.cape codcommission.org/pathways.* This network of walking and hiking trails is composed of a perfect mix of dirt, sand, and gravel, and when completed will link all the towns in Cape Cod. The Cape Cod Commission oversees the trails and produces a detailed map, yours for the asking by calling or writing. Don't miss the Cape Walk in early June, in which hearty souls hike from one end of the cape to another, or the Walking Weekend in late October, when trail guides lead walks and hikes of varying lengths. (Daily) **FREE**

Donald G. Trayser Memorial Museum. *In Old Custom House and Post Office, Main St on Cobb's Hill, Rte 6A (02630).* Phone 508/362-2092. Marine exhibits, scrimshaw, Barnstable silver, historic documents. (July-mid-Oct, Tues-Sat afternoons)

Hyannis Whale Watcher Cruises. *Barnstable Harbor, 269 Mill Way (02630). Contact PO Box 254.* Phone 508/362-6088. View whales aboard the *Whale Watcher,* a 297-passenger super-cruiser, custom designed and built specifically for whale watching. Naturalist on board will narrate. Café on board. (Apr-Oct, daily) Reservations necessary. **$$$$**

Mill Way Fish and Lobster Market. *276 Mill Way (02630).* Phone 508/362-2760. www.millwayfish.com. Mill Way is both a restaurant that specializes in seafood and vegetarian dishes, and a take-out market, offering fried and grilled dishes, pastas, cod cakes, salads, and other on-the-go meals. Try the unique shellfish sausage that's stuffed with shrimp, lobster, and scallops. (Tues-Sun 10 am-8 pm; closed Mon)

Sturgis Library. *3090 Main St (02630).* Phone 508/362-6636. Oldest library building (1644) in US has material on the Cape, including maritime history; genealogical records of Cape Cod families. Research fee for nonresidents. (Mon-Sat; closed holidays; limited hours) **$$**

West Parish Meetinghouse. *2049 Meetinghouse Way, West Barnstable (02668).* Phone 508/362-4385. (1717) Said to be the oldest Congregational church in the country; restored. Congregation established in London, 1616. Regular Sun services are held here all year. **FREE**

B&B/Small Inns

★ ★ ★ **ACWORTH INN.** *4352 Old Kings Hwy, Rte 6A (02637).* Phone 508/362-3330; toll-free 800/362-6363; fax 508/375-0304. www.acworthinn.com. Whether guests come here to relax and unwind or for a romantic getaway, this bed-and-breakfast has everything one needs for both. Guests can enjoy a day of sightseeing, mountain biking, or golf and then return to enjoy a nice cozy evening in the gathering room. 5 rooms. Some A/C, 2 story. No room phones. Children over 12 years only. Complimentary full breakfast. Check-out 11 am, check-in 3-7 pm. TV in common room. Concierge. Farmhouse built in 1860. Totally nonsmoking. **$**

★ ★ ★ **ASHLEY MANOR.** *3660 Main St (02630).* Phone 508/362-8044; toll-free 888/535-2246; fax 508/362-9927. www.ashleymanor.net. A lovely garden and gazebo adorn this beautiful inn. Guests can unwind with a book in the library or relax with afternoon tea in front of the fire. Some activities available to guests include whale watching, beaches, biking, and even off-Cape excursions. 6 rooms, 2 story. Phone available. Children over 14 years only. Complimentary full breakfast. Check-out 11 am, check-in 2 pm. Many fireplaces. Tennis. Lawn games. Restored early 18th-century inn on 2-acre estate. **$**

★ ★ ★ **BEECHWOOD INN.** *2839 Main St (02630). Phone 508/362-6618; toll-free 800/609-6618; fax 508/362-0298. www.beechwoodinn.com.* Situated near Barnstable Village, guests can enjoy biking, whale watching, and golf. For the guest who prefers a relaxing vacation, sit on the porch and enjoy an iced tea or lemonade while you rock on the gliders. 6 rooms, 3 story. No room phones. Complimentary full breakfast. Check-out 11 am, check-in 2 pm. Lawn games. Restored Victorian house (1853); veranda with rocking chairs, glider. Totally nonsmoking. **$**

★ ★ **HONEYSUCKLE HILL B&B.** *591 Old King's Hwy, Rte 6A (02668). Phone 508/362-8418; toll-free 800/444-5522; fax 508/362-8386. www.honeysucklehill.com.* 5 rooms, 2 story. Children over 12 years only. Complimentary full breakfast. Check-out 11 am, check-in 3 pm. Built in 1810. Restored Victorian décor. **$**

Restaurants

★ ★ **BARNSTABLE TAVERN AND GRILLE.** *3176 Main St (02630). Phone 508/362-2355; fax 508/362-9012.* Seafood menu. Closed Dec 24-25. Lunch, dinner. Bar; entertainment. Children's menu. Outdoor seating. Inn and tavern since 1799. **$$**

D

★ ★ **HARBOR POINT.** *Harbor Point Rd (02630). Phone 508/362-2231.* Seafood, steak menu. Closed Feb-Mar. Lunch, dinner, Sun brunch. Bar; entertainment. Children's menu. Fountain. **$$**

D

★ ★ **MATTAKEESE WHARF.** *271 Mill Way (02630). Phone 508/362-4511; fax 508/362-8826.* Seafood menu. Closed late Oct-early May. Lunch, dinner, brunch. Bar; entertainment weekends. Children's menu. Valet parking. **$$**

Bourne

1 hour 40 minutes; 89 miles from Boston
See also Buzzards Bay, Sandwich

Settled 1627 **Pop** 18,721 **Elev** 19 ft **Area code** 508 **Zip** 02532

Information Cape Cod Chamber of Commerce, Rtes 6 and 132, PO Box 790, Hyannis 02601-0790; 508/362-3225 or 888/33-CAPECOD

Web www.capecodchamber.org

Named for Jonathan Bourne, a successful whaling merchant, this town has had a variety of industries since its founding. Originally a center for herring fishing, the town turned to manufacturing stoves, kettles, and later, freight cars. Bourne's current prosperity is derived from cranberries and tourism.

What to See and Do

Aptucxet Trading Post. *24 Aptucxet Rd (02532), off Shore Rd, 1/2 mile W of Bourne Bridge. Phone 508/759-9487.* A replica of a 1627 trading post that may have been the first of its kind in America. Native American artifacts; rune stone believed to be proof of visits to the area by the Phoenicians in 400 BC; artifacts in two rooms. On grounds are herb garden, site of original spring, saltworks; railroad station built for President Grover Cleveland for use at his Gray Gables home, his summer White House; Dutch-style windmill; picnic area adjacent to Cape Cod Canal. (July-Aug, daily; last two weekends in May and June and Sept-mid-Oct, Tues-Sun) **$**

Bourne Scenic Park. *375 Scenic Hwy (02532). North bank of Cape Cod Canal. Phone 508/759-7873.* Playground, picnicking; bike trails; swimming pool, bathhouse; recreation building; camping (fee); store. (Apr-May, weekends; June-Oct, daily) **$$**

Pairpoint Crystal Company. *851 Sandwich Rd (Rte 6A), Sagamore (02561). Phone 508/888-2344.* (est 1837) Handmade lead crystal ware, glassblowing demonstrations. Viewing (Mon-Fri). Store (Daily). **FREE**

Brewster

1 hour 40 minutes; 89 miles from Boston

Settled 1656 **Pop** 10,094 **Elev** 39 ft **Area code** 508 **Zip** 02631

Information Cape Cod Chamber of Commerce, Rtes 6 and 132, PO Box 790, Hyannis 02601-0790; 508/362-3225 or 888/33-CAPECOD

Web www.capecodchamber.org

What to See and Do

Cape Cod Museum of Natural History. *869 Rte 6A (02631). Phone 508/896-3867; toll-free 800/479-3867.* Exhibits on wildlife and ecology of the area; art exhibits; library; lectures; nature trails; field walks; trips to Monomoy Island. Gift shop. (Daily; closed holidays) **$$**

Cape Cod Repertory Theater Company. *3379 Rte 6A (02631). Phone 508/896-1888. www.caperep.org.* Boasting both an indoor and outdoor theater, the Cape Cod Repertory Theater offers a children's theater two mornings per week (Tues and Fri) in July and August. In addition, you'll find productions for the whole family in the outdoor theater, which sits back in the beautiful woods near Nickerson State Park and is open in fair weather. The indoor theater offers plays and musicals year-round. **$$$**

★ **New England Fire & History Museum.** *1439 Main St (02631). 1/2 mile W of MA 137 on Rte 6A. Phone 508/896-5711.* This six-building complex houses an extensive collection of fire-fighting equipment and includes the Arthur Fiedler Memorial Fire Collection; diorama of Chicago fire of 1871; engines dating from the Revolution to the 1930s; world's only 1929 Mercedes Benz fire engine; life-size reproduction of Ben Franklin's firehouse; 19th-century blacksmith shop; largest apothecary shop in the country contains 664 gold-leaf bottles of medicine; medicinal herb gardens; library; films; theater performances. Guided tours. Picnic area. (Memorial Day weekend-mid-Sept, daily; mid-Sept-Columbus Day, weekends) **$$$**

Nickerson State Park. *3488 Rte 6A (02631). Phone 508/896-3491. www.state.ma.us/dem/parks/nick.htm.* Nickerson State Park offers an unusual experience on Cape Cod: densely wooded areas that show no signs of the marshy areas that abound on the Cape. Nickerson offers camping, challenging hiking trails, an 8-mile bike path that connects to the Cape Cod Rail Trail (a 25-mile paved bike trail), fishing, swimming, canoeing, and birdwatching. Also consider areas on the Cape that offer similar activities: Green Briar Nature Center in Sandwich, Lowell Holly Reservation in Mashpee, Ashumet Holly and Wildlife Sanctuary in East Falmouth, Great Island Trail in Wellfleet, Coatue-Coksata-Great Point on Nantucket. (Daily) **FREE**

Ocean Edge Golf Course. *2660 Rte 6A (02631). Phone 508/896-9000. www.oceanedge.com.* This beautiful golf course, just a stone's throw from the ocean, offers 6,665 yards of manicured greens, plus five ponds for challenging play. Play during the week in the off-season, and you'll pay extremely reasonable greens fees. Lessons from PGA pros are available. The course is part of a resort that offers accommodations, tennis courts and lessons, a private beach, and 26 miles of paved bike trails (bike rentals are available). (Daily; closed for snow and enclement weather) **$$$$**

Stoney Brook Mill. *830 Stony Brook Rd (02631). Phone 508/896-1734. Old Grist Mill in West Brewster, on site of one of first gristmills in America.* Museum upstairs includes historical exhibits, weaving. Corn grinding (July and Aug, Thurs-Sat afternoons). **FREE**

Resort

★ ★ ★ OCEAN EDGE RESORT. *2907 Main St (02631). Phone 508/896-9000; toll-free 800/343-6074; fax 508/896-9123. www.oceanedge.com.* Ideally situated on the charming Cape Cod Bay and surrounded by lush gardens, this charming English country manor offers guests an oasis of comfort and privacy, while being surrounded by understated elegance and superb service. Discover the charm and character of this 19th-century mansion and carriage house. From the quiet elegance of their luxurious guest rooms to the championship 18-hole golf course, 11 tennis courts, and premiere health and fitness center, this resort offers timeless tranquility and complete relaxation for a romantic weekend or a quiet business retreat. 406 rooms, 2 story. Check-out 11 am, check-in 3 pm. TV; VCR available (movies). In-room modem link. Fireplaces. Dining room, bar; entertainment. Room service. Supervised children's activities (June-Sept), ages 4-12. In-house fitness room, sauna. Two indoor pools, four outdoor pools, whirlpool, poolside service. Golf on premise, greens fee $68. Outdoor tennis. Lawn games. Bicycle rentals. Hiking. Airport transportation. Business center. Concierge. **$$**

B&B/Small Inns

★ ★ **BRAMBLE INN.** *2019 Main St (02631). Phone 508/896-7644; fax 508/896-9332. www.brambleinn.com.* Family owned and operated, this attractive inn with its pine floors, lovely antiques, and charmingly appointed guest rooms offer guests a truly delightful stay. 8 rooms, 2 story. No room phones. Closed Jan-Apr. Children over 8 years only. Complimentary full breakfast. Check-out 11 am, check-in 2 pm. TV in some rooms; cable (premium). Restaurant. Intimate, country atmosphere. **$**

★ ★ ★ **BREWSTER FARMHOUSE INN.** *716 Main St (02631). Phone 508/896-3910; toll-free 800/892-3910; fax 508/896-4232. www.brewster farmhouseinn.com.* Get away from it all, rejuvenate and relax at this charming and elegant inn. Built in 1846 and set amidst a country-like setting, this inn has been charmingly restored and offers guests a delightful stay. 8 rooms, 2 story. Some rooms with shower only, some share bath. No room phones. Children over 16 years only. Complimentary full breakfast. Check-out 11 am, check-in 3 pm. TV; cable (premium). Outdoor pool, whirlpool. Lawn games. Built in 1850; antiques and reproductions. Totally nonsmoking. **$**

★ ★ **CAPTAIN FREEMAN INN.** *15 Breakwater Rd (02631). Phone 508/896-7481; toll-free 800/843-4664; fax 508/896-5618. www.captainfreeman inn.com.* 12 rooms, 3 story. Some room phones. Children over 10 years only. Complimentary full breakfast. Check-out 11 am, check-in 2 pm. TV; VCR (free movies). Game room. Outdooor pool. Lawn games. Free airport transportation. Concierge. House built in 1866. Totally nonsmoking. **$**

★ ★ **ISAIAH CLARK HOUSE.** *1187 Main St (02631). Phone 508/896-2223; toll-free 800/822-4001; fax 508/896-2138. www.isaiahclark.com.* 7 rooms, 2 story. Children over 10 years only. Complimentary full breakfast. Check-out 11 am, check-in 2-5 pm. TV in most rooms. Many room phones. Former sea captain's house (1780). Totally nonsmoking. **$**

★ ★ **OLD SEA PINES INN.** *2553 Main St (02631). Phone 508/896-6114; fax 508/896-7387. www.oldseapinesinn.com.* 24 rooms, 3 story. No room phones. Children over 8 years only except in family suites. Complimentary full breakfast. Check-out 11 am, check-in 2 pm. Room service. Service bar. Founded in 1907 as School of Charm and Personality for Young Women. On 3 1/2 acres. Breakfast in bed available. Totally nonsmoking. **$**

★ ★ **POORE HOUSE INN.** *2311 Main St (02631). Phone 508/896-0004; toll-free 800/233-6662; fax 508/896-0005. www.capecodtravel.com/poore.* 5 rooms, 2 story. Pets accepted; fee. Children over 8 years only. Complimentary full breakfast. Check-out 11 am, check-in 2 pm. Built in 1837. Totally non-smoking. **$$**

★ ★ **RUDDY TURNSTONE.** *463 Main St (02631). Phone 508/385-9871; toll-free 800/654-1995; fax 508/385-5696. www.ruddyturnstone.com.* 5 rooms, 2 story. No room phones. Children over 10 years only. Complimentary full breakfast. Check-out 11 am, check-in 1 pm. Lawn games. Concierge. Early 19th-century Cape Cod house; antique furnishings. Totally nonsmoking. **$**

Restaurants

★ ★ ★ **BRAMBLE INN.** *2019 Main St (02631). Phone 508/896-7644; fax 508/896-9332. www.brambleinn.com.* This restaurant is located in the charming Bramble Inn (see), in the heart of the historic district. Chef/owner Ruth Manchester delights guests with her creative cuisine and heartwarming hospitality. A perfect choice for a romantic dinner. Closed Mon-Wed off season; also Jan-Apr. Dinner. Built in 1861; four dining areas, including an enclosed porch. Totally nonsmoking. **$$$**

★ ★ ★ **CHILLINGSWORTH.** *2449 Main St (02631). Phone 508/896-3640; fax 508/896-7540. www.chillingsworth.com.* This restaurant is located on the 300-year-old Chillingsworth Foster estate that has 6 acres of lawns and gardens. The nightly seven-course table d'hote menu features creative French cuisine. Menu changes daily. Lunch, dinner, Sun brunch. **$$$**

⎣D⎦

★ ★ ★ **OLD MANSE INN AND RESTAURANT.** *1861 Main St (02631). Phone 508/896-3149; fax 508/896-1546. www.oldmanseinn.com.* The casual restaurant of this inn, located in the heart of Cape Cod's historic district, serves a world menu prepared by the chef/owners, both graduates of the Culinary Institute of America. Closed Mon; Jan-Apr. Dinner. Two dining rooms in early 19th-century inn; antiques. Guest rooms available. Totally nonsmoking. **$$**

Buzzards Bay

1 hour 40 minutes; 89 miles from Boston

Pop 3,549 **Elev** 10 ft **Area code** 508 **Zip** 02532

Information Cape Cod Chamber of Commerce, Rtes 6 and 132, PO Box 790, Hyannis 02601-0790; 508/362-3225 or 888/33-CAPECOD

Web www.capecodchamber.org

Cape Cod is said to face "four seas": Buzzards Bay, Nantucket Sound, the Atlantic Ocean, and Cape Cod Bay. The shore is jagged and irregular, dotted with hundreds of summer resorts, public and private beaches, yacht clubs, and fishing piers.

The area of Buzzards Bay is at the west entrance to the Cape Cod Canal. Among the better-known towns on the mainland shore are Nonquit and South Yarmouth (see), west of New Bedford, and Fairhaven, Crescent Beach, Mattapoisett, Wareham, and Onset, to the east. On the Cape side are Monument Beach, Pocasset, Silver Beach, West Falmouth, Woods Hole, and the string of Elizabeth Islands, which ends with Cuttyhunk.

What to See and Do

Cape Cod Canal Cruises. *Onset Town Pier. 3 miles W via Rtes 6 and 28. Phone 508/295-3883.* Cruises with historical narration. Also evening cocktail and entertainment cruises. (June-Oct, daily; May, Sat and Sun) **$$$$**

Porter's Thermometer Museum. *49 Zarahemla Rd, Onset (02532). Just E of the junction of I-495 and I-195. Phone 508/295-5504.* Heralded as the only museum of its kind in the world, the Porter Thermometer Museum in tiny Onset houses some 2,600 distinct specimens. Varieties include those used by astronauts, ones that can be worn as earrings, and temperature-telling instruments from around the world. One thermometer from Alaska can accurately record temperatures all the way down to -100 degrees! Run by former high school science teacher Richard Porter out of his house, the museum is free, as long as you call ahead. Make sure to admire the world's largest thermometer out front, which can be read from as far away as a mile. **FREE**

Motel/Motor Lodge

★ **BAY MOTOR INN.** *223 Main St (02532). Phone 508/759-3989; fax 508/759-3199. www.capecodtravel.com/baymotorinn.* 17 rooms, 1-2 story. Closed mid-Nov-Mar. Pets accepted, some restrictions; fee. Check-out 11 am. TV; cable (premium). Outdooor pool. **$**

Centerville

1 hour 40 minutes; 89 miles from Boston
See also Hyannis (Cape Cod)

Pop 9,190 **Elev** 40 ft **Area code** 508 **Zip** 02632

Information Cape Cod Chamber of Commerce, Rtes 6 and 132, PO Box 790, Hyannis 02601-0790; 508/362-3225 or 888/33-CAPECOD

Web www.capecodchamber.org

What to See and Do

Centerville Historical Society Museum. *513 Main St (02632). Phone 508/775-0331.* Houses 14 exhibition rooms interpreting Cape Cod's history, art, industry, and domestic life. Displays include early American furniture, housewares, quilts; dolls, costumes; Crowell carved birds, Sandwich glass collection, marine room, tool room, research library. (June-mid-Sept, Wed-Sun; winter by appointment) **$$**

Osterville Historical Society Museum. *155 W Bay Rd, Osterville (02655). 3 miles SW, at junction West Bay and Parker rds. Phone 508/428-5861.* Sea captain's house with 18th- and 19th-century furnishings; Sandwich glass, Chinese porcelain, majolica and Staffordshire pottery; doll collection. Special events throughout the summer. Boat-building museum, ship models; catboat *Cayugha* is on display. Restored Cammett House (circa 1730) is on grounds. (Mid-June-Sept, Thurs-Sun afternoons; other times by appointment) **$$**

Motels/Motor Lodges

★ **CENTERVILLE CORNERS MOTOR LODGE.** *1338 Craigville Beach Rd (02632). Phone 508/775-7223; toll-free 800/242-1137; fax 508/775-4147. www.centervillecorners.com.* 48 rooms, 2 story. Closed Dec-Apr. Pets accepted, some restrictions; fee. Complimentary continental breakfast. Check-out 11 am. TV. Sauna. Indoor pool. Lawn games. **$**

★ **TRADE WINDS INN.** *780 Craigville Beach Rd (02632). Phone 508/775-0365; toll-free 877/444-7966. www.twicapecod.com.* 35 rooms, 2 story. Closed Nov-Mar. Complimentary continental breakfast. Check-out 11 am. TV. Private beach opposite. **$**

B&B/Small Inn

★ ★ **ADAM'S TERRACE GARDENS INN.** *539 Main St (02632). Phone 508/775-4707. www.adamsterrace.com.* 5 rooms, 2 story. No A/C. No room phones. Complimentary full breakfast. Check-out 11 am, check-in 3-6 pm. TV. Built circa 1830. Totally nonsmoking. **$**

Chatham

1 hour 40 minutes; 89 miles from Boston

Settled 1656 **Pop** 6,625 **Elev** 46 ft **Area code** 508 **Zip** 02633

Information Chamber of Commerce, PO Box 793; 800/715-5567; or the Cape Cod Chamber of Commerce, Rtes 6 and 132, PO Box 790, Hyannis 02601-0790; 508/362-3225 or 888/CAPECOD

Web www.capecodchamber.org

Chatham is among the Cape's fashionable shopping centers. Comfortable estates in the hilly country nearby look out on Pleasant Bay and Nantucket Sound. Monomoy Island, an unattached sand bar, stretches 10 miles south into the sea. It was once a haunt of "moon-cussers"—beach pirates who lured vessels aground with false lights and then looted the wrecks.

What to See and Do

Chatham Light. *Bridge and Main sts (02633). Phone 508/862-0700.* Chatham Light is a quintessential Cape Cod lighthouse: gleaming white, with a charming keeper's house attached. Originally built with two towers to distinguish the signal from a single lighthouse farther north, the first pair—built of wood—decayed three decades later. A second pair, made of brick, fell to the beach far below when bad weather eroded the cliff on which they were built. A third pair was built inland, and one was moved to Nauset Beach and forever disconnected from her Chatham sister. Today, the lighthouse offers a superb view of the Atlantic and seals on the beach below, and the Coast Guard uses the keeper's house as its station. (Daily) **FREE**

Clambake Celebrations. *1223 Main St (02633). Phone 508/945-7771. www.clambake-to-go.com.* For the easiest clam and lobster takeout on the Cape, visit Clambake Celebrations for simple packages that you steam and eat. You can also pick up complete meals with complementary side dishes, utensils, and bibs. If, after you leave, you need to taste fresh seafood again, you can have a meal for two or four people FedExed to you anywhere in the United States. (Mon-Sat 9 am-3 pm; closed Sun, Jan 1, July 4, Dec 25)

Gristmill. *Shattuck Pl, off Cross St (02633). W shore of Mill Pond in Chase Park. Phone 508/945-5158.* (1797) (Daily) **FREE**

Monomoy National Wildlife Refuge. *Monomoy Island (02633). Take Rte 6 east to State Rte 137 south to State Rte 28 east to the Coast Guard Station. Take the first left after the Chatham Lighthouse, and then take the first right. Follow signs for the refuge, which is on your left off Morris Island Rd. Phone 508/945-0594 or 508/443-4661.* The Monomoy National Wildlife Refuge is 2,750 acres of birdlover's paradise. You'll spot a wealth of shorebirds all year 'round, although the spectacle is greatest in spring, when birds exhibit bright plumage while breeding. Also visit Sandy Neck Recreation Area in Barnstable, Wellfleet Bay/Audubon Sanctuary in Brewster, Crane Reservation in Mashpee, and Beech Forest in Provincetown. **FREE**

Old Atwood House. *347 Stage Harbor Rd (02633). Phone 508/945-2493.* (1752) Chatham Historical Society. Memorabilia of Joseph C. Lincoln, Cape Cod novelist. Shell collection, murals by Alice Stallknecht, "Portrait of a New England Town." China trade collection. Maritime collection. (Mid-June-Sept, Tues-Fri afternoons; Sat mornings; schedule may vary) **$$**

Railroad Museum. *Depot Rd and Main St (02633). Phone 508/945-5199.* Restored "country railroad depot" houses scale models, photographs, railroad memorabilia, and relics; restored 1910 New York Central caboose. (Mid-June-mid-Sept, Tues-Sat) **DONATION**

Top Rod and Cape Cod Charters. *1082 Orleans Rd (02650). Next to Ryders Cove. Phone 508/945-2256. www.capefishingcharters.com.* Captain Joe Fitzback takes you to Cape Cod's prime saltwater fishing areas, providing tackle, bait, and anything else you need to bring in the big one. Although a day's adventure will cost you a bundle, each additional person adds little to the cost, so plan on bringing a group and splitting the fee. (May-Oct by reservation; closed Nov-Apr) **$$$$**

Special Events

Band Concerts. *Kate Gould Park. Main St (02633). Phone 508/362-3225.* Fri evening. Late June-early Sept.

Monomoy Theatre. *776 Main St (02633). Phone 508/945-1589.* Ohio University Players in comedies, musicals, dramas, classics. Tues-Sat. Late June-late Aug.

Motels/Motor Lodges

★ **CHATHAM HIGHLANDER.** *946 Main St (02633). Phone 508/945-9038; fax 508/945-5731. www.realmass.com/highlander.* 28 rooms. Closed Dec-Apr. Check-out 10:30 am. TV. Outdoor pool. **$**

D ⌾ ⊠

★ **THE CHATHAM MOTEL.** *1487 Main St (02633). Phone 508/945-2630; toll-free 800/770-5545. www.chathammotel.com.* 32 rooms. Closed Nov-Apr. Check-out 11 am. TV; cable (premium). Outdoor pool. Lawn games. In pine grove. **$**

D ⌾ ⊠

★ **CHATHAM SEAFARER.** *2079 Main St (02633). Phone 508/432-1739; toll-free 800/786-2772; fax 508/432-8969. www.chathamseafarer.com.* 20 rooms. Check-out 11 am. TV. Lawn games. **$**

⊠

★ **CHATHAM TIDES WATERFRONT MOTEL.** *394 Pleasant St (02659). Phone 508/432-0379. www.allcapecod.com/chathamtides.* 24 rooms. Some A/C. Check-out 11 am. TV. On private beach. **$**

D

★ ★ **DOLPHIN OF CHATHAM INN AND MOTEL.** *352 Main St (02633). Phone 508/945-0070; toll-free 800/688-5900; fax 508/945-5945. www.dolphininn.com.* Dating from 1805 and amid the treasures of Chatham, this inn charmingly combines old-world nostalgia with modern amenities. Imagine being surrounded by beautifully lush trees and just a brief walk from the beach, fine restaurants, and some divine shops. Guest rooms are all elegantly furnished. Discover the charms of this inn and prepare for a remarkable stay. 38 rooms. Check-out 10 am. TV. Restaurant. Outdoor pool, whirlpool. **$$**

D ⌾ ⊠

★ **THE HAWTHORNE.** *196 Shore Rd (02633). Phone 508/945-0372. www.thehawthorne.com.* 26 rooms. Closed mid-Oct-mid-May. Check-out 11 am. TV. On private beach. **$**

Resorts

★ ★ **CHATHAM BARS INN.** *297 Shore Rd (02633). Phone 508/945-0096; toll-free 800/527-4884; fax 508/945-6785. www.chathambarsinn.com.* Built in 1814, this grand and elegant Cape Cod landmark has managed to maintain all of the historic charm of a bygone era. Beauty and allure are reflected in the charmingly appointed guest rooms, some of which offer private decks along with breathtaking views of Pleasant Bay. With well-maintained gardens and a private beach just steps away, guests can not help but find serenity and peace of mind amidst the luxurious setting. 205 rooms, 1-3 story. No elevator. Check-out 11 am, check-in 3 pm. TV; VCR available (free movies). In-room modem link. Dining room, bar; entertainment (in season). Room service. Free supervised children's activities (Mid-June-Labor Day), ages 4-12. In-house fitness room. Outdoor pool. Outdoor tennis. Lawn games. Complimentary boat shuttle. Concierge. Spacious cottages. Some A/C. On 22 acres; private beach. **$$**

[D] [⌕] [⛷] [⼈]

★ ★ ★ **PLEASANT BAY VILLAGE RESORT.** *1191 Orleans Rd (02633). Phone 508/945-1133; toll-free 800/547-1011; fax 508/945-9701. www.pleasantbayvillage.com.* From the exquisitely arranged rock garden where a waterfall bravely cascades its way down into a stone-edged pool and offers guests a delighted view of colorful and flashing koi, to the lavishly appointed gardens, this woodland retreat welcomes guests to a place of timeless tranquility. 58 rooms. Closed mid-Oct-mid-May. Check-out 11 am. TV. In-room modem link. Restaurant. Room service. Outdoor pool, poolside service. Lawn games. On 6 landscaped acres. **$$**

[⌕] [⛏]

★ ★ ★ **WEQUASSETT INN.** *On Pleasant Bay (02633). Phone 508/432-5400; toll-free 800/225-7125; fax 508/432-5032. www.wequassett.com.* Enjoy the warmth and elegance of this lovely inn located on Chatham's picturesque waterfront. From the quiet luxury of the rooms and suites charmingly furnished in a country house style to the extensive leisure excursions offered, this inn offers a delightful stay and memorable visit. 98 rooms, 1-2 story. Closed mid-Nov-mid-Apr. Check-out 11 am, check-in 3 pm. TV; cable (premium), VCR available. Dining room. Room service. Supervised children's activities (in season), ages 3-12 years. In-house fitness room, massage. Outdoor pool, poolside service. Outdoor tennis. Lawn games; bocce, croquet, shuffleboard. Sailboats, windsurfing, deep-sea fishing charters, whale-watching cruises. Airport transportation available. Business center. **$$**

[D] [⛷] [⌕] [⼈] [⛏] [⼈]

B&B/Small Inns

★ ★ ★ **CAPTAIN'S HOUSE INN.** *369-377 Old Harbor Rd (02633). Phone 508/945-0127; toll-free 800/315-0728; fax 508/945-0866. www.captainshouseinn.com.* Once a sea captain's estate, this charming inn was built in 1839, and features exquisite period wallpapers, Williamsburg antiques, and elegantly refined Queen Anne chairs. Some of the charmingly appointed guests rooms are named after the ships the captain skippered. 16 rooms, 2 story. Complimentary full breakfast. Check-out 11 am, check-in 2 pm. TV in some rooms; VCR available. Fireplaces. Outdoor pool. Lawn games. Bicycles. Concierge. Totally nonsmoking. **$$**

[D] [⌕] [⛏]

★ ★ ★ **CHATHAM TOWN HOUSE INN.** *11 Library Ln (02633). Phone 508/945-2180; toll-free 800/242-2180; fax 508/945-3990. www.chatham townhouse.com.* Once a sea captain's estate, this charming inn has undergone many transformations over the years, yet has still maintained the elegance and style of yesterday. Guests will find some of the old hemlock floors as well as original woodwork characterizing the harpoon and oar motifs still in place. Enjoy any one of the attractively furnished guest rooms offering a picturesque water or garden view, as well as romantic canopies and private balconies. 29 rooms, 2 story. Complimentary full breakfast. Check-out noon, check-in 3 pm. TV; cable (premium). Fireplace in cottages. Pool, whirlpool, poolside service. In Chatham historical district. Totally nonsmoking. **$**

D ⌦ ☒

★ ★ ★ **CRANBERRY INN.** *359 Main St (02633). Phone 508/945-9232; toll-free 800/332-4667; fax 508/945-3769. www.cranberryinn.com.* Built in 1830, and nestled in the heart of the village historic district, this elegant inn offers guests all the comforts of home. Relax in one of the charmingly appointed guest rooms, each uniquely furnished, or enjoy the picturesque view of a windmill while lazying away in one of the Kennedy rocking chairs set along the expansive front porch. 18 rooms, 2 story. Children over 12 years only. Complimentary breakfast buffet. Check-out 11 am, check-in 2 pm. TV. Some fireplaces. Totally nonsmoking. **$**

☒

★ ★ ★ **MOSES NICKERSON HOUSE INN.** *364 Old Harbor Rd (02633). Phone 508/945-5859; toll-free 800/628-6972; fax 508/945-7087. www.mosesnickersonhouse.com.* Built in 1839, this charming inn has managed to blend all of the character and romance of yesterday while lovingly renovated to include all of today's modern amenities. This inn is perfect for that romantic getaway. 7 rooms, 2 story. Children over 14 years only. Complimentary full breakfast. Check-out 10:30 am, check-in 2:30 pm. TV available. Lawn games. Built in 1839. Totally nonsmoking. **$**

☒

★ ★ **OLD HARBOR INN.** *22 Old Harbor Rd (02633). Phone 508/945-4434; toll-free 800/942-4434; fax 508/945-7665. www.chathamoldharbor inn.com.* 8 rooms, 2 story. No room phones. Children over 14 years only. Complimentary breakfast buffet. Check-out 11 am, check-in 3 pm. Fireplace in parlor. Concierge. Built in 1933; former residence of prominent doctor. Renovated and furnished with a blend of antiques and modern conveniences. Outside deck. Totally nonsmoking. **$**

☒

★ ★ **PORT FORTUNE INN.** *201 Main St (02633). Phone 508/945-0792; toll-free 800/750-0792. www.portfortuneinn.com.* 12 rooms, 2 with shower only, 2 story. Children over 8 years only. Complimentary continental breakfast. Check-out 11 am, check-in 2 pm. TV in some rooms. Built in 1910. Totally nonsmoking. **$$**

☒

★ ★ ★ **QUEEN ANNE INN.** *70 Queen Anne Rd (02633). Phone 508/945-0394; toll-free 800/545-4667; fax 508/945-4884. www.queenanneinn.com.* Built in 1840, and named after Queen Anne of England, this charming Victorian-style inn offers guests understated elegance as well as friendly service. Guest rooms are furnished with some antique pieces that date back more than 120 years. Cozy up in front of the fireplace or relax on one of the private verandas; either way, the stay brings serenity to the mind and charm to the heart. 34 rooms, 3 story. Closed Jan. Complimentary continental breakfast. Check-out 11 am, check-in 3 pm. TV; VCR available. Restaurant. Outdoor pool, whirlpool. Outdoor tennis. Lawn games. Boats for excursions. Totally nonsmoking. **$**

Restaurants

★ ★ **CHATHAM SQUIRE.** *487 Main St (02633). Phone 508/945-0945; fax 508/945-4708. www.thesquire.com.* Seafood menu. Lunch, dinner. Bar. Children's menu. **$$**

D

★ ★ **CHRISTIAN'S.** *443 Main St (02633). Phone 508/945-3362; fax 508/945-9058. www.christiansrestaurant.com.* Seafood menu. Lunch, dinner. Bar. Pianist. Built in 1819. Outdoor seating. Two-level dining. **$$**

D

★ ★ **IMPUDENT OYSTER.** *15 Chatham Bars Ave (02633). Phone 508/945-3545; fax 508/945-9319.* Seafood menu. Lunch, dinner. Bar. Children's menu. Reservations required. Cathedral ceilings, stained-glass windows. **$$**

D

Dennis

1 hour 40 minutes; 89 miles from Boston

Settled 1639 **Pop** 15,973 **Elev** 24 ft **Area code** 508 **Zip** 02638

Information Chamber of Commerce, 242 Swan River Rd; 508/398-3568

Web www.dennischamber.com

Dennis heads a group, often called "The Dennises," that includes Dennisport, East Dennis, South Dennis, West Dennis, and Dennis. It was here, in 1816, that Henry Hall developed the commercial cultivation of cranberries. Swimming beaches are located throughout the area.

What to See and Do

Jericho House and Historical Center. *At junction Old Main St and Trotting Park Rd in West Dennis (02638). Phone 508/394-6114.* (1801) Period furniture. Barn museum contains old tools, household articles, model of salt works, photographs. (July-Aug, Wed and Fri) **DONATION**

Josiah Dennis Manse. *77 Nobscusset Rd (02638). Phone 508/385-3528.* (1736) and **Old West School House** (1770). Restored home of minister for whom town was named; antiques, Pilgrim chest, children's room, spinning and weaving exhibit, maritime wing. (July-Aug, Tues and Thurs) **DONATION**

Special Events

Cape Playhouse. *820 Main St (02638). Phone 508/385-3911. www.cape playhouse.com.* The Cape Playhouse offers opportunities to watch both established Broadway stars and up-and-coming actors for two-week runs of musicals, comedies, and other plays. Putting on performances since 1927, the Playhouse is the oldest professional summer theater in the United States—you can sometimes take a backstage tour of this historic facility. On Friday mornings during summer, attend the special children's performance that includes puppetry, storytelling, and musicals. The Playhouse complex also houses the Cape Museum of Fine Arts, the Playhouse Bistro, and the Cape Cinema. (Late June-Labor Day) **$$$$**

Festival Week. *Phone 508/398-3568.* Canoe and road races, antique car parade, craft fair, antique show. (Late Aug)

Motels/Motor Lodges

★ **BREAKERS MOTEL.** *61 Chase Ave (02639). Phone 508/398-6905; toll-free 800/540-6905; fax 508/398-7360. www.capecodtravel.com/breakers.* 36 rooms, 2 story. Closed mid-Oct-Apr. Continental breakfast. Check-out 11 am. TV; cable (premium). Outdoor pool. On beach. **$**

★ **COLONIAL VILLAGE RESORT.** *426 Lower County Rd (02639). Phone 508/398-2071; toll-free 800/287-2071; fax 508/398-2071. www.sunsol.com/ colonial village.* 49 rooms, 1-2 story. Closed mid-Oct-mid-May. Check-out 11 am. TV. Fireplaces. Sauna. Indoor pool, outdoor pool, whirlpool. **$**

★ **CORSAIR OCEANFRONT MOTEL.** *41 Chase Ave (02639). Phone 508/ 398-2279; toll-free 800/889-8037; fax 508/760-6681. www.corsaircrossrip.com.* 25 rooms, 2 story. Closed Dec-Mar. Complimentary continental breakfast. Check-out 11 am. TV; cable (premium), VCR available. Laundry services. Supervised children's activities (in season), ages 5-14. Indoor pool, outdoor pool, whirlpool. Lawn games. **$$**

★ **THE GARLANDS.** *117 Old Wharf Rd (02639). Phone 508/398-6987.* 20 air-cooled rooms, 2 story. Closed mid-Oct-mid-Apr. Children over 5 years only. Check-out 10 am. TV. No credit cards accepted. **$**

★ **HUNTSMAN MOTOR LODGE.** *829 Main St Rte 28, West Dennis (02670). Phone 508/394-5415; toll-free 800/628-0498. www.thehuntsman.com.* 25 rooms, 2 story. Closed Nov-mid-Apr. Check-out 11 am. TV. Outdoor pool. Lawn games. Totally nonsmoking. **$**

★ **SEA LORD RESORT MOTEL.** *56 Chase Ave (02639). Phone 508/398-6900. www.sunsol.com/sealord.* 27 rooms, 1-3 story. Closed Nov-Apr. Check-out 11 am. TV. Beach opposite. **$**

★ **SEA SHELL MOTEL.** *45 Chase Ave (02639). Phone 508/398-8965; toll-free 800/698-8965; fax 508/394-1237. www.virtualcapecod.com/market/seashellmotel.* 17 rooms, some A/C, 1-2 story. Complimentary continental breakfast. Check-out 11 am. TV. **$**

★ **SESUIT HARBOR.** *1421 Main St (02641). Phone 508/385-3326; toll-free 800/359-0097; fax 508/385-3326. www.sesuitharbormotel.com.* 20 rooms, 1-2 story. Complimentary continental breakfast. Check-out 10:30 am. TV. In-room modem link. Outdoor pool. **$**

★ ★ **SOUDINGS SEASIDE RESORT.** *79 Chase Ave (02639). Phone 505/394-6561; fax 508/374-7537. www.thesoundings.com.* 100 rooms, 1-2 story. Closed mid-Oct-late-Apr. Check-out 11 am. TV; cable (premium). In-room modem link. Restaurant. Sauna. Indoor pool, outdoor pool, poolside service. **$**

★ ★ **SPOUTER WHALE MOTOR INN.** *405 Old Wharf Rd (02639). Phone 508/398-8010; fax 508/760-3214.* 38 rooms, 2 story. Closed late-Oct-Mar. Check-out 11 am. TV. Beachside breakfast bar. Outdoor pool, whirlpool. On ocean; private beach. Totally nonsmoking. No credit cards accepted **$**

★ ★ **THREE SEASONS MOTOR LODGE.** *421 Old Wharf Rd (02639). Phone 508/398-6091; fax 508/398-3762. www.threeseasonsmotel.com.* 61 rooms, 2 story. Closed Nov-late May. Check-out 11 am. TV. Restaurant. On private beach. **$**

Resorts

★ ★ **EDGEWATER BEACH RESORT.** *95 Chase Ave (02639). Phone 508/398-6922; fax 508/760-3447. www.edgewatercapecod.com.* 86 rooms, 1-2 story. Closed mid-Nov-mid-Mar. Check-out 11 am. TV; VCR (movies). In-house fitness room, sauna. Indoor pool, outdoor pool, whirlpool. Lawn games. **$**

★ ★ **LIGHTHOUSE INN.** *1 Lighthouse Rd (02670). Phone 508/398-2244; fax 508/398-5658. www.lighthouseinn.com.* 63 rooms. Closed mid-Oct-late-May. Check-out 11 am. TV; VCR available. Restaurant, bar; entertainment. Room service. Supervised children's activities (July-Aug); ages 3-10.

Outdoor pool. Miniature golf. Outdoor tennis. Lawn games. Business center. Large private beach. **$$**

D 🎿 🏊 🏖 🚶

B&B/Small Inns

★ ★ **BY THE SEA GUESTS.** *57 Chase Ave (02639). Phone 508/398-8685; toll-free 800/447-9202; fax 508/398-0334. www.bytheseaguests.com.* 12 rooms, 1 A/C, 3 story. Complimentary continental breakfast. Check-out 11 am, check-in 2 pm. TV. Lawn games. Concierge. On private beach. **$**

D 🏖

★ ★ **FOUR CHIMNEYS INN.** *946 Main St (02638). Phone 508/385-6317; toll-free 800/874-5502; fax 508/385-6285. www.fourchimneysinn.com.* 8 air-cooled rooms, 3 story. No room phones. Complimentary full breakfast. Check-out 11 am, check-in 3 pm. TV in sitting room; cable (premium). Lawn games. **$**

🏖

★ ★ **ISAIAH HALL BED AND BREAKFAST INN.** *152 Whig St (02638). Phone 508/385-9928; toll-free 800/736-0160; fax 508/385-5879. www.isaiahhallinn.com.* 10 rooms, 2 story. No room phones. Nov-mid-Apr. Children over 7 years only. Complimentary continental breakfast. Check-out 2-9:30 pm, check-in 2 pm. TV; VCR. Lawn games. Farmhouse built in 1857. Totally nonsmoking. **$**

🏖

Restaurants

★ ★ **CAPTAIN WILLIAM'S HOUSE.** *106 Depot St (02639). Phone 508/398-3910.* Seafood menu. Closed Jan-Mar. Dinner. Bar. Children's menu. **$$**

D

★ ★ ★ **RED PHEASANT INN.** *905 Main St (02638). Phone 508/385-2133; fax 508/385-2112. www.redpheasantinn.com.* This charming restaurant is situated in a converted 200-year-old barn in the historic part of town. Dinner. Bar. Valet parking. Totally nonsmoking. **$$$**

D

★ ★ **SCARGO CAFE.** *799 Rte 6A (02638). Phone 508/385-8200; fax 508/385-6977. www.scargocafe.com.* Continental menu. Closed Thanksgiving, Dec 25. Lunch, dinner. Bar. Children's menu. Former residence (1865); opposite nation's oldest stock company theater. Totally nonsmoking. **$$**

D

★ **SWAN RIVER.** *5 Lower County Rd (02639). Phone 508/394-4466; fax 508/398-3201. www.swanriverseafoods.com.* Closed mid-Sept-late May. Lunch, dinner. Bar. Children's menu. **$$**

D

Eastham

1 hour 40 minutes; 89 miles from Boston

Settled 1644 **Pop** 5,453 **Elev** 48 ft **Area code** 508 **Zip** 02642

Information Chamber of Commerce, PO Box 1329; 508/240-7211 or 508/255-3444 (summer only); or visit the Information Booth at Rte 6 and Fort Hill

Web www.easthamchamber.com

On the bay side of the Cape, in what is now Eastham town, the *Mayflower* shore party met their first Native Americans. Also in the town is a magnificent stretch of Nauset Beach, which was once a graveyard of ships. Nauset Light is an old friend of mariners.

What to See and Do

Eastham Historical Society. *190 Samoset Rd (02642). Phone 508/255-0788.* 1869 schoolhouse museum; Native American artifacts; farming and nautical implements. (July-Aug, Mon-Fri afternoons) **DONATION** The society also maintains the

> **Swift-Daley House.** *On Rte 6 (02642). Phone 508/255-1766.* (1741) Cape Cod house contains period furniture, clothing, original hardware. (July-Aug, Mon-Fri afternoons or by appointment) **FREE**

Eastham Windmill. *Windmill Green (02642), in town center. Phone 508/240-7211.* Oldest windmill on the Cape (1680); restored in 1936. (Late June-Labor Day, daily) **DONATION**

Motels/Motor Lodges

★ ★ **BLUE DOLPHIN INN.** *5950 Rte 6 (02651). Phone 508/255-1159; toll-free 800/654-0504; fax 508/240-3676. www.bluedolphincapecod.com.* 49 rooms. Closed late-Oct-Mar. Check-out 11 am. TV; cable (premium). Restaurant. Outdoor pool, poolside service. Lawn games. On 7 wooded acres. **$**

[D] [≈] [⊠]

★ **CAPTAIN'S QUARTERS.** *Rte 6 (02651). Phone 508/255-5686; toll-free 800/327-7769; fax 508/240-0280. www.captains-quarters.com.* 75 rooms. Closed mid-Nov-mid-Apr. Complimentary continental breakfast. Check-out 11 am. TV. Outdoor pool. Outdoor tennis. Lawn games. Bicycles. **$**

[D] [↗] [≈] [⊠]

★ **EAGLE WING GUEST MOTEL.** *960 Rte 6 (02642). Phone 508/240-5656; toll-free 800/278-5656; fax 508/240-5657. www.eaglewingmotel.com.* 19 rooms. Closed Nov-May. TV; cable (premium). Outdoor pool. Totally nonsmoking. **$**

[≈] [⊠] [SC]

★ **EASTHAM OCEAN VIEW MOTEL.** *Rte 6 (02642). Phone 508/255-1600; toll-free 800/742-4133; fax 508/240-7104.* 31 rooms, 2 story. Closed Nov-mid-Feb. Check-out 11 am. TV. Outdoor pool. **$**

★ ★ **FOUR POINTS BY SHERATON.** *3800 Rte 6 (02642). Phone 508/255-5000; toll-free 800/533-3986; fax 508/240-1870. www.fourpoints.com.* 107 rooms, 2 story. Check-out 11 am. TV; cable (premium). In-room modem link. Restaurant, bar. Room service. In-house fitness room, sauna. Health club privileges. Game room. Indoor pool, outdoor pool, whirlpool, poolside service. Outdoor tennis. **$$**

★ **MIDWAY MOTEL & COTTAGES.** *5460 Rte 6 (02651). Phone 508/255-3117; toll-free 800/755-3117; fax 508/255-4235. www.midwaymotel.com.* 11 rooms. Closed Nov-Feb. Check-out 11 am. TV; cable (premium), VCR available. Lawn games. Bicycle rentals. **$**

★ ★ **TOWN CRIER MOTEL.** *3620 Rte 6 (02642). Phone 508/255-4000; toll-free 800/932-1434; fax 508/255-7491. www.towncriermotel.com.* 36 rooms. Check-out 11 am. TV; cable (premium). Restaurant. Indoor pool. **$**

★ **VIKING SHORES MOTOR LODGE.** *Rte 6 (02651). Phone 508/255-3200; toll-free 800/242-2131; fax 508/240-0205. www.vikingshores.com.* 40 rooms. Closed early-Nov-mid-Apr. Complimentary continental breakfast. Check-out 11 am. TV; cable (premium). Outdoor pool. Outdoor tennis. Lawn games. **$**

B&B/Small Inns

★ ★ **OVERLOOK INN OF CAPE COD.** *3085 County Rd, Rte 6 (02642). Phone 508/255-1886; fax 508/240-0545. www.overlookinn.com.* 10 rooms, 3 story. Complimentary full breakfast. Check-out 11 am, check-in 2 pm. Lawn games. **$$**

★ ★ **PENNY HOUSE INN.** *4885 County Rd (Rte 6) (02642). Phone 508/255-6632; toll-free 800/554-1751; fax 508/255-4893. www.pennyhouseinn.com.* 12 rooms, 2 story. Children over 8 years only. Complimentary full breakfast. Check-out 11 am, check-in 2 pm. TV; cable (premium), VCR (free movies). Lawn games. Audubon Society bird sanctuary, bicycle trails nearby. Totally nonsmoking. **$$**

Falmouth

1 hour 40 minutes; 89 miles from Boston

Settled circa 1660 **Pop** 32,660 **Elev** 10 ft **Area code** 508 **Zip** 02540

Information Cape Cod Chamber of Commerce, Rtes 6 and 132, PO Box 790, Hyannis 02601-0790; 508/362-3225 or 888/CAPECOD

Web www.capecodchamber.org

What to See and Do

Ashumet Holly & Wildlife Sanctuary. *Ashumet and Currier rds (02540). Just N of Rte 151. Phone 508/362-1426.* (Massachusetts Audubon Society) A 45-acre wildlife preserve with holly trail; herb garden; observation beehive. Trails open dawn to dusk. (Tues-Sun) **$$**

Falmouth Historical Society Museums. Julia Wood House. *55 Palmer Ave (02540). Phone 508/548-4857.* (1790) and **Conant House** (circa 1740). Whaling collection; period furniture; 19th-century paintings; glassware; silver; tools; costumes; widow's walk; memorial park; colonial garden. (Mid-June-mid-Sept, Mon-Thurs; rest of year, by appointment) Katharine Lee Bates exhibit in Conant House honors author of "America the Beautiful." (Mid-June-mid-Sept, Mon-Thurs) On village green. **$$**

Island Queen. *Phone 508/548-4800.* Passenger boat trips to Martha's Vineyard; 600-passenger vessel. (Late May-mid-Oct)

Special Events

Arts & Crafts Street Fair. *Main St (02540). Phone 508/548-8500.* On a midsummer Wednesday each year in Falmouth, more than 200 painters, weavers, glassworkers, woodworkers, potters, and others artisans set up booths along Main Street. The Arts & Crafts Street Fair is a classic summer festival, with food and entertainment for the entire family. The Falmouth Artists Guild also hosts a fundraising art auction during the fair. Mid-July. **FREE**

Barnstable County Fair. *1220 Nathan Ellis Hwy (02536). 8 miles N on Rte 151. Phone 508/563-3200.* Horse and dog shows, horse-pulling contest; exhibits. Last week in July.

College Light Opera Company at Highfield Theatre. *Off Depot Ave, Rte 28 (02540). Phone 508/548-2211.* Nine-week season of musicals and operettas with full orchestra. Mon-Sat. Late June-Labor Day.

Falmouth Road Race. *790 E Main St (race headquarters) (02540). Phone 508/540-7000. www.falmouthroadrace.com.* Starting in scenic Woods Hole and winding back into Falmouth Heights, this hilly and hot course takes you past some of the best scenery in the country. This 7.1-mile race has been called the "Best USA Road Race" by *Runner's World* magazine. The entry is a lottery, which means that far more people try to enter than are allowed in.

Your best bet is to join the over 70,000 spectators who line the course. If you want to race and don't get in, check the Internet for at least a dozen other summer road races on Cape Cod. Third Sun in Aug. **$$$**

Music on the Green. *Main St, Peg Noonan Park (02540). Phone 508/362-0066. www.artsfoundationcapecod.org.* Professional musicians from the Cape Cod area take part in the Music on the Green series, held on the town green in Falmouth. You'll enjoy rock, swing, marches, and folk music, all performed in the breezy park, and you're encouraged to bring a picnic and beach chair or blanket. The town of Hyannis also offers a Jazz by the Sea concert in early August on its town green. Early July-late Aug. **FREE**

Motels/Motor Lodges

★ ★ **ADMIRALTY INN.** *51 Teaticket Hwy, Rte 28 (02541). Phone 508/548-4240; fax 508/457-0535. www.vacationinnproperties.com.* 98 rooms, 3 story. Check-out 11 am. TV; cable (premium), VCR. Restaurant, bar. Supervised children's activities (seasonal), ages 5-12. Indoor pool, outdoor pool, whirlpool, poolside service. **$**

[D] [icon]

★ **BEST WESTERN FALMOUTH MARINA TRADEWINDS.** *26 Robbins Rd (02541). Phone 508/548-4300; toll-free 800/341-5700; fax 508/548-6787. www.bestwestern.com.* 63 rooms, 2 story. Closed Nov-Feb. Check-out 11 am. TV; cable (premium). Outdoor pool. Overlooks Falmouth Harbor. **$**

[icon] [icon]

★ **MARINER MOTEL.** *555 Main St (02540). Phone 508/548-1331; toll-free 800/233-2939; fax 508/457-9470. www.marinermotel.com.* 30 rooms. Check-out 11 am. TV; VCR available. Outdoor pool. **$**

[icon] [icon]

★ ★ **RAMADA INN.** *40 N Main St (02540). Phone 508/457-0606; toll-free 800/272-6232; fax 508/457-9694. www.ramada.com.* 72 rooms, 2 story. Check-out 11 am. TV; VCR (movies). In-room modem link. Restaurant, bar. Indoor pool. Business center. **$**

[D] [icon] [icon]

★ **RED HORSE INN.** *28 Falmouth Hts Rd (02540). Phone 508/548-0053; toll-free 800/628-3811; fax 508/540-6563. www.redhorseinn.com.* 22 rooms, 2 story. Check-out 11 am. TV; cable (premium). In-room modem link. Outdoor pool. **$**

[D] [icon] [icon]

Hotel

★ ★ ★ **NEW SEABURY RESORT AND CONFERENCE CENTER.** *Rock Landing Rd (02649). Phone 508/477-9111; toll-free 800/999-9033; fax 508/477-9790. www.newseabury.com.* This resort, conference center, and residential community sits on 2,300 recreation-filled acres and offers rentals from early March to early January. The resort's villa development began in

1962 and consists of two golf courses, 16 tennis courts, and private beaches. 160 rooms. Check-out 10 am, check-in 4 pm. TV; cable (premium), VCR (movies). In-room modem link. Laundry services. Dining room, bar; entertainment in season. Supervised children's activities (July-Aug). In-house fitness room. Seaside freshwater pool, children's pool. Miniature golf. 16 all-weather tennis courts. Bike trails. Sailboats. Trips to islands, whale watching, deep-sea fishing available. Wind surfing. Airport transportation. Business center. **$**

Resort

★ ★ **SEA CREST RESORT.** *350 Quaker Rd (02556). Phone 508/540-9400; toll-free 800/225-3110; fax 508/548-0556. www.seacrest-resort.com.* 266 rooms, 1-3 story. Check-out 11 am, check-in 3 pm. TV. In-room modem link. Laundry services. Restaurant, bar; entertainment. Room service. Free supervised children's activities (in season), ages over 3. In-house fitness room, sauna. Game room. Indoor pool, outdoor pool, whirlpool, poolside service. Outdoor tennis. Lawn games. Windsurfing. Business center. Concierge. **$$**

B&B/Small Inns

★ ★ **BEACH HOUSE AT FALMOUTH HEIGHTS.** *10 Worcester Ct (02540). Phone 508/457-0310; toll-free 800/351-3426; fax 508/548-7895. www.capecodbeachhouse.com.* 8 rooms, 6 with shower only, 2 story. No room phones. Closed Nov-May. Children over 12 years only. Complimentary continental breakfast. Check-out 11 am, check-in 3-6 pm. Outdoor pool. Hand-painted murals and furniture; unique theme rooms. Totally nonsmoking. **$**

★ ★ ★ **CAPT. TOM LAWRENCE HOUSE.** *75 Locust St (02540). Phone 508/540-1445; toll-free 800/266-8139; fax 508/457-1790. www.captaintomlawrence.com.* Vaulted ceilings, hardwood floors, and a spiral staircase add to the romantic, old-world charm of this intimate inn located within walking distance of the town's main historic street. The name refers to the successful whaler who built the property in 1861. 7 rooms, 2 story. No room phones. Closed Jan. Complimentary full breakfast. Check-out 11 am, check-in 3 pm. TV. Island ferry tickets available. Whaling captain's home (1861). Totally nonsmoking. **$$**

★ ★ **ELM ARCH INN.** *26 Elm Arch Way (02540). Phone 508/548-0133. www.elmarchinn.com.* 24 rooms, 2 story. No room phones. Check-out 11 am, check-in noon. TV in some rooms; cable (premium). Bombarded by British in 1814; dining room wall features cannonball hole. Outdoor pool. Built in 1810; private residence of whaling captain. Screened terrace. No credit cards accepted. **$**

★ ★ ★ **GRAFTON INN.** *261 Grand Ave S (02540). Phone 508/540-8688; toll-free 800/642-4069; fax 508/540-1861. www.graftoninn.com.* Built in the early 1900s and restored in the tradition of a charming Victorian Inn, guests will delight in strolls along the sea while a gentle breeze drifts the tensions of yesterday away. With the tranquility of the ocean right outside the door and romantically furnished private guest rooms, this inn offers the serenity and charm to make for a truly delightful stay. 10 air-cooled rooms, 3 story. No room phones. Children over 16 years only. Complimentary full breakfast. Check-out 11 am, check-in 2-6 pm. TV; cable (premium). Former home of sea captain; built in 1850. On Nantucket Sound. Totally nonsmoking. Free transportation. **$$**

◰

★ ★ **INN ON THE SOUND.** *313 Grand Ave (02540). Phone 508/457-9666; toll-free 800/564-9668; fax 508/457-9631. www.innonthesound.com.* 10 air-cooled rooms, 2 story. No room phones. Children over 16 years only. Complimentary full breakfast. Check-out 11 am, check-in 3-6 pm. TV. Built in 1880. Overlooking Vineyard Sound. Totally nonsmoking. **$$**

◰

★ ★ ★ **LAMAISON CAPPELLARI AT MOSTLY HALL.** *27 Main St (02540). Phone 508/548-3786; fax 508/548-5778. www.mostlyhall.com.* This 1849 plantation-style house, which is the only one of its kind on Cape Cod, offers a secluded location in the heart of the town's historic district. 6 rooms, 3 story. Shower only. No room phones. Closed Nov-mid-May. Children over 16 years only. Complimentary full breakfast. Check-out 11 am, check-in 3 pm. TV in sitting room. Bicycles. Concierge. Totally nonsmoking. **$**

◰

★ ★ ★ **THE PALMER HOUSE INN.** *81 Palmer Ave (02540). Phone 508/548-1230; toll-free 800/472-2632; fax 508/540-1878. www.palmerhouse inn.com.* Perched at the upper end of Cape Cod, this 1901 Queen-Anne style inn and guesthouse welcomes visitors year-round. Beaches, the Shining Sea Bikeway, and ferries to the islands are all nearby. 16 rooms, 3 story. Complimentary full breakfast. Check-out 11 am, check-in 3-9 pm. Some TVs. Concierge. Totally nonsmoking. **$$**

[D] [◰] [SC]

★ ★ ★ **WILDFLOWER INN.** *167 Palmer Ave (02540). Phone 508/548-9524; toll-free 800/294-5459; fax 508/548-9524. www.wildflower-inn.com.* Conveniently located near Martha's Vineyard, guests will enjoy the relaxing and peaceful atmosphere offered at this bed-and-breakfast. 6 rooms, 3 story. No room phones. Complimentary breakfast. Check-out 11 am, check-in 3-6 pm. TV; cable (premium). Game room. Lawn games. Concierge. Built in 1898; wraparound porch. **$$**

◰

Restaurants

★ **THE FLYING BRIDGE.** *220 Scranton Ave (02540). Phone 508/548-2700; fax 508/457-7675. www.capecodrestaurants.org.* Seafood menu. Lunch, dinner. Bar; entertainment Fri. Children's menu. Valet parking. Outdoor seating. **$$$**

D

★ **GOLDEN SAILS CHINESE.** *143-145 Main St (02536). Phone 508/548-3526.* Chinese menu. Closed Thanksgiving. Lunch, dinner. Bar. **$**

D SC

Harwich

1 hour 40 minutes; 89 miles from Boston

Settled circa 1670 **Pop** 12,386 **Elev** 55 ft **Area code** 508 **Zip** 02646

Information Harwich Chamber of Commerce, PO Box 34; 508/432-1600; or the Cape Cod Chamber of Commerce, Rtes 6 and 132, PO Box 790, Hyannis 02601-0790; 508/362-3225 or 888/CAPECOD

Web www.capecodchamber.org

Harwich, whose namesake in England was dubbed "Happy-Go-Lucky Harwich" by Queen Elizabeth, is one of those towns made famous in New England literature. It is "Harniss" in the Joseph C. Lincoln novels of Cape Cod. A local citizen, Jonathan Walker, was immortalized as "the man with the branded hand" in Whittier's poem about helping escaped slaves; Enoch Crosby of Harwich was the Harvey Birch of James Fenimore Cooper's novel, *The Spy.* Today, summer people own three-quarters of the land.

What to See and Do

Brooks Free Library. *739 Main St (02646), Harwich Center. Phone 508/430-7562.* Houses 24 John Rogers' figurines. (Mon-Sat; closed holidays) **FREE**

★ **Cape Cod Baseball League.** *11 North Rd (02645). Phone 508/432-3878. www.capecodbaseball.org.* The Cape Cod Baseball League is baseball as you remember it: local, passionate, affordable, and played only with wooden bats. The ten teams are all drawn from college players from around the country, who live with host families for the summer, visit schools to interact with kids, and host a summer baseball clinic. Spectators sit on wooden benches, pack a picnic lunch or dinner, and cheer for their favorite players during each of the 44 games played each season at venues throughout Cape Cod. Mid-June-mid-Aug. **FREE**

Harwich Historical Society. *80 Parallel St (02646), at Sisson Rd, in Harwich Center. Phone 508/432-8089.* Includes Brooks Academy Building and Revolutionary War Powder House. Native American artifacts, marine exhibit, cranberry industry articles, early newspapers and photographs. Site of one of the first schools of navigation in US. (Usually mid-June-mid-Sept, Tues-Fri; schedule may vary) **DONATION**

Red River Beach. *Deep Hole and Uncle Venies rds (02646). Off Rte 28, S on Uncle Venies Rd in South Harwich.* Sticker fee per weekday. A fine Nantucket Sound swimming beach (water 68°F to 72°F in summer).

Saquatucket Municipal Marina. *715 Main St (02646). Off Rte 28. Phone 508/432-2562.* Boat ramp for launching small craft. (May-mid-Nov) **$$$**

Special Events

Cranberry Harvest Festival. *Rte 58 N and Rochester Rd (02645).* Family Day, antique car show, music, arts and crafts, fireworks, carnival, parade. One weekend in mid-Sept.

Harwich Junior Theatre. *105 Division St (02671). Phone 508/432-2002.* Plays for the family and children through high school age. Reservations required. (July-Aug, daily; Sept-June, monthly)

Motels/Motor Lodges

★ **COACHMAN MOTOR LODGE.** *774 Main St (02646). Phone 508/432-0707; toll-free 800/524-4265; fax 508/432-7951. www.coachmanmotorinn.com.* 28 rooms. Closed mid-Nov-Apr. Check-out 11 am. TV; cable (premium). Restaurant. Outdoor pool. **$**

★ **SEADAR INN.** *Bank St Beach (02646). Phone 508/432-0264; fax 508/430-1916. www.seadarinn.com.* 20 rooms, 1-2 story. No A/C. Closed mid-Oct-late May. Complimentary continental breakfast. Check-out 11 am. TV; VCR. In-room modem link. Lawn games. Main building is an old colonial house (1789). Early American décor; some rooms with bay windows. Near beach. **$**

★ **WYCHMERE VILLAGE.** *767 Main St (02646). Phone 508/432-1434; toll-free 800/432-1434; fax 508/432-8904. www.wychmere.com.* 25 rooms. Check-out 11 am. TV. Outdoor pool. Lawn games. **$**

B&B/Small Inns

★ ★ **AUGUSTUS SNOW HOUSE.** *528 Main St (02646). Phone 508/430-0528; toll-free 800/320-0528; fax 508/432-6638. www.augustussnow.com.* 5 rooms, 2 story. Children over 12 years only. Complimentary full breakfast. Check-out 11 am, check-in 2 pm. TV; cable. Fireplaces. Beach. Free airport transportation. Concierge. Built in 1901; Victorian décor. Totally nonsmoking. **$$**

★ ★ **CAPE COD CLADDAGH INN.** *77 Main St (02671). Phone 508/ 432-9628; toll-free 800/356-9628; fax 508/432-6039. www.capecodcladdagh inn.com.* 9 rooms, 3 story. Closed Jan-Mar. Pets accepted, some restrictions. Complimentary breakfast. Check-out 10:30 am, check-in 2 pm. TV; cable (premium). Dining room. Outdoor pool. Parking. Former Baptist parsonage (circa 1900). **$**

★ ★ **COUNTRY INN.** *86 Sisson Rd (02646). Phone 508/432-2769; toll-free 800/231-1722; fax 508/430-1455. www.countryinncapecod.com.* 6 rooms, 2 story. No room phones. Complimentary continental breakfast. Check-out noon, check-in 2 pm. TV. Dining room (reservations required). Outdoor pool. Built in 1780; colonial décor. On 6 acres. Use of private beach. **$**

★ ★ ★ **DUNSCROFT BY THE SEA.** *24 Pilgrim Rd (02646). Phone 508/432-0810; toll-free 800/432-4345; fax 508/432-5134. www.dunscroftby thesea.com.* Located just steps from the beach, this inn offers white sands and privacy. Guests can also venture to town to enjoy shopping, restaurants, and galleries. Activities include miniature golf, fishing, water sports, clambakes, and whale-watching. 8 rooms, 2 story. Children over 12 years only. Complimentary breakfast. Check-out 11 am, check-in 2 pm. Whirlpool. Near a mile-long beach on Nantucket Sound. **$$**

★ **SEA HEATHER INN.** *28 Sea St (02646). Phone 508/432-1275; toll-free 800/789-7809.* 20 rooms, 1-2 story. Children over 10 years only. Complimentary continental breakfast. Check-out 11 am, check-in 2 pm. TV. Lawn games. Early American décor; porches. Near beach. Totally nonsmoking. **$**

Restaurant

★ ★ **BISHOP'S TERRACE.** *Rte 28 (02671). Phone 508/432-0253.* Dinner, Sun brunch. Bar; entertainment. Children's menu. Restored colonial house. Outdoor seating. **$$**

Hyannis

1 hour 40 minutes; 89 miles from Boston
See also Martha's Vineyard, South Yarmouth

Settled 1639 **Pop** 14,120 **Elev** 19 ft **Area code** 508 **Zip** 02601

Information Chamber of Commerce, 1481 Rte 132; 508/362-5230 or 877/ HYANNIS

Web www.hyannis.com

Hyannis is the main vacation and transportation center of Cape Cod. Recreational facilities and specialty areas abound, including tennis courts, golf courses, arts and crafts galleries, theaters, and antique shops. There are libraries, museums, and the Kennedy Memorial and Compound. Candle-making tours are available. Scheduled airliners and Amtrak stop here, and it is also a port for boat trips to Nantucket Island and Martha's Vineyard. More than 6 million people visit the village every year, and it is within an hour's drive of the many attractions on the Cape.

What to See and Do

Auto Ferry/Steamship Authority. *Ocean St (02601). Phone 508/477-8600. www.steamshipauthority.com.* The Woods Hole, Martha's Vineyard, and Nantucket Steamship Authority conducts trips to Nantucket from Hyannis (year-round); departs from South Street dock.

Cape Cod Crusaders. *35 Winter St (02601). Games are played at Dennis-Yarmouth High School. Rte 6 to exit 8, turn right off the ramp, and the stadium is about 2 miles down on your left. Phone 508/790-4782. www.capecodcrusaders .com.* If you want to see a professional sports team on Cape Cod, the Crusaders are the only team to watch. As members of the USISL (United States Independent Soccer League), the Crusaders play about 12 home games throughout late spring and summer. The Crusaders are the farm team for the New England Revolution, which means that Crusaders' players are often recruited from around the world and start out in Cape Cod. **$$**

Cape Cod Melody Tent. *21 W Main St (02601). Phone 508/775-9100. www.melodytent.com.* Looking for top-notch musical acts? The Cape Cod Melody Tent draws top musicians from around the country—mostly easy listening and country music—plus comedians. The venue is a huge white tent that's been hosting concerts on Cape Cod for over 50 years. Wednesday mornings in July and August bring theater and musical productions for kids. Call, or visit the Web site for all concert dates and times, and if you want to be sure you get tickets, purchase them the day they go on sale. You may be able to pick up tickets left behind by no-shows just before performances begin. (Late May-mid-Sept)

Cape Cod Potato Chip Company. *100 Breed's Hill Rd (02601). Phone 508/ 775-7253. www.capecodchips.com.* Cape Cod Potato Chips, which are now sold all over the world, may be Cape Cod's most recognizable food prod-uct (although Nantucket Nectars, a local brand of juices available on the island and around the world, may take issue with that assessment). Perhaps the best part about taking the ten-minute self-guided tour of the facility is tasting the free samples, although seeing the unique kettles in which these crunchy chips are cooked is a close second. (Mon-Fri 9 am-5 pm, also Sat 10 am-4 pm July-Aug; closed Sun, holidays) **FREE**

Hyannis-Nantucket or Martha's Vineyard Day Round Trip. *Hy-Line, Pier #1, Ocean St Dock (02601). Phone 508/778-2600.* (May-Oct) Also hourly sightseeing trips to Hyannis Port (Late Apr-Oct, daily); all-day or half-day deep-sea fishing excursions. (Late Apr-mid-Oct, daily)

John F. Kennedy Memorial. *Ocean St (02601).* Circular fieldstone wall memorial 12 feet high with presidential seal, fountain, and small pool honors late president who grew up nearby.

Pufferbellies Entertainment Complex. *183 Rear Iyanough Rd (02601). Phone 508/790-4300. www.pufferbellies.com.* Pufferbellies is a unique collection of nightclubs and places to eat. On four separate dance floors, you'll dance the night away to swing, disco, country, and Top 40 music. If you have two left feet, be sure to take an on-site dance lesson. The sports bar entertains you with three big-screen TVs, dart boards, pool tables, and basketball machines, and a beach volleyball court in the Jimmy Buffet Parrothead Bar extends the fun outdoors. (Fri, Sat; closed Sun-Thurs) **$$$**

Swimming. Craigville Beach. Basset Ln. *Phone 508/790-6345.* SW of town center. **Sea St Beach.** Sea St. Overlooking Hyannis Port harbor, bathhouse. **Kalmus Park.** Ocean St, bathhouse. **Veteran's Park.** Ocean St. Picnicking at Kalmus and Veteran's parks. Parking fee at all beaches.

Special Events

Cape Cod Oyster Festival. *20 Independence Dr (02601). Phone 508/778-6500. www.capecodoysterfestival.com.* What you get at the Cape Cod Oyster Festival is oysters—as many as you care to eat—accompanied by wine from local vineyards. Sample raw, baked, and roasted oysters, and also taste oyster stew. Held at the Naked Oyster restaurant under a big tent, the Oyster Festival draws locals and tourists alike. Late Oct. **$$$$**

Fleet Pops by the Sea. *Town Green (02601). Phone 508/362-0066. www.arts foundationcapecod.org.* In early August, the Boston Pops makes its way from Boston to Cape Cod for a once-a-year concert on the Hyannis Town Green. You'll enjoy classics, pops, and Sousa marches. Each year brings a new celebrity guest conductor, from actors to poets to famous chefs. The performance serves as a fundraiser that supports the Arts Foundation of Cape Cod. **$$$$**

Hyannis Harbor Festival. *Waterfront at Bismore Park (02601). Phone 508/362-5230 or 508/775-2201.* Coast Guard cutter tours, sailboat races, marine displays, food, entertainment. Weekend in early June.

Motels/Motor Lodges

★ **BUDGET HOST INN.** *614 Rte 132 (02601). Phone 508/775-8910; toll-free 800/322-3354; fax 508/775-6476. www.capecodtravel.com/hyannismotel.* 41 rooms, 2 story. Check-out 11 am. TV; cable (premium). Outdoor pool. **$**

D ⊠ ⊠

★ ★ **CAPE CODDER RESORT AND SPA.** *1225 Iyanough Rd (02601). Phone 508/771-3000; toll-free 888/297-2200; fax 508/771-6564. www.capecod derresort.com.* 258 rooms, 2 story. Check-out 11 am, check-in 3 pm. TV; cable (premium), VCR available. Internet access. Restaurant, bar; entertainment. Room service. In-house fitness room, spa. Game room. Indoor pool, whirlpool. Outdoor tennis. Airport transportation. Business center. **$**

D ⊠ ⊠ ⊼ ⊠ ⊼

★ **CAPTAIN GOSNOLD VILLAGE.** *230 Gosnold St (02601). Phone 508/775-9111; fax 508/790-9776. www.captaingosnold.com.* 36 rooms. Closed Dec-mid-Apr. Check-out 10:30 am. TV; VCR available (free movies). Outdoor pool. Lawn games. **$**

☐ SC

★ **COMFORT INN.** *1470 Rte 132 (02601). Phone 508/771-4804; toll-free 877/424-6423; fax 508/790-2336. www.comfortinn-hyannis.com.* 104 rooms, 3 story. No elevator. Complimentary continental breakfast. Check-out noon. TV; cable (premium). Sauna. Indoor pool, whirlpool. **$**

D ☐ ☒ SC

★ **DAYS INN.** *867 Rte 132 (02601). Phone 508/771-6100; toll-free 800/368-4667; fax 508/775-3011. www.daysinn.com.* 99 rooms, 2 story. Complimentary continental breakfast. Check-out 11 am. TV. In-room modem link. In-house fitness room. Indoor pool, outdoor pool, whirlpool. **$**

D ☐ ☒ ☒ SC

★ ★ **HERITAGE HOUSE HOTEL.** *259 Main St (02601). Phone 508/775-7000; toll-free 800/352-7189; fax 508/778-5687. www.heritagehousehotel.com.* 143 rooms, 3 story. Check-out 11 am. TV; cable (premium). Restaurant. Sauna. Indoor pool, outdoor pool, whirlpool. **$**

☐ ☒ SC

★ ★ **RAMADA INN.** *1127 Rte 132 (02601). Phone 508/775-1153; toll-free 800/272-6232; fax 508/775-1169. www.ramada.com.* 196 rooms, 2 story. Check-out 11 am. TV. Restaurant, bar. Room service. Game room. Indoor pool. Concierge. **$**

D ☐ ☒

Hotel

★ ★ ★ **INTERNATIONAL INN.** *662 Main St (02601). Phone 508/775-5600; toll-free 877/588-3353; fax 508/775-3933. www.cuddles.com.* With a trademark like "cuddle and bubble," it's obvious romance is the distinguishing feature of this Cape Cod inn conveniently located within walking distance of town and ferries. Geared toward couples, each room or suite has a Jacuzzi built for two. 141 rooms, 2 story. Check-out 11 am. TV; VCR. In-room modem link. Restaurant, bar. Sauna. Indoor pool, outdoor pool. **$**

D ☒ ☐ ☒

Resort

★ ★ ★ **SHERATON HYANNIS RESORT.** *West End Cir (02601). Phone 508/775-7775; toll-free 800/598-4559; fax 508/778-6039. www.sheraton.com.* The property is conveniently located at the island's center within walking distance of shops and restaurants. 224 rooms, 2 story. Check-out 11 am, check-in 4 pm. TV. In-room modem link. Dining room, bar; entertainment. Room service. Supervised children's activities (in season), ages 4-13.

In-house fitness room, spa, sauna, steam room. Game room. Indoor pool, outdoor pool, whirlpool, poolside service. Golf on premise, greens fee $20-$30. Outdoor tennis, lighted courts. Lawn games. Airport transportation. Business center. Concierge. **$**

D

B&B/Small Inns

★ ★ **SEA BREEZE INN.** *270 Ocean Ave (02601). Phone 508/771-7213; fax 508/862-0663. www.seabreezeinn.com.* 14 rooms, 2 story. Complimentary continental breakfast. Check-out 10:30 am, check-in 2 pm. TV. Concierge. Near beach; some rooms with ocean view. **$**

★ ★ **SIMMONS HOMESTEAD INN.** *288 Scudder Ave (02647). Phone 508/778-4999; toll-free 800/637-1649; fax 508/790-1342. www.simmons homesteadinn.com.* 14 rooms, 2 story. No room phones. Pets accepted, some restrictions; fee. Complimentary full breakfast. Check-out 11 am, check-in 1 pm. TV in sitting room. Lawn games. Bicycles. Concierge. Restored sea captain's home built in 1820; some canopied beds. Unique décor; all rooms have different animal themes. **$$**

Restaurants

★ **EGG & I.** *521 Main St (02601). Phone 508/771-1596; fax 508/778-6385.* Closed Dec-Feb; weekends only Mar, Nov. Breakfast. Children's menu. Family dining. **$**

D SC

★ **ORIGINAL GOURMET BRUNCH.** *517 Main St (02601). Phone 508/771-2558; fax 508/778-6052. www.theoriginalgourmetbrunch.com.* Closed Thanksgiving, Dec 25. Breakfast, lunch. Casual attire. **$**

★ ★ **PADDOCK.** *20 Scudder Ave (02601). Phone 508/775-7677; fax 508/771-9517. www.paddockcapecod.com.* Seafood menu. Closed mid-Nov-early Apr. Lunch, dinner. Bar. Children's menu. Victorian décor. Valet parking. **$$**

D

★ ★ **PENGUINS SEA GRILL.** *331 Main St (02601). Phone 508/775-2023; fax 508/778-6999.* Closed Thanksgiving, Dec 25. Dinner. Bar. Children's menu. **$$**

D

★ ★ **RISTORANTE BAROLO.** *297 North St (02601). Phone 508/778-2878; fax 508/862-8050.* Italian menu. Closed Jan 1, Dec 25. Dinner. Bar. Reservations required. Outdoor seating. **$$**

D

★ ★ **ROADHOUSE CAFE.** *488 South St (02601). Phone 508/775-2386; fax 508/778-1025. www.roadhousecafe.com.* Continental menu. Closed Dec 24-25. Dinner. Bar; entertainment. In 1903 house. Valet parking. **$$**

D

★ **SAM DIEGO'S.** *950 Hyannis Rd (Rte 132) (02601). Phone 508/771-8816. www.caperestaurantassociation.com.* Mexican menu. Closed Easter, Thanksgiving, Dec 25. Lunch, dinner. Bar. Children's menu. Outdoor seating. **$$**

D

★ **STARBUCKS.** *668 Rte 132 (02601). Phone 508/778-6767; fax 508/790-0036. www.starbuckscapecod.com.* Mexican menu. Closed Dec 25. Dinner. Bar; entertainment. Children's menu. Outdoor seating. **$$$**

D

Orleans

1 hour 40 minutes; 89 miles from Boston

Settled 1693 **Pop** 6,341 **Elev** 60 ft **Area code** 508 **Zip** 02653

Information Cape Cod Chamber of Commerce, Rtes 6 and 132, PO Box 790, Hyannis 02601-0790; 508/362-3225 or 888/CAPECOD

Web www.capecodchamber.org

Orleans supposedly was named in honor of the Duke of Orleans after the French Revolution. The settlers worked at shipping, fishing, and salt production. Its history includes the dubious distinction of being the only town in America to have been fired upon by the Germans during World War I. The town is now a commercial hub for the summer resort colonies along the great stretch of Nauset Beach and the coves behind it. A cable station, which provided direct communication between Orleans and Brest, France, from 1897 to 1959, is restored to its original appearance and open to the public.

What to See and Do

Academy of Performing Arts. *120 Main St (box office) (02653). Phone 508/255-1963.* Theater presents comedies, drama, musicals, dance. Workshops for all ages.

French Cable Station Museum. *41 S Orleans Rd (02653). Phone 508/240-1735.* Built in 1890 as American end of transatlantic cable from Brest, France. Original equipment for submarine cable communication on display. (July-Labor Day, Tues-Sat afternoons) **$$**

Nauset Beach. *44 Main St (02643). About 3 miles E of Rte 6 on marked roads. Phone 508/255-1386.* One of the most spectacular ocean beaches on the Atlantic Coast is now within the boundaries of Cape Cod National Seashore. Swimming, surfing, fishing; lifeguards. Parking fee.

Motels/Motor Lodges

★ **THE COVE.** *13 State Rte 28 (02653). Phone 508/255-1203; toll-free 800/343-2233; fax 508/255-7736. www.thecoveorleans.com.* 47 rooms, 1-2 story. Check-out 11 am. TV; VCR. Outdoor pool. Lawn games. Float boat rides available. Business center. On town cove. **$**

⌖ ⌖ ⌖ ⌖

★ **NAUSET KNOLL MOTOR LODGE.** *237 Beach Rd, East Orleans (02643). Phone 508/255-3348; fax 508/247-9184. www.capecodtravel.com.* 12 rooms. No room phones. Closed late Oct-mid-Apr. Check-out 11 am. TV. **$**

D

★ **OLDE TAVERN MOTEL AND INN.** *151 Rte 6A (02653). Phone 508/255-1565; toll-free 800/544-7705. www.capecodtravel.com/oldetavern.* 29 rooms. Closed Dec-Mar. Complimentary continental breakfast. Check-out 11 am. TV; cable (premium). Outdoor pool. Main building is restored inn and tavern visited by Thoreau in 1849, Daniel Webster, and other personalities of the day. 18 deck rooms. **$**

⌖ ⌖

★ **RIDGEWOOD MOTEL AND COTTAGES.** *10 Quanset Rd (02662). Phone 508/255-0473. www.ridgewoodmotel.com.* 12 rooms. No room phones. Complimentary continental breakfast. Check-out 10 am. TV. Outdoor pool. Lawn games. Totally nonsmoking. **$**

⌖ ⌖

★ **SEASHORE PARK MOTOR INN.** *24 Canal Rd (02653). Phone 508/255-2500; toll-free 800/772-6453; fax 508/255-9400. www.seashoreparkinn.com.* 62 rooms, 2 story. Closed Nov-mid-Apr. Complimentary continental breakfast. Check-out 11 am. TV. Sauna. Indoor pool, outdoor pool, whirlpool. Totally nonsmoking. **$**

⌖ ⌖

★ **SKAKET BEACH MOTEL.** *203 Cranberry Hwy (02653). Phone 508/255-1020; toll-free 800/835-0298; fax 508/255-6487. www.skaketbeachmotel.com.* 46 rooms, 1-2 story. Closed Dec-Mar. Complimentary continental breakfast. Check-out 11 am. TV; cable (premium). Laundry services. Outdoor pool. Lawn games. **$**

⌖ ⌖

B&B/Small Inns

★ ★ **KADEE'S GRAY ELEPHANT.** *216 Main St (06243). Phone 508/255-7608.* 10 rooms, 2 story. Complimentary breakfast. Check-out 10:30 am, check-in 3 pm. TV; VCR available. Restaurant, bar. Parking lot. **$$**

D ⌖ ⌖ ⌖

★ ★ **THE PARSONAGE INN.** *202 Main St (02643)*. Phone 508/255-8217; toll-free 888/422-8217; fax 508/255-8216. *www.parsonageinn.com*. 8 rooms, 2 story. No room phones. Children over 6 years only. Complimentary full breakfast. Check-out 11 am, check-in 2 pm. TV. Originally a parsonage (1770) and cobbler's shop. Totally nonsmoking. **$**

★ ★ **SHIPS KNEES INN.** *186 Beach Rd (02643)*. Phone 508/255-1312; fax 508/240-1351. *www.capecodtravel.com/shipskneesinn*. 16 air-cooled rooms, 2 story. No room phones. Children over 12 years only. Complimentary continental breakfast. Check-out 10:30 am, check-in 1 pm. TV. Outdoor pool. Outdoor tennis. Rooms individually decorated in nautical style; many antiques, some four-poster beds. Restored sea captain's house (circa 1820). Near ocean, beach. Totally nonsmoking. **$**

Restaurants

★ ★ **BARLEY NECK INN.** *5 Beach Rd (02653)*. Phone 508/255-0212; fax 508/255-3626. *www.barleyneck.com*. Continental menu. Dinner. **$$**

★ ★ ★ **CAPTAIN LINNELL HOUSE.** *137 Skaket Beach Rd (02653)*. Phone 508/255-3400; fax 508/255-5377. *www.linnell.com*. Chef/owner Bill Conway delivers a delightful dining experience at this charming and romantic restaurant. Take a walk out to the Victorian gazebo and enjoy the smell of lavender and the refreshing ocean breeze, then settle in for a cozy candlelit dinner. Seafood menu. Dinner. Children's menu. Outdoor seating. Totally nonsmoking. **$$$**

★ **DOUBLE DRAGON INN.** *Rtes 6A and 28 (02653)*. Phone 508/255-4100. Chinese, Polynesian menu. Closed Thanksgiving. Lunch, dinner. **$$**

★ **LOBSTER CLAW.** *Rte 6A (02653)*. Phone 508/255-1800. *www.capecod.com/lobclaw*. Closed mid-Nov-Mar. Lunch, dinner. Bar. Children's menu. Former cranberry packing factory. **$$**

★ ★ **NAUSET BEACH CLUB.** *222 E Main St, East Orleans (02643)*. Phone 508/255-8547; fax 508/255-8872. *www.nausetbeachclub.com*. Regional Italian menu. Closed Sun, Mon (off-season). Dinner. Bar. Totally nonsmoking. **$$$**

★ ★ **OLD JAILHOUSE TAVERN.** *28 West Rd (02653)*. Phone 508/255-5245. *www.legalseafoods.com*. Seafood menu. Closed Thanksgiving, Dec 25. Lunch, dinner. Bar. Part of old jailhouse. **$$$**

Provincetown

1 hour 40 minutes; 89 miles from Boston

Settled circa 1700 **Pop** 3,431 **Elev** 40 ft **Area code** 508 **Zip** 02657

Information Chamber of Commerce, 307 Commercial St, PO Box 1017; 508/487-3424

Web www.capecodaccess.com/provincetownchamber

Provincetown is a startling mixture of heroic past and easygoing present. The Provincetown area may have been explored by Leif Ericson in AD 1004. It is certain that the *Mayflower* anchored first in Provincetown Harbor while the Mayflower Compact, setting up the colony's government, was signed aboard the ship. Provincetown was where the first party of Pilgrims came ashore. A bronze tablet at Commercial Street and Beach Highway marks the site of the Pilgrims' first landing. The city attracts many tourists who come each summer to explore the narrow streets and rows of picturesque old houses.

What to See and Do

Commercial Street. *Commercial St (02657).* To view a shopping district that's steeped in history and still thriving today, visit Provincetown's Commercial Street. Stretching more than 3 miles in length, the narrow street sports art galleries, shops, clubs, restaurants, and hotels. When the street was constructed in 1835, the houses that backed up to it all faced the harbor, which was the principle area of business activity. As you tour the street, note that many of those homes were turned 180 degrees to face the street or had a new "front" door crafted in the back of the house.

Expedition Whydah's Sea Lab & Learning Center. *16 MacMillan Wharf (02657). Phone 508/487-7955.* Archaeological site of sunken pirate ship *Whydah,* struck by storms in 1717. Learn about recovery of the ship's pirate treasure, the lives and deaths of pirates, and the history of the ship and its passengers. (Apr-mid-Oct, daily; mid-Oct-Dec, weekends and school holidays)

⭐ **Pilgrim Monument & Museum.** *High Pole Hill (02657). Phone 508/487-1310.* A 252-foot granite tower commemorating the Pilgrims' 1620 landing in the New World; provides an excellent view. (Summer, daily) **$$$** Admission includes

> **Provincetown Museum.** *High Pole Hill (02657). Phone 508/487-1310.* Exhibits include whaling equipment, scrimshaw, ship models, artifacts from shipwrecks; Pilgrim Room with scale model diorama of the merchant ship *Mayflower;* Donald MacMillan's Arctic exhibit; antique fire engine and firefighting equipment; theater history display. (Summer, daily)

Provincetown Art Association & Museum. *460 Commercial St (02657). Phone 508/487-1750.* Changing exhibits; museum store. (Late May-Oct, daily; rest of year, weekends) **DONATION**

Recreation. Swimming at surrounding beaches, including Town Beach, W of the village, Herring Cove and Race Point, on the ocean side. Tennis, cruises, beach buggy tours, and fishing available.

Town Wharf (MacMillan Wharf). *Commercial and Standish sts (02657).* Center of maritime activity. Also here is

> **Portuguese Princess Whale Watch.** *Phone 508/487-2651; toll-free 800/ 442-3188 (New England).* 100-foot boats offer 3 1/2-hour narrated whale watching excursions. Naturalist aboard. (Apr-Oct, daily)

Whale-watching. *306 Commercial St (02657). Dolphin Fleet of Provincetown. Phone 508/349-1900; toll-free 800/826-9300.* Offers 3 1/2-4-hour trips (Mid-Apr-Oct, daily). Research scientists from the Provincetown Center for Coastal Studies are aboard each trip to lecture on the history of the whales being viewed. **$$$$**

Special Event

Provincetown Portuguese Festival. *MacMillian Wharf (02657). Phone 508/487-3424.* Provincetown's fisherman of Portuguese ancestry started this enduring festival over 50 years ago. Each year in late June, the local bishop says Mass at St. Peter's Church and then leads a procession to MacMillan Wharf, where he blesses a parade of fishing boats. The festival that follows features fireworks, concerts, dancing, Portuguese art, and delightful food choices. If you aren't in town for the Provincetown Blessing, check out similar events in Falmouth (July 4) and Hyannis (early July). Last week in June.

Motels/Motor Lodges

★ **BEST WESTERN CHATEAU MOTOR INN.** *105 Bradford St W (02657). Phone 508/487-1286; toll-free 800/780-7234; fax 508/487-3557. www.bwprovincetown.com.* 54 rooms, 1-2 story. Closed Nov-Apr. Complimentary continental breakfast. Check-out 11 am. TV; cable (premium). In-room modem link. Outdoor pool. Harbor view. **$**

★ ★ **BEST WESTERN TIDES BEACHFRONT MOTOR INN.** *837 Commercial St (02657). Phone 508/487-1045; toll-free 800/780-7234; fax 508/ 487-3557. www.bwprovincetown.com.* 64 rooms, 1-2 story. Closed mid-Oct-mid-May. Check-out 11 am. TV; cable (premium). In-room modem link. Laundry services. Restaurant. Outdoor pool. On private beach. **$**

★ **BLUE SEA MOTOR INN.** *696 Shore Rd (02657). Phone 508/487-1041; toll-free 888/768-7666. www.blueseamotorinn.com.* 43 rooms, 1-2 story. Closed Nov-Apr. Check-out 10 am. TV. In-room modem link. Laundry services. Indoor pool, whirlpool. **$**

Resorts

★ ★ **THE MASTHEAD RESORT.** *31-41 Commercial St (02657). Phone 508/487-0523; toll-free 800/395-5095; fax 508/481-9251. www.capecodtravel.com/masthead.* 10 rooms, 2 story. Check-out 10 am. TV. In-shore and deepwater moorings; launch service. On private beach. **$**

D 🖾

★ ★ **PROVINCETOWN INN.** *1 Commericial St (02657). Phone 508/487-9500; toll-free 800/942-5388; fax 508/487-2911. www.provincetowninn.com.* 100 rooms, 1-2 story. Complimentary continental breakfast. Check-out 11 am. TV. Restaurant, bar. Outdoor pool. Private beach. **$**

🖾 🖾

All Suite

★ ★ **WATERMARK INN.** *603 Commercial St (02657). Phone 508/487-0165; fax 508/487-2383. www.watermark-inn.com.* 10 rooms, 2 story. Check-out 11 am, check-in 3 pm. TV. In-room modem link. On beach. **$**

B&B/Small Inns

★ ★ **FAIRBANKS INN.** *90 Bradford St (02657). Phone 508/487-0386; toll-free 800/324-7265; fax 508/487-3540. www.fairbanksinn.com.* 14 rooms, 2 story. No room phones. Children over 15 years only. Complimentary continental breakfast. Check-out 11 am, check-in 2 pm. TV; cable (premium). Concierge. Built in 1776; courtyard. Totally nonsmoking. **$**

🖾

★ ★ ★ **SNUG COTTAGE.** *178 Bradford St (02657). Phone 508/487-1616; fax 508/487-5123. www.snugcottage.com.* This romantic inn offers the perfect relaxing vacation spot. Guests will enjoy the colorful gardens and original paintings. Guest rooms are individually decorated. 8 rooms, 1-2 story. Complimentary breakfast. Check-out 11 am, check-in 3 pm. TV; VCR (free movies). Fireplaces. Built in 1820. **$$**

🖾

★ ★ **SOMERSET HOUSE.** *378 Commercial St (02657). Phone 508/487-0383; toll-free 800/575-1850; fax 508/487-4746. www.somersethouseinn.com.* 13 rooms, 2-3 story. Complimentary full breakfast. Check-out 11 am, check-in 3 pm. TV; cable. Opposite beach. Restored 1850s house. Totally nonsmoking. **$$**

🖾

★ ★ **WATERSHIP INN.** *7 Winthrop St (02657). Phone 508/487-0094; toll-free 800/330-9413. www.watershipinn.com.* 15 rooms, 3 story. Some A/C. No room phones. Complimentary continental breakfast. Check-out 11:30 am, check-in 2 pm. TV. Lawn games. Built in 1820. **$**

★ ★ **WHITE WIND INN.** *174 Commercial St (02657). Phone 508/487-1526; toll-free 888/49-WIND; fax 508/487-4792. www.whitewindinn.com.*

12 rooms, 8 with shower only, 3 story. No elevator. No room phones. Pets accepted, some restrictions; fee. Complimentary continental breakfast. Check-out 11 am, check-in 2 pm. TV; VCR available (movies). Concierge. Built in 1845; former shipbuilder's home. Opposite the harbor. Totally nonsmoking. **$**

Restaurants

★ ★ **CAFE EDWIGE.** 333 Commercial St (02657). Phone 508/487-2008. Closed Oct 31; also late May. Breakfast, dinner. Outdoor seating. Cathedral ceilings, skylights. Totally nonsmoking. **$$**

★ ★ **DANCING LOBSTER CAFE.** 373 Commercial St (02657). Phone 508/487-0900. Mediterranean menu. Closed Mon; also Dec-May. Dinner. Bar. **$$**

D

★ ★ **FRONT STREET.** 230 Commercial St (02657). Phone 508/487-9715. www.capecod.net/frontstreet. Italian, continental menu. Closed Jan-Apr. Dinner. Bar. Totally nonsmoking. **$$**

D

★ ★ **LOBSTER POT.** 321 Commercial St (02657). Phone 508/487-0842; fax 508/487-4863. www.provincetown.com/lobsterpot. Closed Jan. Lunch, dinner. Bar. Lobster and chowder market on premises. **$$**

D

★ ★ **NAPI'S.** 7 Freeman St (02657). Phone 508/487-1145; fax 508/487-7123. www.provincetown.com. Continental menu. Dinner. Bar. Children's menu. **$$**

D

★ **PUCCI'S HARBORSIDE.** 539 Commercial St (02657). Phone 508/487-1964. Seafood menu. Closed Nov-mid-Apr. Lunch, dinner. Bar. **$$**

D

★ ★ ★ **RED INN RESTAURANT.** 15 Commercial St (02657). Phone 508/487-0050; fax 508/487-6253. Located on the edge of the harbor, this historic inn restaurant features continental cuisine with an emphasis on seafood and prime beef. The views are stunning and the service is friendly. Continental menu. Closed Dec 25. Lunch, dinner, Sun brunch. Three dining rooms in a restored colonial building. **$$**

D

★ ★ **SAL'S PLACE.** 99 Commercial St (02657). Phone 508/487-1279; fax 508/487-1279. www.salsplaceprovincetown.com. Southern Italian menu. Closed Nov-Apr. Dinner. Children's menu. Outdoor seating. **$$**

D

Sandwich

1 hour 3 minutes; 57.5 miles from Boston

Settled 1637 **Pop** 20,136 **Elev** 20 ft **Area code** 508 **Zip** 02563

Information Cape Cod Canal Region Chamber of Commerce, 70 Main St, Buzzards Bay 02532; 508/759-6000

Web www.capecodcanalchamber.org

The first town to be settled on Cape Cod, Sandwich made the glass that bears its name. This pressed glass was America's greatest contribution to the glass industry.

What to See and Do

⭐ **Heritage Plantation.** *67 Grove St (02563). Phone 508/888-3300. www. heritageplantation.org.* The Heritage Plantation offers an eclectic mix of beautiful gardens, folk art, antique cars, and military paraphernalia. Visit the Old East Windmill from 1800 and the restored 1912 carousel that's great fun for young and old. Call ahead to find out about unique exhibits, displays, and concerts. Note that the Heritage Plantation is located in the town of Sandwich, the oldest town on the Cape. (Daily, mid-May-mid-Oct) **$$**

Hoxie House & Dexter Gristmill. *Water St (02563). Phone 508/888-1173.* Restored mid-17th-century buildings. House, operating mill; stone-ground corn meal sold. (Mid-June-mid-Oct, daily)

Sandwich Glass Museum. *129 Main St (02563). Phone 508/888-0251.* Internationally renowned collection of exquisite Sandwich Glass (circa 1825-1888). (Apr-Oct, daily) **$$**

Scusset Beach. *3 miles NW on MA 6A across canal, then 2 miles E at junction MA 3 and US 6. Phone 508/362-3225.* Swimming beach, fishing pier; camping (fee).

Shawme-Crowell State Forest. *42 Main St (02563). 3 miles W on MA 130, off US 6. Phone 508/888-0351.* Approximately 2,700 acres. Primitive camping. Standard fees.

Motels/Motor Lodges

⭐ **COUNTRY ACRES MOTEL.** *187 Rte 6A (02563). Phone 508/888-2878; toll-free 888/860-8650; fax 508/888-8511. www.countryacresmotel.com.* 17 rooms. Check-out 11 am. TV; cable (premium). Outdoor pool. Lawn games. **$**
🔲 🔲

⭐ **EARL OF SANDWICH MOTEL.** *378 Rte 6A (02537). Phone 508/888-1415; toll-free 800/442-3275; fax 508/833-1039. www.earlofsandwich.com.* 24 rooms. Pets accepted, some restrictions. Complimentary continental breakfast. Check-out 11 am. TV. Tudor motif. **$**
D 🔲 🔲

★ **OLD COLONY MOTEL.** *436 Rte 6A (02537). Phone 508/888-9716; toll-free 800/786-9716. www.oldcolonymotel.com.* 10 rooms. Complimentary continental breakfast. Check-out 11 am. TV. Outdoor pool. Lawn games. **$**

★ **SANDY NECK MOTEL.** *669 Rte 6A (02537). Phone 508/362-3992; toll-free 800/564-3992; fax 508/362-5170. www.sandyneck.com.* 12 rooms. Closed Jan. Check-out 11 am. TV; cable (premium). **$**

★ **SHADY NOOK INN & MOTEL.** *14 Old Kings Hwy (02563). Phone 508/888-0409; toll-free 800/338-5208; fax 508/888-4039. www.shadynookinn.com.* 30 rooms. Check-out 11 am. TV; cable (premium). In-room modem link. Laundry services. Outdoor pool. **$**

★ **SPRING HILL MOTOR LODGE.** *351 Rte 6A (02537). Phone 508/888-1456; toll-free 800/646-2514; fax 508/833-1556. www.sunsol.com/springhill.* 24 rooms. Check-out 11 am. TV; cable (premium). Outdoor pool. Outdoor tennis. **$**

B&B/Small Inns

★★★ **BAY BEACH BED & BREAKFAST.** *3 Bay Beach Ln (02563). Phone 508/888-8813; toll-free 800/475-6398; fax 508/888-5416. www.baybeach.com.* Overlooking Cape Cod Bay, this private, beachfront bed-and-breakfast offers guests a quiet haven from their busy lives. Visitors will enjoy the elegant guest room amenities such as fresh flowers, wine and cheese, and fresh fruit in their refrigerator. 6 rooms, 3 story. Closed Nov-mid-May. Children over 16 years only. Complimentary full breakfast. Check-out noon, check-in 2-6 pm. TV; cable (premium). In-house fitness room. Concierge. On beach. Totally nonsmoking. **$$$**

★★ **THE BELFRY INN & BISTRO.** *6-8 Jarves St (02563). Phone 508/888-8550; toll-free 800/844-4542; fax 508/888-3922. www.belfryinn.com.* 14 air-cooled rooms, 3 with shower only, 3 story. No elevator. Children over 10 years only. Complimentary full breakfast. Check-out 11 am, check-in 3 pm. TV in common room; cable (premium), VCR available (movies). In-room modem link. Fireplaces. Laundry services. Restaurant. Room service 24 hours. Lawn games. Business center. Concierge. Former rectory built in 1882; belfrey access. Totally nonsmoking. **$$**

★★ **CAPTAIN EZRA NYE HOUSE BED & BREAKFAST.** *152 Main St (02563). Phone 508/888-6142; toll-free 800/388-2278; fax 508/833-2897. www.captainezranyehouse.com.* 6 rooms, 2 story. No A/C. No room phones.

Children over 10 years only. Complimentary full breakfast. Check-out 11 am, check-in 2 pm. TV in sitting room. Built in 1829. Totally nonsmoking. **$**

★ ★ ★ **DAN'L WEBSTER INN.** *149 Main St (02563). Phone 508/888-3622; toll-free 800/444-3566; fax 508/888-5156. www.danlwebsterinn.com.* Enjoy candlelit evenings by the fire in the award-winning restaurant at this comfortable inn. Modern comfort and old-world charm unite to offer a memorable stay in the heart of New England. 54 rooms, 1-3 story. Check-out 11 am, check-in 3 pm. TV; cable (premium). In-room modem link. Dining room (see DAN'L WEBSTER INN). Bar; entertainment. Room service. Outdoor pool. Whirlpool in suites. Modeled on an 18th-century house. **$$**

★ ★ ★ **ISAIAH JONES HOMESTEAD.** *165 Main St (02563). Phone 508/888-9115; toll-free 800/526-1625; fax 508/888-9648. www.isaiahjones.com.* An American flag and flower-lined porch beckon guests inside this 1849 Victorian home. The guest rooms, decorated with antiques and country-patterned fabrics, are a great resting stop when visiting this Cape Cod town's many historic sites. 7 rooms, 2 story. No A/C. No room phones. Children over 16 years only. Complimentary full breakfast. Check-out 11 am, check-in 3-6 pm. TV in sitting room. Concierge. Totally nonsmoking. **$**

★ ★ **VILLAGE INN.** *4 Jarves St (02563). Phone 508/833-0363; toll-free 800/922-9989; fax 508/833-2063. www.capecodinn.com.* 8 rooms, 3 story. No A/C. No room phones. Children over 8 years only. Complimentary full breakfast. Check-out 11 am, check-in 3-6 pm. Federal-style house (1837) with wrap-around porch, gardens. Totally nonsmoking. **$**

Restaurants

★ **BOBBY BYRNE'S PUB.** *Rte 6A and Tupper Rd (02563). Phone 508/888-6088; fax 508/833-1614. www.bobbybyrnes.com.* Seafood, steak menu. Closed Thanksgiving, Dec 25. Lunch, dinner. Bar. Children's menu. **$$**

Ⓓ

★ ★ **BRIDGE RESTAURANT.** *21 MA 6A (02561). Phone 508/888-8144.* Continental, Italian, seafood menu. Closed Thanksgiving, Dec 25. Lunch, dinner. Bar. Children's menu. **$**

Ⓓ

★ ★ ★ **DAN'L WEBSTER INN.** *149 Main St (02563). Phone 508/888-3623; fax 508/888-5156. www.danlwebsterinn.com.* Dinner in the dining room of the historic Cape Cod inn is a romantic affair, complete with candlelight and a wood-burning fireplace. The updated continental menu ranges from prime rib and filet mignon to pan-seared monkfish. Seafood menu. Breakfast, lunch, dinner, Sun brunch. Bar. Children's menu. Valet parking. Conservatory dining overlooks garden. Reproduction of a 1700s house. **$$**

D

★ **HORIZONS.** *98 Town Neck Rd (02563). Phone 508/888-6166; fax 508/ 888-9209.* Seafood, steak menu. Closed Jan-Apr. Lunch, dinner. Bar; entertainment Sat. Children's menu. Outdoor seating. **$**

D

South Yarmouth

1 hour 20 minutes; 75 miles from Boston

Pop 11,603 **Elev** 20 ft **Area code** 508 **Zip** 02664

Information Yarmouth Area Chamber of Commerce, PO Box 479; 800/732-1008; or the Cape Cod Chamber of Commerce, US 6 and MA 132, PO Box 790, Hyannis 02601-0790; 508/362-3225 or 888/CAPECOD

Web www.capecodchamber.org

Much of the area of the Yarmouths developed on the strength of seafaring and fishing in the first half of the 19th century. South Yarmouth is actually a village within the town of Yarmouth. Well-preserved old houses line Main Street to the north in Yarmouth Port, architecturally among the choicest communities in Massachusetts. Bass River, to the south, also contains many fine estates.

What to See and Do

Captain Bangs Hallet House. *11 Strawberry Ln (02664). Off MA 6A, near Yarmouth Port Post Office. Phone 508/362-3021.* Early 19th-century sea captain's home. (June-Oct, Thurs-Sun afternoons; rest of year, by appointment) Botanic trails (all year; donation). Gate house (June-mid-Sept, daily). **$$**

Swimming. *265 Sisson Rd (02645). Phone 508/430-7553.* Nantucket Sound and bayside beaches. Parking fee.

Winslow Crocker House. *250 Rte 6A (02675). On Old King's Hwy, US 6A, in Yarmouth Port. Phone 508/362-4385.* (Circa 1780) Georgian house adorned with 17th-, 18th-, and 19th-century furnishings collected in early 20th century. Includes furniture made by New England craftsmen in the colonial and Federal periods; hooked rugs, ceramics, pewter. (June-mid-Oct, Tues, Thurs, Sat, and Sun) **$$**

Motels/Motor Lodges

★ ★ **ALL SEASON MOTOR INN.** *1199 Rte 28 (02664). Phone 508/394-7600; toll-free 800/527-0359; fax 508/398-7160. www.allseasons.com.* 114 rooms, 2 story. Check-out 11 am. TV; cable (premium), VCR (movies).

Laundry services. Restaurant. In-house fitness room, sauna. Game room. Outdoor pool, whirlpool. **$**

D 〜 🕱 🏊

★ **AMERICANA HOLIDAY MOTEL.** *99 Main St (02673). Phone 508/ 775-5511; toll-free 800/445-4497; fax 508/790-0597. www.americanaholiday .com.* 153 rooms, 2 story. Closed Nov-Feb. Check-out 11 am. TV. Sauna. Game room. One indoor pool, two outdoor pools, whirlpool. Lawn games. **$**

D 〜 🏊 SC

★ **BEACH 'N TOWNE MOTEL.** *1261 Rte 28 (02664). Phone 508/398- 2311; toll-free 800/987-8556. www.sunsol.com/beachntowne.* 21 rooms. Closed Jan. Check-out 11 am. TV. Outdoor pool. Lawn games. **$**

〜 🏊

★ ★ **BEST WESTERN BLUE ROCK RESORT.** *39 Todd Rd (02664). Phone 508/398-6962; fax 508/398-1830. www.bestwestern.com.* 44 rooms, 1-2 story. Closed late-Oct-Mar. Check-out 11 am. TV. Restaurant, bar. Outdoor pool, whirlpool. Golf on premise, greens fee $31. Outdoor tennis. **$**

D 🕱 🏌 〜 🏊

★ ★ **BEST WESTERN BLUE WATER ON THE OCEAN.** *291 S Shore Dr (02664). Phone 508/398-2288; toll-free 800/367-9393; fax 508/398- 1010. www.bestwestern.com.* 106 rooms, 1-2 story. Check-out 11 am. TV. Restaurant, bar; entertainment Fri-Sat. Free supervised children's activities (July-Labor Day), ages 6-15. Sauna. Indoor pool, outdoor pool, whirlpool, poolside service. Outdoor tennis. Lawn games. On 600-foot private ocean beach. **$$**

D 🏌 〜

★ **CAVALIER MOTOR LODGE.** *881 Main St (02664). Phone 508/394- 6575; toll-free 800/545-3536; fax 508/394-6578. www.cavaliermotorlodge .com.* 66 rooms, 1-2 story. Closed Nov-late-Mar. TV; VCR available (movies). Sauna. Game room. Indoor pool, outdoor pool, children's pool, whirlpool. Lawn games. **$**

〜 🏊

★ ★ **GULL WING SUITES.** *822 Main St (Rte 28) (02664). Phone 508/ 394-9300; fax 508/394-1190. www.ccrh.com.* 136 rooms, 2 story. Check-out 11 am. TV; cable (premium). Sauna. Game room. Indoor pool, outdoor pool, whirlpool. **$**

D 〜 🏊 SC

★ **HUNTERS GREEN MOTEL.** *553 Main St (02673). Phone 508/771- 1169; toll-free 800/775-5400. www.capecodmotel.com.* 74 rooms, 2 story. Closed Nov-mid-Apr. Check-out 11 am. TV; cable (premium). Indoor/ outdoor pool, whirlpool. Lawn games. **$**

D 〜

★ **LEWIS BAY LODGE.** *149 Rte 28 (02673). Phone 508/775-3825; toll-free 800/882-8995; fax 508/778-2870. www.lewisbaylodge.com.* 68 rooms, 2 story. Closed Nov-late-Apr. Complimentary continental breakfast. Check-out 11 am. TV; cable (premium). In-house fitness room. Indoor pool, outdoor pool, whirlpool. **$**

D ⌦ 🏃 ⌦

★ **MARINER MOTOR LODGE.** *573 Rte 28 (02673). Phone 508/771-7887; toll-free 800/445-4050; fax 508/771-2811. www.mariner-capecod.com.* 100 rooms, 2 story. Continental breakfast. Check-out 11 am. TV; cable (premium). Sauna. Game room. Indoor pool, outdoor pool, whirlpool. **$**

D ⌦ ⌦ SC

★ ★ ★ **RED JACKET BEACH.** *1 S Shore Dr (02664). Phone 508/398-6941; toll-free 800/672-0500; fax 508/398-1214. www.redjacketbeach.com.* Found steps away from the coast, this Cape Cod oceanfront resort has private balconies or porches for each room to enjoy the view. Indoor and outdoor heated pools and complete recreation facilities including spas, sailing, tennis, and many more are available. 150 rooms, 1-2 story. Closed late Oct-Mar. Check-out 11 am. TV. Laundry services. Restaurant, bar. Room service. Supervised children's activities (July-Labor Day), ages 4-12. In-house fitness room, sauna. Game room. Indoor pool, outdoor pool, whirlpool, poolside service. Outdoor tennis. Lawn games. Sailing. **$$**

D ⌦ ⌦ 🏃 ⌦

★ **TIDEWATER MOTOR LODGE.** *135 Main St (02673). Phone 508/775-6322; fax 508/778-5105. www.tidewaterml.com.* 100 rooms, 1-2 story. Check-out 11 am. TV. Sauna. Game room. Indoor pool, outdoor pool, whirlpool. Lawn games. On 4 acres; view of Mill Creek Bay. **$**

⌦ ⌦

Resorts

★ ★ **RIVIERA BEACH RESORT–BASS RIVER.** *327 S Shore Dr (02664). Phone 508/398-2273; toll-free 800/CAPECOD; fax 508/398-1202.* 125 rooms, 2 story. Closed late Oct-mid-Apr. Check-out 11 am. TV; VCR available (movies). Restaurant, bar. Free supervised children's activities (July-Labor Day), ages 4-11. Indoor pool, outdoor pool, whirlpool. Lawn games. Sailing, waterbikes, sailboards in season. On 415-foot private beach. **$$**

D ⌦ ⌦

★ ★ **YARMOUTH RESORT.** *343 Rte 28 (02673). Phone 508/775-5155; fax 508/790-8255. www.yarmouthresort.com.* 138 rooms, 2 story. Check-out 11 am. TV. In-room modem link. Sauna. Game room. Indoor pool, outdoor pool, whirlpool. **$**

D ⌦ ⌦

B&B/Small Inns

★ ★ ★ **CAPTAIN FARRIS HOUSE BED & BREAKFAST.** *308 Old Main St (02664). Phone 508/760-2818; toll-free 800/350-9477; fax 508/398-1262. www.captainfarris.com.* With its beautifully landscaped lawns and breathtaking views, this bed-and-breakfast will surely please everyone. Guests can enjoy sailing, canoeing, kayaking, and windsurfing. Antique shopping, birdwatching, and The John F. Kennedy Museum are also nearby. 10 rooms. Children over 10 years only. Complimentary full breakfast. Check-out 11 am, check-in 3 pm. TV; VCR. In-room modem link. Fireplaces. Dining room by reservation. Whirlpool. Lawn games. Concierge. Two buildings (1825 and 1845). Near Bass River. **$**

★ ★ **COLONIAL HOUSE INN & RESTAURANT.** *277 Main St (Rte 6A) (02675). Phone 508/362-4348; fax 508/362-8034.* 21 rooms, 3 story. Pets accepted; fee. Complimentary breakfast. Check-out noon, check-in 2 pm. TV; VCR available. In-room modem link. Dining room, bar. Massage. Indoor pool, whirlpool. Lawn games. Business center. Old mansion (1730s); many antiques, handmade afghans. **$**

★ ★ ★ **INN AT LEWIS BAY.** *57 Maine Ave (02673). Phone 508/771-3433; toll-free 800/962-6679; fax 508/790-1186. www.innatlewisbay.com.* Located in a quiet seaside neighborhood just one block from Lewis Bay, this Dutch colonial bed-and-breakfast offers guests a relaxing place to vacation. The guest rooms are individually decorated. A bountiful breakfast is served each morning and afternoon refreshments each afternoon. 6 rooms, 2 story. No room phones. Children over 12 years only. Complimentary full breakfast. Check-out 11 am, check-in 3-8 pm. Lawn games. Concierge. Beach house built in the 1920s. Totally nonsmoking. **$**

★ ★ ★ **LIBERTY HILL INN.** *77 Main St (MA 6A) (02675). Phone 508/362-3976; toll-free 800/821-3977; fax 508/362-6485. www.libertyhillinn.com.* Built in 1825, this charming bed-and-breakfast features individually appointed rooms, all unique in their décor and feel; many feature fireplaces and canopy beds. 9 rooms, 3 story. No room phones. Complimentary breakfast. Check-out 11 am, check-in 3-9 pm. TV. Free airport transportation. Concierge. Totally nonsmoking. **$**

Restaurants

★ ★ **ABBICCI.** *43 Main St (02675). Phone 508/362-3501; fax 508/362-7802. www.abbiccirestaurant.* Italian menu. Dinner. Bar. **$$$**

★ ★ **RIVERWAY LOBSTER HOUSE.** *MA 28 (02664). Phone 508/398-2172.* Seafood menu. Closed Dec 25. Dinner. Bar. Children's menu. **$**

D

★ **SKIPPER RESTAURANT.** *152 S Shore Dr (02664). Phone 508/394-7406; fax 508/394-0627. www.skipper-restaurant.com.* Seafood, steak menu. Closed Oct-Mar. Breakfast, lunch, dinner. Bar. Children's menu. A/C upstairs only. **$$**

D

Truro and North Truro

2 hours 5 minutes; 105 miles from Boston

Settled Truro: circa 1700 **Pop** 2,087 **Elev** 20 ft **Area code** 508 **Zip** Truro 02666; North Truro 02652

Information Cape Cod Chamber of Commerce, Rtes 6 and 132, PO Box 790, Hyannis 02601-0790; 508/362-3225 or 888/CAPECOD

Web www.capecodchamber.org

Truro, named for one of the Channel towns of England, is today perhaps the most sparsely settled part of the Cape—with great stretches of rolling moorland dotted only occasionally with cottages. On the hill above the Pamet River marsh are two early 19th-century churches; one is now the town hall. The countryside is a favorite resort of artists and writers.

What to See and Do

Fishing. *Pamet and Depot rds.* Surf casting on Atlantic beaches. Boat ramp at Pamet and Depot roads; fee for use, harbor master on duty.

Pilgrim Heights Area. *Cape Cod National Seashore (see). Off Rte 6. Phone 508/487-1256.* Interpretive display, self-guided nature trails, picnicking; rest rooms. **FREE**

Swimming. **Head of the Meadow.** *N on Rte 6 and W of Chamber of Commerce booth.* **Corn Hill Beach.** *On the bay (fee). S on Rte 6, then E.* A sticker for all beaches must be purchased from National Park Service Visitor Center or at beach entrances. No lifeguards. Mid-June-Labor Day.

Truro Historical Society Museum. *6 Highland Light Rd, North Truro (02652). Phone 508/487-3397.* Collection of artifacts from the town's historic past, including shipwreck mementos, whaling gear, ship models, 17th-century firearms, pirate chest, and period rooms. (June-Sept, daily) **$$**

Motels/Motor Lodges

★ **CROW'S NEST MOTEL.** *496 Shore Rd, North Truro (02652). Phone 508/487-9031; toll-free 800/499-9799. www.capecodtravel.com.* 33 rooms, 2 story. No A/C. Closed Dec-Mar. Check-out 10 am. TV. On beach. **$**

★ **EAST HARBOUR MOTEL & COTTAGES.** *618 Shore Rd, North Truro (02652). Phone 508/487-0505; fax 508/487-6693. www.eastharbour.com.* 9 rooms. No A/C. Closed late Oct-mid-Apr. Check-out 10 am. TV. Laundry services. Private beach. **$**

★ **HARBOR VIEW VILLAGE.** *168 Shore Rd, North Truro (02652). Phone 508/487-1087; fax 508/487-6269. www.harborviewvillage.com.* 17 rooms. No A/C. No room phones. Children over 7 years only (in season). Check-out 10 am. TV. Overlooks a private beach. **$**

Restaurants

★ **ADRIAN'S.** *535 Rte 6 (02652). Phone 508/487-4360; fax 508/487-6510. www.capecod.com/adrians.* Regional Italian menu. Closed mid-Oct-mid-May. Breakfast, dinner. Bar. Children's menu. Outdoor seating. **$$**

[D]

★ ★ **BLACKSMITH SHOP RESTAURANT.** *17 Truro Center Rd (02666). Phone 508/349-6554.* Seafood menu. Closed Dec 25; also Mon-Wed in the off-season. Breakfast, dinner, Sun brunch. Bar. Children's menu. **$$**

[D]

★ **MONTANO'S.** *481 Rte 6 (02652). Phone 508/487-2026; fax 508/487-4913. www.montanos.com.* American, Italian menu. Closed Dec 24-25. Dinner. Children's menu. **$$**

Concord, NH

1 hour 10 minutes; 68 miles from Boston

Settled 1727 **Pop** 40,687 **Elev** 288 ft **Area code** 603 **Zip** 03301

Information Chamber of Commerce, 40 Commercial St; 603/224-2508

Web www.concordnhchamber.com

New Hampshire, one of the original 13 colonies, entered the Union in 1788—but its capital was in dispute for another 20 years. Concord finally won the honor in 1808. The state house, begun immediately, was finished in 1819. The legislature is the largest (more than 400 seats) of any state. Concord is the financial center of the state and a center of diversified industry as well.

What to See and Do

Canterbury Shaker Village. *288 Shaker Rd (03301). 15 miles N on I-93 to exit 18, then follow signs. Phone 603/783-9511.* Historic Shaker buildings; living museum of Shaker crafts, architecture, and inventions. Guided tour of six historic buildings and a museum. Restaurant. Gift shop. (May-Oct, daily; Apr and Nov-Dec, Sat, Sun) **$$$**

Capitol Center for the Arts. *44 S Main St (03301). Phone 603/225-1111. www.ccanh.com.* Renovated historic theater (1920s) is the state's largest. Presents nationally touring Broadway and popular family entertainment all year.

Christa McAuliffe Planetarium. *2 Institute Dr (03301). I-93, exit 15 E. Phone 603/271-7827. www.starhop.com.* Official state memorial to the nation's first teacher in space. Changing programs. (Daily except Mon; closed some major holidays, also Apr 12) **$$**

⭐ **Concord Arts & Crafts.** *36 N Main St (03301). Phone 603/228-8171.* High-quality traditional and contemporary crafts by some of New Hampshire's finest craftsmen; monthly exhibits. (Daily except Sun; closed most holidays)

League of New Hampshire Craftsmen. *205 N Main St (03301). Phone 603/224-1471. www.nhcrafts.org.* Six retail galleries throughout the state. Library and resource center for League Foundation members. (Mon-Fri; closed holidays) **FREE**

Museum of New Hampshire History. *6 Eagle Sq (03301). Phone 603/226-3189.* Historical museum (founded 1823) with permanent and changing exhibits, including excellent examples of the famed Concord Coach; museum store. (Tues-Sat, also Sun afternoons) **$$**

Pat's Peak Ski Area. *8 miles N on I-89 to US 202, then 8 miles W to NH 114, then 3 miles S, near Henniker. Phone 603/428-3245; toll-free 800/728-7732.* Triple, two double chairlifts, two T-bars, J-bar, pony lift; patrol, school, rentals, ski shop; snowmaking; cafeteria, lounge; nursery. Night skiing. (Dec-late Mar, daily; closed Dec 25)

Pierce Manse. *14 Penacook St (03301), 1 mile N of State House. Phone 603/224-0094, 603/224-7668 or 603/225-2068.* Home of President Franklin Pierce from 1842 to 1848. Reconstructed and moved to the present site; contains many original furnishings and period pieces. (Mid-June-mid-Sept, Mon-Fri; also by appointment; closed July 4, Labor Day) **$**

State House. *107 N Main St (03301). Phone 603/271-2154.* Hall of Flags; statues, portraits of state notables. (Mon-Fri; closed holidays) **FREE**

Motels/Motor Lodges

★ **CAPITOL INN.** *406 S Main St (03301). Phone 603/224-2511; toll-free 877/224-2511; fax 603/224-6032. www.capitolinnconcord.com.* 40 rooms, 2 story. Complimentary continental breakfast. Check-out 11 am. TV; cable (premium). Outdoor pool. **$**

🛏 🏊

★ **COMFORT INN.** *71 Hall St (03301). Phone 603/226-4100; toll-free 877/424-6423; fax 603/228-2106. www.comfortinn.com.* 100 rooms, 3 story. Pets accepted, some restrictions; fee. Complimentary continental breakfast. Check-out noon. TV. In-room modem link. Sauna. Game room. Indoor pool, whirlpool. **$**

D 🐾 🐕 ♿ 🛏 🏊 SC

★ **HAMPTON INN.** *515 South St (03304). Phone 603/224-5322; fax 603/224-4282. www.hamptoninn.com.* 145 rooms, 4 story. Complimentary continental breakfast. Check-out noon. TV; cable (premium), VCR available. Indoor pool, whirlpool. **$**

[D] [⚊] [⚊]

B&B/Small Inn

★ ★ ★ **COLBY HILL INN.** *The Oaks (03242). Phone 603/428-3281; toll-free 800/531-0330; fax 603/428-9218. www.colbyhillinn.com.* This classic New England country inn offers individually decorated rooms and a fine-dining restaurant in a beautiful, wooded setting. 16 rooms, 2 story. Children over 7 years only. Complimentary full breakfast. Check-out 11 am, check-in 3 pm. TV in library. In-room modem link. Some fireplaces. Dining room. Outdoor pool. Downhill, cross-country ski 1 1/2 miles. Lawn games. Historic farmhouse (circa 1800) used as a tavern, church, meeting house, and private school. On 5 acres. Totally nonsmoking. **$$**

[⚊] [⚊] [⚊]

Restaurant

★ **MARIA'S ITALIAN RESTAURANT.** *346 Suncook Valley Rd (03258). Phone 603/435-7370.* Italian menu. Closed Mon-Tues. Lunch, dinner. Bar. Children's menu. Casual attire. **$$**

[D]

Gloucester

42 minutes; 35 miles from Boston

Settled 1623 **Pop** 30,273 **Elev** 50 ft **Area code** 978 **Zip** 01930

Information Cape Ann Chamber of Commerce, 33 Commercial St; 978/283-1601 or 800/321-0133

Web www.capeannvacations.com

It is said that more than 10,000 Gloucester men have been lost at sea in the last three centuries, which emphasizes how closely the community has been linked with seafaring. Today it is still a leading fishing port—although the fast schooners made famous in *Captains Courageous* and countless romances have been replaced by diesel trawlers. Gloucester is also the center of an extensive summer resort area that includes the famous artists' colony of Rocky Neck.

What to See and Do

Beauport, the Sleeper-McCann House. *75 Eastern Point Blvd (01930). Phone 978/283-0800.* (1907-1934) Henry Davis Sleeper, early 20th-century interior designer, began by building a 26-room house, continually adding rooms with the help of Halfdan Hanson, a Gloucester architect, until there were 40 rooms; 25 are now on view, containing extraordinary collections of antique furniture, rugs, wallpaper, ceramics, and glass; American and European decorative arts. Many artists, statesmen, and businessmen were entertained here. (Mid-May-mid-Sept, Mon-Fri; mid-Sept-mid-Oct, daily) **$$$**

Cape Ann Historical Museum. *27 Pleasant St (01930). Phone 978/283-0455.* Paintings by Fitz Hugh Lane; decorative arts and furnishings; Federal-style house (circa 1805). Emphasis on Gloucester's fishing industry; fisheries/maritime galleries and changing exhibitions depict various aspects of Cape Ann's history. (Tues-Sat; closed holidays, also Feb) **$$**

Gloucester Fisherman. *On Stacy Blvd on the harbor.* Bronze statue by Leonard Craske, a memorial to anglers lost at sea.

Hammond Castle Museum. *80 Hesperus Ave (01930), off MA 127. Schedule may vary. Phone 978/283-2081.* (1926-1929) Built like a medieval castle by inventor Dr. John Hays Hammond, Jr.; contains a rare collection of art objects. The great Hall contains a pipe organ with 8,200 pipes; concerts (selected days throughout the year). (Memorial Day-Labor Day, daily; after Labor Day-Columbus Day, Thurs-Sun; rest of year, Sat and Sun; closed Jan 1, Thanksgiving, Dec 25). **$$**

Sargent House Museum. *49 Middle St (01930). Phone 978/281-2432.* Late 18th-century Georgian residence, built for Judith Sargent, an early feminist writer and sister of Governor Winthrop Sargent; also the home of her second husband, John Murray, leader of Universalism. Period furniture, china, glass, silver, needlework, early American portraits, and paintings by John Singer Sargent. (Memorial Day-Columbus Day, Mon, Fri-Sun; closed holidays) **$**

Special Events

Schooner Festival. *33 Commercial St (01930). Phone 978/283-1601.* Races and a parade of sail and maritime activities. Labor Day weekend.

St. Peter's Fiesta. *Phone 978/283-1601.* A four-day celebration with sports events, fireworks; procession; Blessing of the Fleet. Last weekend in June.

Waterfront Festival. *33 Commercial St (01930). Phone 978/283-1601.* Arts and crafts show, entertainment, food. Third weekend in Aug.

Whale-watching. *33 Commercial St (01930). Phone 978/283-1601.* Half-day trips, mornings and afternoons. May-Oct.

Motels/Motor Lodges

★ **ATLANTIS MOTOR INN.** *125 Atlantic Rd (01930). Phone 978/283-0014; toll-free 800/732-6313; fax 978/281-8994. www.atlantismotorinn.com.* 40 rooms, 2 story. No A/C. Closed rest of year. Check-out noon. TV. Outdoor pool. **$**

D ⌆ ⌧

★ **BEST WESTERN BASS ROCKS OCEAN INN.** *107 Atlantic Rd (01930). Phone 978/283-7600; toll-free 800/780-7234; fax 978/281-6489. www.bestwestern.com/bassrocksoceaninn.* 48 rooms, 2 story. Complimentary breakfast buffet. Check-out noon. TV; VCR available. In-room modem link. Outdoor pool. Bicycles available. **$$**

★ ★ **CAPTAIN'S LODGE MOTEL.** *237 Eastern Ave (01930). Phone 978/281-2420; fax 978/283-1608. www.seecapeann.com.* 47 rooms. Check-out 11 am. TV; cable (premium). Restaurant. Outdoor pool. Outdoor tennis. **$**

★ **THE MANOR INN.** *141 Essex Ave (01930). Phone 978/283-0614; fax 978/283-3154. www.themanorinnofgloucester.com.* 10 rooms. Closed Nov-Mar. Pets accepted, some restrictions; fee. Complimentary continental breakfast. Check-out 11 am, check-in 2 pm. TV. Victorian manor house. Some rooms overlook the river. **$**

★ **VISTA MOTEL.** *22 Thatcher Rd (01930). Phone 978/281-3410; fax 978/283-7335. www.vistamotel.com.* 40 rooms, 2 story. Continental breakfast in summer. Check-out 11 am. TV; cable (premium). Outdoor pool. Ocean opposite, beach privileges. **$**

Resort

★ ★ **OCEAN VIEW INN AND RESORT.** *171 Atlantic Rd (01930). Phone 978/283-6200; toll-free 800/315-7557; fax 978/283-1852. www.oceanviewinnandresort.com.* 62 rooms, 3 story. Pets accepted, some restrictions. Check-out 11 am, check-in 2 pm. TV; VCR available. In-room modem link. Restaurant. Two outdoor pools. Lawn games. Several buildings have accommodations, including a turn-of-the-century English manor house. **$**

Restaurants

★ **CAMERON'S.** *206 Main St (01930). Phone 978/281-1331; fax 978/281-2480. www.camerons-restaurant.com.* Italian menu. Closed Dec 25. Lunch, dinner. Bar; entertainment Wed-Sun. Children's menu. **$$**

★ ★ **GLOUCESTER HOUSE RESTAURANT.** *7 Seas Wharf (01930). Phone 978/283-1812; fax 978/281-0369. www.lobster-express.com.* Seafood menu. Closed Thanksgiving, Dec 25. Lunch, dinner. Bar; entertainment Thurs-Sun. Children's menu. Outdoor seating. **$$**

★ ★ **OCEAN'S EDGE RESTAURANT & PUB.** *171 Atlantic Rd (01930). Phone 978/283-6200; fax 978/282-7723. www.oceanviewinnandresort.com.* Breakfast, lunch, dinner. Bar. Casual attire. **$$$**

Hartford, CT

1 hour 40 minutes; 101 miles from Boston

Settled 1633 **Pop** 121,578 **Elev** 50 ft **Area code** 860

Information Greater Hartford Convention & Visitors Bureau, One Civic Center Plaza, Suite 300, 06103; 860/728-6789 or 800/446-7811 (outside CT)

Web www.enjoyhartford.com

The capital of Connecticut and a major industrial and cultural center on the Connecticut River, Hartford is headquarters for many of the nation's insurance companies.

Roots of American democracy are deep in Hartford's history. The city was made virtually independent in 1662 by Charles II, but an attempt was made by Sir Edmund Andros, governor of New England, to seize its charter. The document was hidden by Joseph Wadsworth in a hollow tree since known as the Charter Oak. The tree was blown down in 1856; a plaque on Charter Oak Avenue marks the spot.

Hartford has what is said to be the oldest continuously published newspaper in the United States, the *Courant*. Founded in 1764, it became a daily in 1837. Trinity College (1823), the American School for the Deaf, Connecticut Institute for the Blind, and the Institute of Living (for mental illness) are located in the city.

Transportation

AIRPORT
Hartford-Bradley International Airport. Information 860/627-3000; lost and found 860/627-3340; cash machines, Terminal B, Concourse A.

CAR RENTAL AGENCIES
See IMPORTANT TOLL-FREE NUMBERS.

PUBLIC TRANSPORTATION
Buses (Connecticut Transit), phone 860/525-9181.

RAIL PASSENGER SERVICE
Amtrak 800/872-7245.

What to See and Do

Bushnell Park. *Downtown, between Jewell, Elm, and Trinity sts. Phone 860/ 246-7739.* The 41-acre park contains 150 varieties of trees and a restored 1914 carousel (schedule varies; fee); concerts and special events (spring-fall). **FREE**

Butler-McCook Homestead and Main Street History Center. *396 Main St (06103). Phone 860/522-1806; toll-free 860/247-8996.* (1782) Preserved house, occupied by four generations of one family (1782-1971), has possessions dating back 200 years; collection of Victorian toys; Japanese armor; Victorian garden. (Wed-Sun; closed holidays) **$$**

Center Church and Ancient Burying Ground. *60 Gold St (06103). Phone 860/247-4080.* Church (1807) is patterned after London's St. Martin-in-the-Fields, with Tiffany stained-glass windows. Cemetery contains markers dating back to 1640.

Connecticut Audubon Society Holland Brook Nature Center. *1361 Main St (06103). Phone 860/633-8402.* On 48 acres adjacent to the Connecticut River, the center features a variety of natural history exhibits and includes a discovery room. Many activities. (Tues-Sun; closed holidays) **$**

Connecticut Historical Society. *1 Elizabeth St (06105). Phone 860/236-5621.* The library contains more than 3 million books and manuscripts. (Tues-Sat; closed holidays). The museum has nine galleries featuring permanent and changing exhibits on state history (Tues-Sun). **$$$**

Connecticut River Cruise. *152 River St (06108). Departs from Charter Oak Landing. Phone 860/526-4954.* The *Silver Star*, a reproduction of an 1850s steam yacht, makes 1- to 2 1/2-hour trips on the Connecticut River. (Memorial Day-Labor Day, daily; after Labor Day-Oct, Sat-Sun) **$$$**

Elizabeth Park. *Prospect and Asylum aves. Phone 860/242-0017.* Public gardens feature 900 varieties of roses and more than 14,000 other plants; first municipal rose garden in country; greenhouses (all year). Outdoor concerts in summer; ice skating in winter. (Daily) **FREE**

Harriet Beecher Stowe House. *77 Forest St (06105). Phone 860/522-9258. www.harrietbeecherstowe.org.* (1871) The restored Victorian cottage of the author of *Uncle Tom's Cabin* contains original furniture, memorabilia. Tours. (Tues-Sat, also Sun afternoons; also Mon June-Columbus Day and Dec) **$$$**

Heritage Trails Sightseeing. *Departs from Hartford hotels. Phone 860/677-8867.* Guided and narrated tours of Hartford and Farmington. (Daily) **$$$$**

Mark Twain House. *351 Farmington Ave (06105). Phone 860/247-0998.* (1874) *Tom Sawyer, Huckleberry Finn*, and other books were published while Samuel Clemens (Mark Twain) lived in this three-story Victorian mansion featuring the decorative work of Charles Comfort Tiffany and the Associated Artists; Tiffany-glass light fixtures, windows, and Tiffany-designed stencilwork in gold and silver leaf. Tours. (May-Oct and Dec, daily; rest of year, Mon, Wed-Sun; closed holidays) **$$$**

Museum of American Political Life. *200 Bloomfield Ave (06117). In the Harry Jack Gray Center. Phone 860/768-4090.* Exhibits include life-size mannequins re-creating political marches from the 1830s to the 1960s; 70-foot wall of historical pictures and images; political television commercials since 1952. (Tues-Sun afternoons; closed holidays) **FREE**

Noah Webster Foundation and Historical Society. *227 S Main St, West Hartford (06107). Phone 860/521-5362.* This 18th-century homestead was the birthplace of America's first lexicographer, writer of the *Blue-Backed*

Speller (1783) and the *American Dictionary* (1828). Period furnishings, memorabilia; costumed guides; period gardens. (Mon, Thurs-Sun; closed holidays) **$$**

Old State House. *800 Main St (06103). Phone 860/522-6766.* (1796) Oldest state house in the nation, designed by Charles Bulfinch; restored Senate chamber with Gilbert Stuart portrait of Washington; displays and rotating exhibitions. Tourist information center; museum shop. Guided tours by appointment. (Mon-Sat; closed holidays) **FREE**

Raymond E. Baldwin Museum of Connecticut History. *Connecticut State Library, 231 Capitol Ave (06106), opposite the Capitol. Phone 860/737-6535.* Exhibits include Colt Collection of Firearms; Connecticut artifacts, including original 1662 Royal Charter; portraits of Connecticut's governors. Library features law, social sciences, history, genealogy collections, and official state archives. (Daily; closed holidays) **FREE**

Science Center of Connecticut. *950 Trout Brook Dr, West Hartford (06119). Phone 860/231-2824.* Computer lab; UTC Wildlife Sanctuary; physical sciences discovery room; walk-in replica of sperm whale; "KaleidoSight," a giant walk-in kaleidoscope; planetarium shows; changing exhibits. (Tues-Sat, also Sun afternoons, Mon during summer; closed holidays) **$$$**

State Capitol. *210 Capitol Ave (06106), at Trinity St. Phone 860/240-0222.* (1879) Guided tours (1 hour) of the restored, gold-domed capitol building and the contemporary legislative office building (Mon-Fri; closed holidays, also Dec 25-Jan 1); includes historical displays. **FREE**

Talcott Mountain State Park. *8 miles NW via US 44, off CT 185, near Simsbury. Phone 860/677-0662.* The 557-acre park features the 165-foot Heublein Tower, on a mountaintop 1,000 feet above Farmington River; considered the best view in the state. Picnicking, shelters. (Third Sat Apr-Labor Day, Thurs-Sun; after Labor Day-first weekend in Nov, daily)

University of Hartford. *4 miles W, at 200 Bloomfield Ave, West Hartford (06117). Phone 860/768-4100.* (1877) 6,844 students. Independent institution on 320-acre campus. Many free concerts, operas, lectures, and art exhibits.

⭐ **Wadsworth Atheneum Museum of Art.** *600 Main St (06103). Phone 860/278-2670.* One of the nation's oldest continuously operating public art museums with more than 40,000 works of art, spanning 5,000 years: 15th- to 20th-century paintings, American furniture, sculpture, porcelains, English and American silver, the Amistad Collection of African-American art; changing contemporary exhibits. (Tues-Sun; closed holidays) Free admission Thurs and Sat mornings.

Special Events

Christmas Crafts Expo I & II. *1 Civic Center Plz (06103). Phone 860/249-6333.* Exhibits and demonstrations of traditional and contemporary craft media. First and second weekends in Dec.

Mark Twain Days. *351 Farmington Ave (06105). Phone 860/247-0998.* Celebration of Twain's legacy and Hartford's cultural heritage with more than 100 events. Concerts, riverboat rides, medieval jousting, tours of Twain House, entertainment. Aug.

Riverfest. *Charter Oak Landing and Constitution Plz. Phone 860/713-3131.* Celebration of America's independence and the Connecticut River. Family entertainment, concerts, food, fireworks display over river. Early July.

Taste of Hartford. *Main St, downtown. Phone 860/920-5337.* Four-day event features specialties of more than 50 area restaurants; continuous entertainment. June.

Motels/Motor Lodges

★ ★ **HOLIDAY INN.** *363 Roberts St (06108). Phone 860/528-9611; toll-free 800/465-4329; fax 860/289-0270. www.holiday-inn.com.* 130 rooms, 5 story. Pets accepted; fee. Check-out noon. TV; cable (premium). In-room modem link. Laundry services. Restaurant, bar. Room service. In-house fitness room. Indoor pool. **$**

★ **RAMADA INN.** *440 Asylum St (06103). Phone 860/246-6591; toll-free 800/272-6232; fax 860/728-1382. www.ramada.com.* 96 rooms, 9 story. Check-out noon. TV; cable (premium). Free valet parking. **$**

Hotels

★ ★ **CROWNE PLAZA.** *50 Morgan St (06120). Phone 860/549-2400; toll-free 800/227-6963; fax 860/549-7844. www.crowneplaza.com.* Located in the heart of downtown Hartford, this popular hotel offers guests all the convenient amenities they might expect, including oversized guest rooms. It is within walking distance of Hartford's popular theater district. 350 rooms, 18 story. Pets accepted, some restrictions; fee. Check-out noon, check-in 3 pm. TV; cable (premium), VCR available. In-room modem link. Restaurant, bar. In-house fitness room. Outdoor pool, poolside service. Free airport transportation. Business center. **$**

★ ★ ★ **GOODWIN HOTEL.** *1 Haynes St (06013). Phone 860/246-7500; toll-free 800/922-5006; fax 860/247-4576. www.goodwinhotel.com.* If travelers are looking for luxurious comfort with impeccable service, this beautiful hotel is the place to stay. Guest suites include mahogany sleigh beds and marble baths. 124 rooms, 6 story. Check-out noon. TV; cable (premium), VCR available. In-room modem link. Fireplaces. Restaurant, bar. Room service. In-house fitness room. Valet parking. Concierge. Small, European-style luxury hotel in a red-brick, Queen Anne-style building (1881) built for J. P. Morgan. **$**

★ ★ ★ **HILTON HARTFORD.** *315 Trumbull St (06103). Phone 860/728-5151; toll-free 800/774-1500; fax 860/240-7246. www.hartford.hilton.com.* For business and leisure travelers alike, this hotel is conveniently located in downtown Hartford and is connected to the Hartford Civic Center and

Civic Center Mall. 388 rooms, 22 story. Check-out noon. TV; cable (premium), VCR available. In-room modem link. Restaurant, bar. In-house fitness room, sauna. Indoor pool, whirlpool. **$$**

D ⊷ 🛉 🛉 ⊠

★ ★ ★ **MARRIOTT HARTFORD ROCKY HILL AT CORPORATE RIDGE.** *100 Capital Blvd (06067). Phone 860/257-6000; toll-free 800/228-9290. www.marriott.com.* 247 rooms, 4 story. Check-out 1 pm. TV; cable (premium). In-room modem link. Restaurant, bar. In-house fitness room. Indoor pool, whirlpool. Business center. Concierge. **$$$**

⊷ 🛉 🛉

★ ★ ★ **SHERATON HARTFORD HOTEL.** *100 E River Dr (06108). Phone 860/528-9703; toll-free 888/530-9703; fax 860/289-4728. www.sheraton.com.* 199 rooms, 8 story. Pets accepted, some restrictions; fee. Check-out 11 am. TV; cable (premium). In-room modem link. Laundry services. Restaurant, bar. Room service. Health club privileges. Indoor pool. **$$**

D 🐾 🐟 ⊷ ✈ ⊠

Restaurants

★ ★ **APP'S.** *451 Franklin Ave (06114). Phone 860/296-2777. www.appshartford.com.* International menu. Closed Mon. Lunch, dinner. Bar. **$$$**

★ ★ ★ **CARBONE'S.** *588 Franklin Ave (06114). Phone 860/296-9646; fax 860/296-2785.* Italian menu. Closed Sun; major holidays. Lunch, dinner. Bar. **$$**

D

★ **HOT TOMATOES.** *1 Union Pl (06103). Phone 860/249-5100; fax 860/524-8120.* Eclectic menu. Lunch, dinner, late night. Bar. Casual attire. Outdoor seating. **$$**

D

★ ★ **MAX DOWNTOWN.** *185 Asylum St (06103). Phone 860/522-2530; fax 860/246-5279. www.maxrestaurantgroup.com.* Closed most major holidays. Lunch, dinner. Bar. Children's menu. **$$**

D

★ ★ ★ **PASTIS.** *201 Ann St (06103). Phone 860/278-8852; fax 860/278-8854. www.pastisbrasserie.com.* Guests can enjoy intimate dining at this authentic French-style bistro. Steak menu. Closed Sun. Lunch, dinner. **$$**

D

★ ★ **PEPPERCORN'S GRILL.** *357 Main St (06106). Phone 860/547-1714; fax 860/724-7612. www.peppercornsrestaurant.com.* Italian menu. Closed Sun; major holidays. Lunch, dinner. Bar. Children's menu. **$$**

D

Lenox

2 hours 11 minutes; 130 miles from Boston

Settled circa 1750 **Pop** 5,077 **Elev** 1,200 ft **Area code** 413 **Zip** 01240

Information Chamber of Commerce, 65 Main St, PO Box 646; 413/637-3646

Web www.lenox.org

This summer resort became world-famous for music when the Boston Symphony began its Berkshire Festival here in 1939. Nearby is Stockbridge Bowl, one of the prettiest lakes in the Berkshires.

What to See and Do

★ **Edith Wharton Restoration (The Mount).** *2 Plunkett St (01240). Plunkett St at S junction of US 7 and MA 7A. Phone 413/637-1899.* Edith Wharton's summer estate; was planned from a book she coauthored in 1897, *The Decoration of Houses,* and built in 1902. This Classical Revival house is architecturally significant; ongoing restoration. On 49 acres, with gardens. Tour of house and gardens (early June-early Nov, daily). (See SPECIAL EVENTS) **$$$$**

Pleasant Valley Wildlife Sanctuary. *472 Mountain Rd (01240). On West Mountain Rd, 1 1/2 miles W of US 7/20. Phone 413/637-0320.* Sanctuary of the Massachusetts Audubon Society. 1,500 acres with 7 miles of trails; beaver colony; office. No dogs. (Mid-June-Columbus Day) **$$**

★ **Tanglewood.** *197 West St (02140). On West St, 1 1/2 miles SW on MA 183. Phone 413/637-1600 (summer) or 617/266-1492 (rest of year).* Where Nathaniel Hawthorne lived and wrote. Here he planned *Tanglewood Tales.* Many of the 526 acres, developed into a gentleman's estate by William Aspinwall Tappan, are in formal gardens. Well known today as the summer home of the Boston Symphony Orchestra and the Tanglewood Music Center, the symphony's training academy for young musicians. (See SPECIAL EVENTS) Grounds (daily; free except during concerts).

Chamber Music Hall. *197 West St (02140).* Small chamber music ensembles, lectures, seminars, and large classes held here. Designed by Eliel Saarinen, who also designed the

Formal Gardens. *197 West St (02140).* Manicured hemlock hedges and lawn, tall pine. Picnicking.

Hawthorne Cottage. *197 West St (02140).* Replica of the "Little Red House" where Hawthorne lived 1850-1851, now contains music studios, Hawthorne memorabilia. (Open before each festival concert.)

Koussevitzky Music Shed. *197 West St (02140).* (1938) The so-called "Shed," where Boston Symphony Orchestra concerts take place; holds 5,121.

Main Gate Area. *197 West St (02140).* Friends of Tanglewood, box office, music and bookstore; cafeteria; gift shop.

Maron House. *197 West St (02140).* Original mansion, now the Boston Symphony Orchestra Visitors Center and the Community Relations Office. Excellent view of Lake Mahkeenac, Monument Mountain.

Seiji Ozawa Concert Hall. *197 West St (02140).* (1941) Festival chamber music programs, Tanglewood Music Center activities; seats 1,200.

Special Events

Apple Squeeze Festival. *65 Main St (01240). Phone 413/637-3646.* Celebration of apple harvest; entertainment, food, music. Usually the third weekend in Sept.

House Tours of Historic Lenox. *65 Main St (01240). Phone 413/637-3646.* Fall.

Shakespeare & Company. *70 Kemble St (01240). Phone 413/637-3353 (box office) or 413/637-1199 (info).* Professional theater company performs plays by Shakespeare and Edith Wharton, as well as other events. Four stages, one outdoor. Tues-Sun. Late May-Dec.

Tanglewood Music Festival. *1277 Main St (02115). Phone 617/266-1200.* Tanglewood Boston Symphony Orchestra. Concerts performed on Fri and Sat evenings and Sun afternoons. Inquire for other musical events. July-Aug.

Motels/Motor Lodges

★ **HOWARD JOHNSON.** *462 Pittsfield Rd (01240). Phone 413/442-4000; toll-free 800/446-4656; fax 413/443-7954. www.hojo.com.* 44 rooms, 2 story. Complimentary continental breakfast. Check-out 11 am. TV. Outdoor pool. Business center. **$**

[D] [≈] [≈] [SC] [⅍]

★ **YANKEE INN.** *461 Pittsfield Rd (01240). Phone 413/499-3700; toll-free 800/835-2364; fax 413/499-3634. www.yankeeinn.com.* 96 rooms, 1-2 story. Continental breakfast. Check-out 11 am. TV. Fireplaces. Indoor pool. Downhill, cross-country ski 1 mile. Business center. On 7 1/2 acres with a pond. **$**

[D] [≈] [≈] [⅍]

Hotels

★ ★ ★ ★ **BLANTYRE.** *16 Blantyre Rd (01240). Phone 413/637-3556; fax 413/637-4282. www.blantyre.com.* Listen closely and you can still hear the laughter of Gilded Age garden parties at Blantyre. A private home in the early 1900s, this Tudor-style mansion set on 100 acres in the Berkshire Mountains now welcomes guests seeking to live out a splendid pastoral fantasy. Blantyre's rooms maintain a decidedly British country style of floral fabrics and overstuffed furniture. Fireplaces are available in many rooms to warm the often-chilly evenings. Country pursuits like croquet, tennis, and swimming entice many, while the cultural festivals of Tanglewood and Jacob's Pillow attract others. Dining at Blantyre is a special occasion, whether you're lingering over breakfast in the conservatory or enjoying the romantic ambience of a candlelit dinner. The chef even packs gourmet picnics for lazy summer afternoons that guests spend lounging within Blantyre's grounds or exploring the beautiful countryside. *Secret Inspector's Notes:* Blantyre is like stepping out of the real world and into the past. It harkens back to a place from perhaps Scotland or Wales; the mansion is a re-creation of a famous Scottish castle built by the original owner for his homesick wife. It is an idyllic setting for a wedding or special event and is perfect for a romantic weekend getaway. 23 rooms, 2 story. Closed mid-Nov-mid-May. Children over 12 years only. Complimentary continental breakfast. Check-out noon, check-in 3 pm. TV; VCR available. In-room modem link. Some fireplaces. Dining room. Room service. Massage, sauna. Outdoor pool, whirlpool, poolside service. Outdoor tennis. Airport transportation. Formal croquet lawns. **$$$**

★ ★ ★ **CRANWELL RESORT AND GOLF CLUB.** *55 Lee Rd (01240). Phone 413/637-1364; toll-free 800/272-6935; fax 413/637-0571. www.cranwell.com.* This historic 100-year-old country hotel is set on a hill and has a 60-mile view of the southern Berkshires. Situated on 380 acres, the property has a fantastic 18-hole championship golf course that is host to Beecher's golf school. 105 rooms in 7 buildings, 2-3 story. Complimentary continental breakfast. Check-out 11 am. TV; VCR available. In-room modem link. Fireplaces. Restaurant (see THE WYNDHURST RESTAURANT). Bar; entertainment Fri, Sat. In-house fitness room. Indoor pool, poolside service. Golf on premise, greens fee $25-$85. Tennis. Downhill ski 7 miles, cross-country ski on site. Heliport. Country Tudor mansion. **$$**

★ ★ ★ **WHEATLEIGH.** *Hawthorne Rd (01240). Phone 413/637-0610; fax 413/637-4507. www.wheatleigh.com.* Wheatleigh is a country house hotel of the finest order. This 19th-century Italianate palazzo is gloriously set on 22 acres of rolling hills and lush gardens in the Berkshire Mountains. The magical estate shares in the grand Gilded Age heritage of this celebrated region. This bucolic retreat, with a Frederick Law Olmstead-designed private park as its backyard, maintains an urbane spirit. The interiors present a crisp, contemporary approach to classic sensibilities. Lacking the formality of the past and avoiding the starkness of modern style, the guest rooms are comfortably elegant. Details make the difference here, from the dazzling Tiffany windows to the ornate fireplace in the Great Hall. The restaurant is a great source of pride, and its updated French dishes draw gourmets. 19 rooms, 2 story. Children over 9 years only. Check-out noon, check-in 3 pm. TV; VCR. Many fireplaces. Dining room (see also WHEATLEIGH). Room service. Massage. Outdoor pool. Outdoor tennis. Downhill ski 9 miles. Valet parking. Concierge. Built in 1893; abstract sculptures. **$$**

B&B/Small Inns

★ ★ **APPLE TREE INN.** *10 Richmond Mountain Rd (01240). Phone 413/637-1477; fax 413/637-2528. www.appletree-inn.com.* 35 rooms, 2 share bath, 3 story. No room phones. Complimentary continental breakfast. Check-out 11:30 am, check-in 2 pm. TV in some rooms. Restaurant (see APPLE TREE). Outdoor pool. Tennis. Cross-country ski 1 mile. Built in 1885; situated on 22 hilltop acres. **$**

★ ★ **BIRCHWOOD INN.** *7 Hubbard St (01240). Phone 413/637-2600; toll-free 800/524-1646; fax 413/637-4604.* 12 rooms, 8 with shower only, 2 share bath, 3 story. Children over 12 years only. Complimentary full breakfast. Check-out 11:30 am, check-in 2 pm. TV in some rooms. Downhill ski 5 miles, cross-country ski adjacent. Built in 1767; many antiques, gardens. Totally nonsmoking. **$**

★ ★ ★ **BROOK FARM INN.** *15 Hawthorne St (01240). Phone 413/637-3013; toll-free 800/285-7638; fax 413/637-4751. www.brookfarm.com.* The interior of this Victorian inn has a very literary feel perfectly suited to its historic location. Visit nearby cultural venues, including Tanglewood music center, or curl up with a treasure from the impressive library of poetry, fiction, and history. 12 rooms, 3 story. Children over 15 years only. Complimentary full breakfast. Check-out 11 am, check-in 3 pm. Outdoor pool. Downhill ski 4 miles, cross-country ski 1 mile. Built in 1870. **$$**

★ ★ **CANDLELIGHT INN AND RESTAURANT.** *35 Walker St (01240). Phone 413/637-1555; toll-free 800/428-0580. www.candlelightinn-lenox.com.* 8 rooms, 3 story. No room phones. Children over 10 years only. Complimentary continental breakfast. Check-out 11 am, check-in 2 pm. TV in sitting room. Dining room, bar in season. Downhill ski 5 miles, cross-country ski 1/2 mile. Built in 1885. **$$**

★ ★ ★ **THE GABLES INN.** *81 Walker St (01240). Phone 413/637-3416; toll-free 800/382-9401. www.gableslenox.com.* Built in the Queen Anne style in 1885, this classic Berkshire home is 1 mile from Tanglewood Music Center. The owners' collection of artwork and rare books and manuscripts lends an authentic touch to the 19 rooms and suites. 19 rooms, 3 story. No room phones. Children over 12 years only. Complimentary breakfast. Check-out noon, check-in 2 pm. TV; VCR (free movies). Some fireplaces. Indoor pool. Outdoor tennis. Downhill ski 5 miles, cross-country ski 1/4 mile. Once the home of writer Edith Wharton. **$**

★ ★ ★ **GARDEN GABLES INN.** *135 Main St (01240). Phone 413/637-0193; fax 413/637-4554. www.lenoxinn.com.* This bed-and-breakfast has been welcoming guests since the late 1940s. Originally built as a private estate in 1780, the inn now offers 14 main-house rooms and 4 cottages and is just 1 mile from Tanglewood Music Center. 18 rooms, 2 story. Children over 12 years only. Complimentary full breakfast. Check-out 11 am, check-in 2 pm. TV in some rooms. In-room modem link. Fireplaces. Outdoor pool. Downhill ski 4 miles, cross-country ski 1/4 mile. Business center. **$$**

★ ★ **GATEWAYS INN.** *51 Walker St (01240). Phone 413/637-2532; toll-free 888/492-9466; fax 413/637-1432. www.gatewaysinn.com.* 12 rooms, 2 story. Children over 12 years only. Continental breakfast. Check-out 11 am, check-in 1 pm. TV. Many fireplaces. Restaurant (see GATEWAYS INN). Room service. Downhill ski 5 miles, cross-country ski 1/4 mile. Restored mansion (1912). **$**

★ ★ ★ **HARRISON HOUSE.** *174 Main St (01240). Phone 413/637-1746; fax 413/637-9957. www.harrison-house.com.* The circular drive and immaculate porch of this country inn are directly across from Kennedy Park and overlook Tanglewood. Rooms vary in size and décor. 7 rooms, 2 story. Children over 12 years only. Complimentary continental breakfast. Check-out 11 am, check-in 2 pm. TV. Fireplaces. Downhill ski 4 miles, cross-country ski adjacent. Victorian inn. Free transportation. Totally non-smoking. **$**

★ ★ ★ **KEMBLE INN.** *2 Kemble St (01240). Phone 413/637-4113; toll-free 800/353-4113. www.kembleinn.com.* Located on 3 acres in the center of historic Lenox, this inn features magnificent views of the Berkshire Mountains. The guest rooms are named after American authors. 15 rooms, 3 story. Children over 12 years only. Complimentary continental breakfast. Check-out 11 am, check-in 2 pm. TV. Fireplaces. Panoramic mountain views; quiet, elegant atmosphere in restored mansion (1881). Totally nonsmoking. **$$**

★ ★ **ROOKWOOD INN.** *11 Old Stockbridge Rd (01240). Phone 413/637-9750; toll-free 800/223-9750; fax 413/637-1532.* 20 rooms, 3 story. Complimentary full breakfast. Check-out 11 am, check-in 3 pm. TV in sitting room and suites. Fireplaces. Downhill ski 5 miles, cross-country ski 1 mile. Victorian inn (1885) furnished with English antiques. Phones in suites. Totally nonsmoking. **$**

★ ★ **THE SUMMER WHITE HOUSE.** *17 Main St (01240). Phone 413/637-4489; toll-free 800/382-9401. www.summerwhitehouse.com.* Located in the heart of historic Lenox, only 1 mile from Tanglewood, summer home of the Boston Symphony, this inn is an original Berkshire cottage built in 1885. Guest rooms feature private baths and air conditioning. 7 rooms. No room phones. Closed Nov-Apr. Children over 16 years only. Complimentary continental breakfast. Check-out 11 am, check-in 2 pm. TV. Totally non-smoking. **$$**

★★**THE VILLAGE INN.** *16 Church St (01240). Phone 413/637-0020; toll-free 800/253-0917; fax 413/637-9756. www.villageinn-lenox.com.* 32 rooms, 3 story. Check-out 11 am, check-in 1 pm. TV room. Fireplaces. Restaurant, bar. Downhill ski 4 miles, cross-country ski 1 mile. Has been an inn since 1775. **$**

D ⬛ ⬛

★**WALKER HOUSE.** *64 Walker St (01240). Phone 413/637-1271; toll-free 800/235-3098; fax 413/637-2387. www.walkerhouse.com.* 8 rooms, 2 story. No room phones. Pets accepted; fee. Children over 12 years only. Complimentary continental breakfast. Check-out noon, check-in 2 pm. TV in sitting room; VCR available. Downhill ski 6 miles, cross-country ski 1/2 mile. Built in 1804. Rooms named after composers. Totally nonsmoking. **$**

⬛ ⬛ ⬛

★★**WHISTLER'S INN.** *5 Greenwood St (01240). Phone 413/637-0975; fax 419/637-2190. www.whistlersinnlenox.com.* 14 rooms, 2 story. Complimentary full breakfast. Check-out noon, check-in 3 pm. TV; VCR available. Fireplaces. Downhill ski 5 miles, cross-country ski 1/2 block. Lawn games. Tudor-style mansion built in 1820. Music room with Steinway grand piano, Louis XVI furniture. Free transportation. **$**

⬛ ⬛

Restaurants

★★ **APPLE TREE.** *10 Richmond Mountain Rd (01240). Phone 413/637-1477; fax 413/637-2528. www.appletree-inn.com.* Continental menu. Closed Mon-Wed in the off-season. Dinner, brunch. Bar. Outdoor seating. Totally nonsmoking. **$$**

★★★ **BISTRO ZINC.** *56 Church St (01240). Phone 413/637-8800.* French menu. Lunch, dinner. Bar. Children's menu. Casual attire. **$$**

D

★★★ **BLANTYRE.** *16 Blantyre Rd (01240). Phone 413/637-3556; fax 413/637-4282. www.blantyre.com.* Dining at this 1902 mansion is a special experience. Antique glassware and place settings, candlelight, and harp music all combine for a romantic atmosphere. Contemporary French menu. Closed Mon; also Nov-Apr. Lunch, dinner. Harpist (dinner). Jacket required. Reservations required. Valet parking (dinner). Outdoor seating (lunch). **$$$**

D

★★ **CAFE LUCIA.** *80 Church St (01240). Phone 413/637-2640; fax 413/243-9161.* Italian menu. Closed Mon; Easter, Thanksgiving, Dec 25; also Sun Nov-June. Dinner. Outdoor seating. **$$$**

D

★ **CAROL'S.** *8 Franklin St (01240). Phone 413/637-8948.* Closed Tues, Wed (Sept-June); Thanksgiving, Dec 25. Breakfast, lunch. Children's menu. **$**

D

★ ★ **CHURCH STREET CAFE.** *65 Church St (01240). Phone 413/ 637-2745; fax 413/637-2050.* Regional American menu. Closed Jan 1, Thanksgiving, Dec 25; also Sun, Mon Nov-May. Lunch, dinner. Bar. Outdoor seating. **$$**

D

★ ★ ★ **GATEWAYS INN.** *51 Walker St (01240). Phone 413/637-2532; fax 413/637-1432. www.gatewaysinn.com.* The restaurant at this charming inn features Italian cuisine with international influences. The chefs use locally grown produce and dairy products and the menu changes seasonally. Choose to sit in the main room that has French doors and terra cotta painted walls, or, for a more private experience, dine in the Rockwell Room. American menu. Closed Mon, Tues in winter. Dinner. Outdoor seating. **$$**

★ ★ ★ **LENOX 218 RESTAURANT.** *218 Main St (01240). Phone 413/637-4218. www.lenox218.com.* A convenient place to dine when visiting Tanglewood, this contemporary restaurant specializes in Italian and American dishes and can handle banquets for up to 100 people. Don't miss the incredible Sunday brunch. American, Italian menu. Dinner, brunch. Bar. Children's menu. Casual attire. **$$**

D

★ **PANDA HOUSE CHINESE RESTAURANT.** *506 Pittsfield Rd (01240). Phone 413/499-0660; fax 413/499-0786.* Chinese menu. Closed Thanksgiving, Dec 25. Lunch, dinner, Sun brunch. Bar. **$$**

D

★ ★ ★ **WHEATLEIGH.** *Hawthorne Rd (01240). Phone 413/637-0610; fax 413/637-4507. www.wheatleigh.com.* Polished mahogany doors lead to this historic hotel's elegant restaurant. The dining room's design is just as regal as the building itself, which was modeled in 1893 after a 16th-century Florentine palazzo. Guests dine on contemporary French cuisine (degustation menu available) in a beautiful sun-drenched room filled with oil paintings, hand-carved Chippendale chairs, and sparkling crystal chandeliers. French menu. Dinner, Sun brunch. Reservations required. Valet parking. **$$$$**

D

★ ★ ★ **THE WYNDHURST RESTAURANT.** *55 Lee Rd (01240). Phone 413/637-1364; fax 413/637-4364. www.cranwell.com.* The dining room of the Cranwell Resort is situated on the main floor of the 100-year-old Tudor mansion. Large windows offer vistas of the Berkshire Hills. The cuisine highlights local produce, including game and cheeses. Dinner. Bar; entertainment Fri, Sat. Children's menu. Totally nonsmoking. **$$$**

D

Pittsfield

2 hours 21 minutes; 136 miles from Boston

Settled 1743 **Pop** 45,793 **Elev** 1,039 ft **Area code** 413 **Zip** 01201

Information Berkshire Visitors Bureau, Berkshire Common; 413/443-9186 or 800/237-5747

Web www.berkshires.org

Beautifully situated in the Berkshire Hills vacation area, this is also an old and important manufacturing center. It is the home of the Berkshire Life Insurance Company (chartered in 1851) and of industries that make machinery, plastics, gauges, and paper products.

What to See and Do

Arrowhead. *780 Holmes Rd (01201). Phone 413/442-1793.* (1780) Herman Melville wrote *Moby Dick* while living here from 1850 to 1863; historical exhibits, furniture, costumes; gardens. Video presentation. Gift shop. Headquarters of Berkshire County Historical Society. (Memorial Day weekend-Oct, daily) **$$**

Berkshire Hills. *www.berkshires.org.* This western Massachusetts resort area is just south of Vermont's Green Mountains, but has neither the ruggedness nor the lonesomeness of the range to its north. The highest peak, Mt. Greylock (elevation: 3,491 feet), is cragless and serene. Farms and villages dot the landscape. The area is famous for its variety of accommodations, culture, and recreation. There are also countless summer homes and camps for children by the lakes, ponds, and brooks. Berkshire County is about 45 miles long from north to south, and half that from east to west. It has 90 lakes and ponds, 90,000 acres of state forest, golf courses, ski areas, ski touring centers, numerous tennis facilities, and campsites. The area first became famous when Nathaniel Hawthorne wrote *Tanglewood Tales,* and it has since become distinguished for its many summer cultural activities, including the Tanglewood Music Festival at Tanglewood (see LENOX) and the Berkshire Theatre Festival (see STOCKBRIDGE & WEST STOCKBRIDGE).

Berkshire Museum. *39 South St (US 7) (01201). Phone 413/443-7171.* Museum of art, natural science, and history, featuring American 19th- and 20th-century paintings; works by British, European masters; artifacts from ancient civilizations; exhibits on Berkshire County history; aquarium; changing exhibits; films, lectures, children's programs. (July-Aug, daily; rest of year, Tues-Sun; closed holidays) **$$$**

Bousquet. *2 miles S on US 7, then 1 mile W, on Dan Fox Dr. Phone 413/442-8316 or 413/442-2436 for snow conditions. www.bousquets.com.* Two double chairlifts, three rope tows; snowmaking, patrol, school, rentals; cafeteria, bar, daycare. Longest run 1 mile; vertical drop 750 feet. Night skiing. (Dec-Mar, daily) **$$$$**

Brodie Mountain. *10 miles N on US 7 in New Ashford. Phone 413/443-4752. www.skibrodie.com.* Four double chairlifts, two rope tows; patrol, school, rentals, snowmaking; bar, cafeteria, restaurant; nursery. (Nov-Mar, daily) Cross-country trails with rentals and instruction. Half-day rates. Tennis, racquetball, winter camping. **$$$$**

Canoe Meadows Wildlife Sanctuary. *472 W Mountain Rd (01201). Phone 413/637-0320.* Two hundred sixty-two acres with 3 miles of trails, woods, open fields, ponds; bordering the Housatonic River. (Tues-Sun) **$$**

Hancock Shaker Village. *Rtes 20 and 41. 5 miles W on US 20, at junction Rte 41. Phone 413/443-0188.* An original Shaker site (1790-1960); now a living history museum of Shaker life, crafts, and farming. Large collection of Shaker furniture and artifacts in 20 restored buildings, including the Round Stone Barn, set on 1,200 scenic acres in the Berkshires. Exhibits; seasonal craft demonstrations, Discovery Room activities, café (seasonal); farm animals, heirloom herb and vegetable gardens; museum shop; picnicking. **$$$$**

Jiminy Peak. *9 miles N, then W, between US 7 and MA 43 at 37 Corey Rd in Hancock (01237). Phone 413/738-5500. www.jiminypeak.com.* One six-passanger, three double chairlifts, J-bar, two quads, three triples; patrol, school, rentals, restaurant, two cafeterias, bar, lodge. Longest run 2 miles; vertical drop 1,140 feet. (Thanksgiving-Apr 1, daily) Night skiing. Half-day rates. Also trout fishing; 18-hole miniature golf; Alpine slide and tennis center (Memorial Day-Labor Day); fee for activities. **$$$$**

Special Event

South Mountain Concerts. *South St. 2 miles S on US 7, 20 (01201). Phone 413/442-2106.* Chamber music concerts. Sept-Oct. Sun.

Motels/Motor Lodges

★ **ECONO LODGE.** *US 7 (01237). Phone 413/458-5945; toll-free 800/277-0001; fax 413/458-4351. www.econolodge.com.* 40 rooms, 1-2 story. Check-out 11:30 am. TV; VCR available (movies). Restaurant, bar; entertainment Sat. Room service. Game room. Outdoor pool. Outdoor tennis. Downhill, cross-country ski opposite. **$**

⊡ ⊠ ⊠ ⊠ ⊠

★ **TRAVELODGE.** *16 Cheshire Rd (01201). Phone 413/443-5661; toll-free 800/578-7878; fax 413/443-5866.* 47 rooms, 2 story. Check-out 11 am. TV. Laundry services. Downhill ski 5 miles, cross-country ski 12 miles. **$**

⊠ ⊠ SC

Hotel

★ ★ ★ **CROWNE PLAZA.** *1 West St (01201). Phone 413/499-2000; toll-free 800/227-6963; fax 413/442-0449.* 179 rooms, 12 story. Check-out noon.

TV; cable (premium). Restaurant, bar. In-house fitness room, sauna. Health club privileges. Indoor pool, whirlpool. Free covered parking. **$**

⊠ 大 ⊠ SC

Resort

★ ★ **JIMINY PEAK MOUNTAIN RESORT.** *Corey Rd (01237). Phone 413/738-5500; toll-free 888/4JIMINY; fax 413/738-5513. www.jiminypeak.com.* 96 rooms, 3 story. Check-out 10:30 am, check-in 4 pm. TV; VCR available. Laundry services. Dining room; entertainment weekends (seasonal). Supervised children's activities (Dec-Mar). In-house fitness room, sauna. Game room. Two pools; whirlpool. Outdoor tennis. Downhill ski on site. Hiking. Alpine slide. **$**

⊠ 大 ⊠ 大

Restaurant

★ ★ **DAKOTA.** *1035 South St (01201). Phone 413/499-7900; fax 413/499-8610. www.dakotarestaurant.com.* Seafood menu. Closed Thanksgiving, Dec 25. Lunch, dinner, Sun brunch. Bar. Children's menu. **$$**

D

Lowell

33 minutes; 30 miles from Boston

Settled 1655 **Pop** 105,167 **Elev** 102 ft **Area code** 978

Information Greater Lowell Chamber of Commerce, 77 Merrimack St, 01852; 978/459-8154

Web www.greaterlowellchamber.org

In the 19th century, the powerful Merrimack River and its canals transformed Lowell from a handicraft center to a textile industrial center. The Francis Floodgate, near Broadway and Clare Streets, was called "Francis's Folly" when it was built in 1848, but it saved the city from flood in 1936. Restoration of the historic canal system is currently in progress.

What to See and Do

American Textile History Museum. *491 Dutton St (01854). Phone 978/441-0400. www.athm.org.* Permanent exhibit, "Textiles in America," features 18th- to 20th-century textiles, artifacts, and machinery in operation, showing the impact of the Industrial Revolution on labor. Collections of cloth samples, books, prints, photographs, and preindustrial tools may be seen by appointment. Tours; activities. Library; education center. Restaurant; museum store. (Tues-Sun; closed Jan 1, Thanksgiving, Dec 25) **$$**

Lowell Heritage State Park. *246 Market St (01852). Phone 978/453-0592.* Six miles of canals and associated linear parks and 2 miles of park on the bank of the Merrimack River offers boating, boathouse; concert pavilion, interpretive programs. (Schedule varies) **FREE**

Lowell National Historical Park. *246 Market St (01852). Contact Visitor Center.* Established to commemorate Lowell's unique legacy as the most important planned industrial city in America. The nation's first large-scale center for the mechanized production of cotton cloth, Lowell became a model for 19th-century industrial development. Park includes mill buildings, and a 5 1/2-mile canal system. Visitor center at Market Mills, includes audiovisual show and exhibits (daily; closed Jan 1, Thanksgiving, Dec 25). Free walking and trolley tours (Mar-Nov). Tours by barge and trolley (May-Columbus Day weekend; fee), reservations suggested. Located here are

> **Boott Cotton Mills Museum.** *400 Foot of John St (01852). Phone 978/970-5000.* Industrial history museum with operating looms (ear plugs supplied). Interactive exhibits, video presentations. (Daily; closed Jan 1, Thanksgiving, Dec 24-25) **$$**

> **Patrick J. Mogan Cultural Center.** *40 French St (01852).* Restored 1836 boarding house of the Boott Cotton Mills, including a re-created kitchen, keeper's room, parlor, and mill girls' bedroom; exhibits on working people, immigrants, and labor history; also local history. (Daily)

New England Quilt Museum. *18 Shattuck St (01852). Phone 978/452-4207. www.nequiltmuseum.org.* Changing exhibits feature antique, traditional, and contemporary quilts. Museum shop. (Tues-Sat; closed holidays) **$**

University of Massachusetts-Lowell. *1 University Ave (01854). Phone 978/934-4000.* 15,500 students. State-operated university formed by the 1975 merger of Lowell Technological Institute (1895) and Lowell State College (1894). Music ensembles at Durgin Hall Performing Arts Center.

Whistler House Museum of Art. *243 Worthen St (01852). Phone 978/452-7641. www.whistlerhouse.org.* Birthplace of the painter James Abbott McNeill Whistler. Exhibits include several of his etchings. Collection of 19th- and early 20th-century American art. (Wed-Sun; closed holidays) **$**

Special Events

Lowell Celebrates Kerouac Festival. *PO Box 1111 (01852). Phone toll-free 877/KER-OUAC. www.lckorg.tripod.com.* Tours, music, poetry competition, book signings, and panel discussions. First weekend in Oct.

Lowell Folk Festival. *246 Market St (01852). Phone 978/970-5000.* Concerts, crafts, demonstrations, ethnic food, and street parade. Last full weekend in July.

Motels/Motor Lodges

★ **BEST WESTERN CHELMSFORD INN.** *187 Chelmsford St (01824). Phone 978/256-7511; toll-free 888/770-9992; fax 978/250-1401. www.bestwestern.com/chelmsfordinn.* 120 rooms, 5 story. Check-out noon. TV; cable (premium), VCR available. In-room modem link. Laundry services. In-house fitness room, sauna. Outdoor pool, whirlpool, poolside service. **$**

[D] [≈] [✕] [≈] [SC]

★ ★ **COURTYARD BY MARRIOTT.** *30 Industrial Ave E (01852). Phone 978/458-7575; toll-free 800/321-2211; fax 978/458-1302. www.courtyard.com.* 120 rooms, 3 story. Check-out 1 pm. TV; cable (premium). In-room modem link. Laundry services. Restaurant, bar. Room service. In-house fitness room. Outdoor pool. Airport transportation. **$**

[D] [≈] [✕] [≈]

Hotels

★ ★ **DOUBLETREE HOTEL.** *50 Warren St (01852). Phone 978/452-1200; toll-free 800/876-4586; fax 978/453-4674. www.doubletree.com.* 252 rooms, 9 story. Check-out 11 am. TV; cable (premium), VCR available. In-room modem link. Laundry services. Restaurant, bar. In-house fitness room, sauna. Indoor pool, children's pool, whirlpool, poolside service. Free garage parking. **$**

[D] [≈] [✕] [≈] [SC]

★ ★ ★ **RADISSON HOTEL AND SUITES CHELMSFORD.** *10 Independence Dr (01824). Phone 978/256-0800; toll-free 800/333-3333; fax 978/256-0750. www.radisson.com.* Friendly staff, attentive service, and well-appointed guest rooms are what guests will discover at this hotel. Perfectly suited to assist the business traveler and well maintained to relax the leisure traveler, this hotel offers something for everyone. 194 rooms, 5 story. Check-out 11 am, check-in 2 pm. TV; cable (premium), VCR in suites. In-room modem link. Restaurant, bar. Room service. In-house fitness room, sauna. Indoor pool. **$**

[D] [≈] [✕] [≈] [SC]

★ ★ ★ **WESTFORD REGENCY INN AND CONFERENCE CENTER.** *219 Littleton Rd (01886). Phone 978/692-8200; toll-free 800/543-7801; fax 978/692-7403. www.westfordregency.com.* Take in the joys of New England at this inn and conference center with 20,000 square feet of meeting space. Every Thursday from June through August, there's a classic lobster boil and clambake hosted outdoors under a 6,000-square-foot tent. 193 rooms, 4 story. Pets accepted, some restrictions; fee. Check-out noon. TV; cable (premium). In-room modem link. Restaurant, bar; entertainment. In-house fitness room, sauna. Indoor pool, whirlpool. **$$**

[D] [🐾] [≈] [✕] [≈]

Resort

★ ★ ★ **STONEHEDGE INN.** *160 Pawtucket Blvd (01879). Phone 978/649-4400; fax 978/649-9256. www.stonehedgeinn.com.* This contemporary inn is an American imitation of an English country manor. It has an intimate feel, and the staff is eager to meet guests' needs. Large, comfortable guest rooms feature spacious bathrooms and heated towel racks. Set on the grounds of a horse farm, this out-of-the-way inn is perfect for a romantic rendezvous or a corporate retreat. 30 rooms, 2 story. Check-out noon, check-in 3 pm. TV; VCR available. Laundry services. Restaurant, bar. Room service 24 hours. In-house fitness room. Indoor/outdoor pool, whirlpool. Golf on premise. Outdoor tennis. Downhill skiing. Bike rentals. Hiking trail. Valet parking available. Concierge. **$$**

D ⬛ ⬛ ⬛ ⬛ ⬛ ⬛

Restaurants

★ ★ **COBBLESTONES.** *91 Dutton St (01852). Phone 978/970-2282; fax 978/970-0266. www.cobblestonesoflowell.com.* For guests who appreciate the wilderness, this restaurant is sure to please. Seasonal game dishes include ostrich, antelope, and kangaroo, and the property is set within the Lowell National Historic Park. For dessert, be sure to try the bananas flambé. Progressive American menu. Closed Sun; major holidays. Lunch, dinner. Bar. In a restored 1859 building. **$$$**

★ ★ **FORTUNATO'S ITALIAN STEAKHOUSE.** *44 Palmer St (01852). Phone 978/454-9800. www.fortunatosrestaurant.com.* Italian steakhouse menu. Closed Sun. Lunch, dinner. Bar. Casual attire. Outdoor seating. **$$**

D

★ ★ ★ **LA BONICHE.** *143 Merrimack St (01852). Phone 978/458-9473.* Though the food is upscale, the dress is casual at this fine restaurant. French menu. Menu changes seasonally. Closed Sun, Mon; major holidays. Lunch, dinner. Bar. Musicians Sat. Children's menu. **$$$**

D

★ ★ ★ ★ **SILKS.** *160 Pawtucket Blvd (01879). Phone 978/649-4400; fax 978/649-9256. www.stonehedgeinn.com.* If you are searching for a little hideaway in the country for dinner and are hoping to find a place that happens to have one of the world's most impressive wine caves, schedule a visit to Silks. Secreted away in 36 acres of New England horse country, Silks is located in the Stonehedge Inn, a charming old English-style manor house. This enchanted spot has not only an incredible international wine collection (there are over 90,000 bottles in the cave, with about 2,000 wines offered daily), but also a talented team of chefs in the kitchen cooking up a spectacular selection of very French, very haute cuisine. Although the food plays second fiddle to the wine, the menu offers exciting, modern riffs on classic French dishes. Herbs and spices are borrowed from around the globe, successfully bringing flavor, style, and flair to the extensive selection of cold and hot appetizers, fish, and meats. The green and burgundy room is warm, comfortable, and romantic. Considering the size of the wine list, several toasts should be made; this is a great spot for a special occasion. While the service is impeccable and European in style, it is free from pretension. Closed Mon. Breakfast, lunch, dinner, Sun brunch. Piano (Sat). Outdoor seating. **$$$**

D

Nashua, NH

50 minutes; 46 miles from Boston

Settled 1656 **Pop** 86,605 **Elev** 169 ft **Area code** 603

Information Greater Nashua Chamber of Commerce, 146 Main St, 2nd flr, 03060; 603/881-8333

Web www.nashuachamber.com

Originally a fur trading post, Nashua's manufacturing began with the development of Merrimack River water power early in the 19th century. The city, second-largest in New Hampshire, has more than 100 diversified industries ranging from computers and tools to beer.

What to See and Do

Anheuser-Busch, Inc. *221 Daniel Webster Hwy (US 3), Merrimack (03054), Everett Tpke exit 10.* Phone 603/595-1202. Guided tours of brewery; sampling room; gift shop. Children only with adult; no pets. **FREE**

Clydesdale Hamlet. *221 Daniel Webster Hwy, Merrimack (03054).* Phone 603/595-1202. Buildings modeled after a 19th-century European-style farm are the living quarters for the famous Clydesdales (at least 15 are here at all times); carriage house contains vintage wagons. **FREE**

Silver Lake State Park. *Silver Lake Rd. 8 miles W on NH 130 to Hollis, then 1 mile N off NH 122.* Phone 603/465-2342. 1,000-foot sand beach on a 34-acre lake; swimming, bathhouse; picnicking. (Late June-Labor Day) Standard fees.

Special Event

American Stage Festival. *14 Court St, Milford (03060). 5 miles NW off NH 101.* Phone 603/886-7000. Five plays; music events, children's series. June-Sept.

Motels/Motor Lodges

★ **COMFORT INN.** *10 St. Laurent St (03060).* Phone 603/883-7700; toll-free 800/228-5150; fax 603/595-2107. www.comfortinn.com. 104 rooms, 3 story. Complimentary continental breakfast. Check-out noon. TV; cable (premium), VCR available (movies). Bar. Health club privileges. Outdoor pool. **$**

D 🛍 🔄

★ **FAIRFIELD INN.** *4 Amherst Rd (03054).* Phone 603/424-7500; toll-free 800/228-2800. www.fairfieldinn.com. 116 rooms, 3 story. Complimentary continental breakfast. Check-out noon. TV; cable (premium). In-room modem link. Outdoor pool. **$**

D 🛍 🔄 SC

★ ★ **HOLIDAY INN.** *9 Northeastern Blvd (03062). Phone 603/888-1551; toll-free 888/801-5661; fax 603/888-7193. www.holiday-inn.com.* 208 rooms, 3-4 story. Pets accepted; fee. Check-out noon. TV; cable (premium), VCR available. Laundry services. Restaurant, bar; entertainment. Room service. In-house fitness room. Outdoor pool. **$**

D 🐾 ⚐ 🛉 ⚐

★ **RED ROOF INN.** *77 Spit Brook Rd (03060). Phone 603/888-1893; fax 603/888-5889. www.redroof.com.* 115 rooms, 3 story. Pets accepted. Check-out noon. TV; cable (premium). **$**

D 🐾 ⚐ SC

Hotels

★ ★ ★ **CROWNE PLAZA.** *2 Somerset Pkwy (03063). Phone 603/886-1200; toll-free 800/962-7482; fax 603/595-4199. www.crowneplaza.com.* Just 15 miles from Manchester Airport or 40 miles from Boston's Logan Airport, this full-service hotel is in the heart of the high-tech "southern tier." 250 rooms, 8 story. Check-out noon. TV. In-room modem link. Restaurant, bar. In-house fitness room, massage, saunas. Indoor pool, whirlpool. Free airport transportation. Luxury level. 48-seat amphitheater. **$**

D ⚐ 🛉 ✈ ⚐ SC

★ ★ ★ **MARRIOTT NASHUA.** *2200 Southwood Dr (03063). Phone 603/880-9100; toll-free 800/362-0962; fax 603/886-9489. www.marriott.com.* Fully renovated in 1997, this medium-sized hotel is close to the high-tech industrial corridor and outfitted for conducting business. 241 rooms, 4 story. Pets accepted, some restrictions. Check-out 1 pm. TV; cable (premium). In-room modem link. Restaurant, bar; entertainment. In-house fitness room. Indoor pool, whirlpool. Lawn games. Airport transportation. Business center. Concierge. Luxury level. Czechoslovakian chandeliers and Oriental *objets d'art* accent lobby. **$**

D 🐾 ⚐ 🛉 ✈ ⚐ 🛉

★ ★ ★ **SHERATON NASHUA HOTEL.** *11 Tara Blvd (03062). Phone 603/888-9970; toll-free 800/325-3535; fax 603/888-4112. www.sheraton.com.* Central to the high-tech business in the area and recreational facilities, this contemporary hotel offers a comfortable stay for business or leisure travelers. 337 rooms, 7 story. Check-out noon. TV; cable (premium), VCR available. In-room modem link. Restaurant, bar; entertainment (Fri, Sat). Supervised children's activities. In-house fitness room, sauna, steam room. Indoor pool, outdoor pool, whirlpool, poolside service. Lawn games. Business center. Luxury level. **$**

D ⚐ 🛉 ⚐ SC 🛉

Extended Stay

★ ★ **RESIDENCE INN BY MARRIOTT.** *246 Daniel Webster Hwy (03054). Phone 603/424-8100; toll-free 800/331-3131; fax 603/424-3128.*

www.residenceinn.com. 129 rooms, 2 story. Pets accepted, some restrictions; fee. Complimentary continental breakfast. Check-out noon. TV; cable (premium). In-room modem link. Health club privileges. Outdoor pool, whirlpool. Sport court. **$**

Restaurants

★ **DEPOT SQUARE STEAKHOUSE.** *1 E Broadway (3038). Phone 603/437-4200; fax 603/437-4202. www.depot-square.com.* American menu. Closed Thanksgiving, Dec 25. Lunch (weekdays), dinner. Bar. Children's menu. Casual attire. Outdoor seating. **$$**

D

★ **HANNAH JACK TAVERN.** *Greeley St and Daniel Webster Hwy (03054). Phone 603/424-4171; fax 603/424-4172.* American menu. Closed July 4, Dec 25. Lunch, dinner. Bar. Children's menu. In a 200-year-old colonial building. **$$**

★ **NEWICK'S.** *696 Daniel Webster Hwy (03054). Phone 603/429-0262; toll-free 800/640-0262; fax 603/429-0675. www.newicks.com.* Seafood menu. Closed Thanksgiving, Dec 25. Lunch, dinner. Bar. Children's menu. **$$**

D SC

Providence, RI

52 minutes; 50 miles from Boston

Settled 1636 **Pop** 173,618 **Elev** 24 ft **Area code** 401

Information Providence Warwick Convention & Visitors Bureau, One W Exchange St, 02903; 401/274-1636 or 800/233-1636

Web www.providencevb.com

Grateful that God's providence had led him to this spot, Roger Williams founded a town and named it accordingly. More than three-and-one-half centuries later, Providence is the capital and largest city of the State of Rhode Island and Providence Plantations, the state's official title.

In its early years Providence was a farm center. Through the great maritime epoch of the late 18th century and first half of the 19th century, clipper ships sailed from Providence to China and the West Indies. During the 19th century, the city became a great industrial center which today still produces widely known Providence jewelry and silverware. Providence is also an important port of entry.

Providence's long history has created a blend of old and new: modern hotels and office buildings share the streets with historic houses. Benefit Street, overlooking Providence's modern financial district, has one of the largest concentrations of colonial houses in America. The city's location along the upper Narragansett Bay and numerous cultural opportunities each provide many varied attractions for the visitor. In addition, Providence is the southern point of the Blackstone River Valley National Heritage Corridor, a 250,000-acre region that extends to Worcester, Massachusetts.

What to See and Do

The Arcade. *Westminster St. Phone 401/598-1049.* (1828) First indoor shopping mall with national landmark status. More than 35 specialty shops; restaurants.

Brown University. *45 Prospect St (02912). Phone 401/863-1000.* (1764) 7,500 students. Founded as Rhode Island College; school was renamed for Nicholas Brown, a major benefactor and son of a founder, in 1804. Brown is the seventh-oldest college in the US. Pembroke College for Women (1891), named for the Cambridge, England *alma mater* of Roger Williams, merged with the men's college in 1971. Here are

Annmary Brown Memorial. *21 Brown St (02912), N of Charlesfield St. Phone 401/863-1994.* (1907) Paintings; Brown family memorabilia. (Mon-Fri afternoons, by appointment)

David Winton Bell Gallery. *64 College St (02912), in List Art Center. Phone 401/863-2932.* (1971) Historical and contemporary exhibitions. (Late Aug-May, Tues-Sun; closed holidays)

John Carter Brown Library. *George and Brown sts (02912). S side of campus green. Phone 401/863-2725.* (1904) Library houses exhibits, books, and maps relating to the exploration and settlement of America. (Mon-Sat; closed school vacations) **FREE**

John Hay Library. *20 Prospect St (02912), across from Van Wickle gates. Phone 401/863-3723.* (1910) Named for Lincoln's secretary, John Hay (Brown, 1858); library houses extensive special collections, including Lincoln manuscripts, the Harris collection of American poetry and plays, and university archives. (Mon-Fri) **FREE**

Rockefeller Library. *10 Prospect St (02912). Phone 401/863-2167 or 401/863-2162.* (1964) Named for John D. Rockefeller, Jr. (Brown, 1897), library houses collections in the social sciences, humanities, and fine arts. (Daily; closed school vacations) **FREE**

University Hall. (1770) The original "college edifice" serves as the main administration building.

Wriston Quadrangle. *On Brown St near John Carter Brown Library.* (1952) Square named for president-emeritus Henry M. Wriston.

Cathedral of St. John. *271 N Main St (02903), at Church St. Phone 401/331-4622.* (1810) This Georgian structure with Gothic detail was built on the site of King's Church (1722). (Daily) **FREE**

First Baptist Church in America. *75 N Main St (02903), at Waterman St. Phone 401/454-3418.* Oldest Baptist congregation in America, established in 1638; the present building was erected by Joseph Brown in 1775. Sun morning service. (Mon-Fri; closed holidays)

First Unitarian Church. *1 Benevolent St (02906). Phone 401/421-7970.* (1816) Organized as First Congregational Church in 1720, the church was designed by John Holden Greene and has the largest bell ever cast by Paul Revere. **FREE**

Governor Stephen Hopkins House. *15 Hopkins St (02903). Opposite courthouse. Phone 401/421-0694.* (1707) House of signer of Declaration of Independence and ten-time governor of Rhode Island; 18th-century garden; period furnishings. (Apr-Dec, Wed and Sat afternoons, also by appointment) Children only with adult. **DONATION**

Johnson & Wales University. *8 Abbott Park Pl (02903). Phone 401/598-1000; toll-free 800/DIAL-JWU.* (1914) 8,000 students. Two- and four-year degree programs are offered in business, hospitality, food service, and technology. Tours available by appointment (free). On campus is the

> **Culinary Archives & Museum.** *315 Harborside Blvd (02903). Trade Center at Harborside Campus. Phone 491/598-2805.* Dubbed the "Smithsonian of the food service industry," this museum contains over 200,000 items related to the fields of culinary arts and hospitality collected and donated by Chicago's Chef Louis Szathmary. Includes rare US Presidential culinary autographs; tools of the trade from the third millennium BC; Egyptian, Roman, and Asian spoons over 1,000 years old; gallery of chefs; original artwork; hotel and restaurant silver; and periodicals related to the field. Guided tours. (Tues-Sat by appointment; closed holidays) **$$**

Lincoln Woods State Park. *2 Manchester Print Works Rd (02865). 5 miles N via Rte 146, S of Breakneck Hill Rd. Phone 401/723-7892.* More than 600 acres. Swimming, bathhouse, freshwater ponds, fishing, boating; hiking and bridle trails, ice skating, picnicking, concession. Fees for some activities. **$**

Museum of Rhode Island History at Aldrich House. *110 Benevolent St (02906). Phone 401/331-8575.* Exhibits on Rhode Island's history. Headquarters for Rhode Island Historical Society. (Tues-Fri; closed Jan 1, Thanksgiving, Dec 25) **$$$**

John Brown House. *52 Power St (02906), at Benefit St. Phone 401/331-8575.* (1786) Georgian masterpiece by Joseph Brown, brother of John. George Washington was among the guests entertained in this house. Museum of 18th-century china, glass, Rhode Island antiques, and paintings; John Brown's chariot (1782), perhaps the oldest American-made vehicle extant. Guided tours. (Jan, Feb, Fri-Sun; rest of year, Tues-Sun; closed holidays) **$$$** The historical society also maintains a

> **Library.** *121 Hope St (02906), at Power St.* One of the largest genealogical collections in New England; Rhode Island imprints dating from 1727; newspapers, manuscripts, photographs, films. (Tues-Sat) **FREE**

North Burial Ground. *1 mile N of Market Sq on N Main (US 1).* Graves of Roger Williams and other settlers.

Old State House. *150 Benefit St (02903). Phone 401/222-2678.* Where the General Assembly of Rhode Island met between 1762 and 1900. Independence was proclaimed in the Old State House two months before the Declaration was signed in Philadelphia. (Mon-Fri; closed holidays) **FREE**

Providence Athenaeum Library. *251 Benefit St (02903). Phone 401/421-6970.* (1753) One of the oldest subscription libraries in the US; housed in a Greek Revival building designed by William Strickland in 1836. Rare book room includes original Audubon elephant folios; small art collection. (Daily; summer, Mon-Fri; closed holidays, also two weeks in early Aug) Tours. **FREE**

Providence Children's Museum. *100 South St (02903). Phone 401/273-KIDS.* Many hands-on exhibits, including a time-travel adventure through Rhode Island's multicultural history, wet-and-wild exploration of water, and hands-on geometry lab. Traveling exhibits. Weekly programs. Gift shop. (Sept-June, Tues-Sun; rest of year, daily) **$$**

Providence Preservation Society. *21 Meeting St (02903). Phone 401/831-7440.* The Providence Preservation Society offers brochures and tour booklets for several historic Providence neighborhoods. (Mon-Fri) **$$**

Rhode Island School of Design. *2 College St (02903). Phone 401/454-6100.* (1877) 1,960 students. One of the country's leading art and design schools. Tours. On campus are

RISD Museum. *224 Benefit St (02903). Phone 401/454-6500.* Collections range from ancient to contemporary. (Tues-Sun; closed holidays) **$$**

Woods-Gerry Gallery. *62 Prospect St (02906). Phone 401/454-6141.* Mansion built 1860-1863 has special exhibits by students, faculty, and alumni. Call for schedule.

Rhode Island State House. *82 Smith St (02903). Phone 401/222-2357.* Capitol by McKim, Mead, and White was completed in 1901. Building contains a Gilbert Stuart full-length portrait of George Washington and the original parchment charter granted to Rhode Island by Charles II in 1663. *Independent Man* statue on dome. Guided tours. Building (Mon-Fri; closed holidays and second Mon in Aug). **FREE**

Roger Williams National Memorial. *282 N Main St (02903). Phone 401/521-7266.* This 4 1/2-acre park, at the site of the old town spring, commemorates founding of Providence and contributions made by Roger Williams to civil and religious liberty; slide presentation, exhibit. Visitor information. (Daily; closed Jan 1, Dec 25) **FREE**

Roger Williams Park. *1000 Elmwood Ave (02905). 3 miles S on Elmwood Ave. Phone 401/785-9450.* The park has 430 acres of woodlands, waterways, and winding drives. Japanese garden, Betsy Williams' cottage, and greenhouses. (Daily; closed Jan 1, Thanksgiving, Dec 25) **FREE** Also in the park are

Museum of Natural History and Cormack Planetarium. *1000 Elmwood Ave (02905). Phone 401/785-9450.* Anthropology, geology, astronomy, and biology displays; educational and performing arts programs. (Daily; closed Jan 1, Thanksgiving, Dec 25) **$**

Zoo. *1000 Elmwood Ave (02907). Phone 401/785-3510.* Children's nature center, tropical building, African plains exhibit; Marco Polo exhibits; over 600 animals. Educational programs; tours. (Daily; closed Dec 25) **$$$**

Special Events

Spring Festival of Historic Houses. *21 Meeting St (02903). Phone 401/831-7440. Sponsored by the Providence Preservation Society.* Tours of selected private houses and gardens. Second weekend in June.

WaterFire. *Waterplace Park, 101 Regent Ave (02908). Phone 401/272-3111.* Floating bonfires in the Providence River accompanied by music. Call for schedule.

Hotels

★ ★ **JOHNSON & WALES INN.** *213 Taunton Ave (02771). Phone 508/336-8700; toll-free 800/232-1772; fax 508/336-3414. www.jwu.edu/jwinn.* 86 rooms, 5 story. Check-out 11 am. TV; cable (premium), VCR available. Restaurant, bar. Room service. Health club privileges. Business center. **$**

[D] [✈] [⊷] [🏃]

★ ★ ★ **MARRIOTT PROVIDENCE.** *1 Orms St (02904). Phone 401/272-2400; toll-free 800/937-7768; fax 401/273-2686. www.marriott.com.* 345 rooms, 6 story. Check-out noon. TV; cable (premium), VCR available. In-room modem link. Restaurant, bar; entertainment. Room service. In-house fitness room, sauna. Game room. Indoor pool, outdoor pool, whirlpool, poolside service. Airport transportation. Business center. **$**

[D] [⊷] [🏃] [⊷] [SC] [🏃]

★ ★ ★ **PROVIDENCE BILTMORE.** *11 Dorrance St (02903). Phone 401/421-0700; toll-free 800/294-7709; fax 401/455-3050. www.providencebiltmore.com.* Operating since 1922, this historic building is listed on the National Preservation Register and houses spacious guest rooms and suites. The beautiful grand staircase, ornate lobby, and 19,000 square feet of meeting space attract many special events to this landmark property. 290 rooms, 18 story. Check-out noon. TV; cable (premium). In-room modem link. Restaurant, bar. In-house fitness room. Valet parking. Business center. **$$**

[D] [🏃] [⊷] [SC] [🏃]

★ ★ **RADISSON HOTEL PROVIDENCE HARBOR.** *220 India St (02903). Phone 401/272-5577; toll-free 800/333-3333; fax 401/272-0251. www.radisson.com.* 136 rooms, 6 story. Check-out 11 am. TV; cable (premium). In-room modem link. Restaurant, bar. In-house fitness room. Airport transportation. Business center. Overlooks the harbor. **$**

[D] [🏃] [⚙] [⊷] [🏃]

★ ★ ★ **WESTIN HOTEL.** *1 W Exchange St (02903). Phone 401/598-8000; toll-free 800/228-3000; fax 401/598-8200. www.westin.com.* At the convention center and adjacent to the Providence Place Mall, this hotel has business-friendly guest rooms and an indoor rooftop pool. 363 rooms, 25 story. Pets accepted, some restrictions; fee. Check-out noon. TV; cable (premium), VCR available (movies). In-room modem link. Restaurant, bar. In-house fitness room, sauna. Indoor pool, whirlpool. Business center. Concierge. **$$**

[D] [⊷] [⊷] [🏃] [⊷] [🏃]

B&B/Small Inns

★ ★ **OLD COURT BED & BREAKFAST.** *144 Benefit St (02903). Phone 401/751-2002; fax 401/272-4830. www.oldcourt.com.* 10 rooms, 3 story. Complimentary full breakfast. Check-out 11:30 am, check-in 2-11 pm. TV; cable; VCR available. Built in 1863 as a rectory. Overlooks the Old State House. Antique furnishings, chandeliers, and memorabilia from the 19th century. **$$**

★ **STATE HOUSE INN.** *43 Jewett St (02908). Phone 401/351-6111; fax 401/351-4261. www.providence-inn.com.* 10 rooms, 3 story. Complimentary full breakfast. Check-out 11 am, check-in 3 pm. TV; cable; VCR available. Fireplaces. Built in 1890. Totally nonsmoking. **$**

Restaurants

★ ★ **ADESSO.** *161 Cushing St (02906). Phone 401/521-0770; fax 401/521-1777.* Contemporary Italian menu. Closed July 4, Thanksgiving, Dec 25. Dinner. Bar. **$$**

[D]

★ **THE CACTUS GRILLE.** *800 Allens Ave (02905). Phone 401/941-0004; fax 401/941-0175.* Mexican menu. Closed Dec 25. Lunch, dinner. Bar. Children's menu. Casual attire. **$$**

[D]

★ ★ **HEMENWAY'S SEAFOOD GRILL.** *1 Providence-Washington Plz (02903). Phone 401/351-8570; fax 401/351-8594.* Seafood menu. Closed Thanksgiving, Dec 25. Lunch, dinner. Bar. Children's menu. Valet parking. Outdoor seating. **$$$**

[D]

★ ★ **INDIA.** *123 Dorrance St (02903). Phone 401/278-2000; fax 401/778-7001.* Indian menu. Lunch, dinner. Bar. Casual attire. **$$**

★ ★ **OLD GRIST MILL TAVERN.** *390 Fall River Ave (02771). Phone 508/336-8460; fax 508/336-6713.* Closed Thanksgiving, Dec 25. Lunch, dinner. Bar. Children's menu. In a restored mill (1745); antiques; fireplace. Gardens, pond, wooden bridge over waterfall. **$$**

[D]

★ ★ **PANE E VINO.** *365 Atwells Ave (02903). Phone 401/223-2230; fax 401/223-4322.* Italian menu. Closed Sat; major holidays. Dinner. Bar. Casual attire. Outdoor seating. **$$**

[D]

★ ★ ★ **POT AU FEU.** *44 Custom House St (02903). Phone 401/273-8953; fax 401/273-8963.* This restaurant features casual, bistro-style dining downstairs and a more formal upstairs. French menu. Closed Sun; most major holidays. Lunch, dinner. Bar. **$$$**

Salem

30 minutes; 15 miles from Boston

Settled 1626 **Pop** 40,407 **Elev** 9 ft **Area code** 978 **Zip** 01970

Information Chamber of Commerce, 63 Wharf St; 978/744-0004

Web www.salem-chamber.org

In old Salem, the story of early New England life is told with bricks, clapboards, carvings, and gravestones. The town had two native geniuses to immortalize it: Samuel McIntire (1757-1811), master builder, and Nathaniel Hawthorne (1804-1864), author. History is charmingly entangled with the people and events of Hawthorne's novels. Reality, however, could be far from charming. During the witchcraft panic of 1692, 19 persons were hanged on Gallows Hill, another "pressed" to death; at least two others died in jail. Gallows Hill is still here; so is the house of one of the trial judges.

Early in the 18th century, Salem shipbuilding and allied industries were thriving. Salem was a major port. The Revolution turned commerce into privateering. Then began the fabulous China trade and Salem's heyday. The captains came home, and Sam McIntire built splendid houses for them that still stand. Shipping declined after 1812. Salem turned to industry, which, together with tourism, is the present-day economic base.

What to See and Do

Chestnut Street. Architecturally, one of the most beautiful streets in America; laid out in 1796.

House of Seven Gables. *54 Turner St (01970), off Derby St on Salem Harbor. Phone 978/744-0991. www.7gables.org.* Nathaniel Hawthorne's 1851 novel is said to have been inspired by this home, although he never lived there. You'll enjoy the tour most if you've read the book, because you'll recognize furnishings and areas of the home from Hawthorne's descriptions. Even if you haven't read it, however, you're sure to enjoy the well-preserved estate that dates back to 1669, as well as the guide in period clothing. (Daily; closed first three weeks in Jan) **$$**

Peabody Museum & Essex Institute. *East India Sq (01970). Phone 978/745-9500.* The Peabody Museum, founded by sea captains in 1799, features five world-famous collections in 30 galleries. Large collections of marine art, Asian export art. Essex Institute features historical interpretations of area. Peabody Museum (daily; closed Jan 1, Thanksgiving, Dec 25). Essex Institute (Daily) Admission includes

> **Crowninshield-Bentley House.** *Essex St and Hawthorne Blvd (01970).* (1727) Reverend William Bentley, minister and diarist, lived here from 1791 to 1819. Period furnishings. (June-Oct, daily; rest of year, Sat-Sun, and holidays)

A Walk through Salem

Salem is a fascinating old port city with a walkable downtown. Begin at the National Park Visitors Center at 2 Liberty Street across from the Museum Place garage. Just around the corner on the pedestrian stretch of Essex Street is the Peabody Essex Museum, New England's ultimate treasure chest of exotica, all of it brought from the farthest points of the globe by Salem sea captains in the decades after the Revolution. The Essex Institute part of the museum houses a collection of portraits and archives, including the actual records of the 1692 witch trials for which Salem is infamous; a short film puts the trials in their historical context. Historic homes on the grounds include the Gardner-Pingree House, showcasing the work of Samuel McIntire. Salem's famous architect, McIntire, is known for creating airy Federal-era mansions with elegant carved detailing, arches, and stairways. You might want to detour to see Chestnut Street, famous because it is lined with McIntire mansions (walk west up Essex Street and south on Cambridge Street; return the same route).

West of the museums turn south off Essex Street to Derby Square, site of Salem's Old Town Hall, a graceful brick building dating from 1816 that is now a hospitable visitor center for the Salem Chamber of Commerce. Continue down the square (it's really a mini-park) to Front Street and follow the red line on the sidewalk (the Salem Heritage Trail) down Charter and Liberty streets, past the Old Burying Point Cemetery and the Salem Wax Museum.

Continue down along Derby Street to the Salem Maritime National Historic site on Salem Harbor. *The Friendship,* a fully-rigged tall ship, is berthed at Central Wharf. The handsome brick Custom House (1819), where Nathaniel Hawthorne worked, is next door at the head of Derby Wharf. Here, too, is the Elias Hasket Derby House, built by the man who pioneered a new sailing route around the Cape of Good Hope, and is said to have been America's first millionaire. The House of Seven Gables, immortalized by Hawthorne, is a few blocks east, overlooking the harbor. Retrace your steps (following the red line) up Derby Street and turn up Hawthorne Boulevard to Salem Common. Look for the Salem Witch Museum (Washington Square North), which dramatizes the tale of the witch trials with computerized sound and light. This tour is slightly under 2 miles, but you can hop a trolley—also a good way to gain an overview of sites to begin with—if you tire along the way. Return down Brown Street to your starting point.

Gardner-Pingree House. *128 Essex St (01970).* (1804) Designed by McIntire; restored and handsomely furnished. (June-Oct, daily; rest of year, Sat-Sun and holidays)

John Ward House. *161 Essex St (01970). Behind Essex Institute.* (1684) Seventeenth-century furnishings. (June-Oct, daily; rest of year, Sat-Sun and holidays)

Peirce-Nichols House. *80 Federal St (01970). Phone 978/745-9500.* (1782) One of the finest examples of McIntire's architectural genius; authentically furnished. (By appointment only)

Pickering Wharf. *174 Derby St (01970). Adjacent to Salem Maritime National Historic Site.* This 6-acre commercial and residential village by the sea includes shops, restaurants, and a marina.

Pioneer Village: Salem in 1630. *Forest River Park, off West St (01970). Phone 978/744-0991 or 978/745-0525.* Reproduction of early Puritan settlement, includes dugouts, wigwams, and thatched cottages; costumed interpreters. Guided tours. (Last weekend May-Oct, daily) **$$$$**

Ropes Mansion and Garden. *318 Essex St (01970). Phone 978/745-9500.* (Late 1720s) Gambrel-roofed, Georgian and colonial mansion; restored and furnished with period pieces. The garden (laid out in 1912) is nationally known for its beauty and variety. (June-Oct, daily; limited hours Sun) **$$**

⭐ **Salem Maritime National Historic Site.** *Orientation Center, Central Wharf Warehouse, 174 Derby St (01970). Phone 978/740-1660.* Nine acres of historic waterfront. Self-guided and guided tours. (Daily; Thanksgiving, closed Dec 25, Jan 1). **$$** The site includes

Custom House. *174 Derby St (01970). Derby St, opposite wharf. Phone 978/745-0799.* (1819) Restored offices. (Daily; closed Jan 1, Thanksgiving, Dec 25)

Derby House. *174 Derby St (01970). Phone 978/745-0799.* (1761-1762) Home of maritime merchant Elias Hasket Derby, one of the country's first millionaires. In back are the Derby House Gardens, featuring roses, herbs, and 19th-century flowers. Inquire at Orientation Center for tour information.

Derby Wharf. *Off Derby St. Phone 978/740-1660.* Once a center of Salem shipping (1760-1810).

Narbonne House. *Phone 978/745-0799.* A 17th-century house with archaeological exhibits. Inquire at Orientation Center for tour information.

Scale House. *174 Derby St (01970). Phone 978/745-0799.* (1829) and **Bonded Warehouse** (1819). Site of 19th-century customs operations. (Daily)

Visitor Information. *2 New Liberty St (01970). Phone 978/744-0004.* In Orientation Center and downtown visitor center at Museum Place, Essex St.

West India Goods Store. *164 Derby St (01970).* (1800) Coffee, teas, spices, and goods for sale. (Daily; closed Jan 1, Thanksgiving, Dec 25)

Winfisky Art Gallery. Photographs, paintings, graphics, and sculpture by national and local artists. (Sept-May, Mon-Fri) **FREE**

Salem State College. *352 Lafayette St. Phone 978/542-6200.* (1854) 9,300 students.

Chronicle of Salem. *Meier Hall.* Mural, 60 feet by 30 feet, depicts Salem history from settlement to present in 50 sequences. (Mon-Fri; closed holidays)

Library Gallery. Art exhibits by local and national artists. (Mon-Sat) **FREE**

Main Stage Auditorium. *352 Lafayette St (01970). Phone 978/744-3700.* This 750-seat theater presents musical and dramatic productions (Sept-Dec, Jan-Apr).

Salem Witch Museum. *19 1/2 Washington Sq (01970). Follow Hawthorne Blvd to the NW corner of Salem Common. Phone 978/744-1692. www. salemwitchmuseum.com.* The Salem Witch Museum re-creates the Salem Witch Trials of 1692 with a 30-minute narrated presentation that uses special lighting and life-size figures. The museum may be too frightening for young children. If you're traveling in October, also visit Salem's Haunted Happenings, a Halloween festival that begins in early October and runs through Halloween and features street merchants, plays, witchy games, and haunted houses. (Jul-Aug: daily 10 am-7 pm, Sept-June: daily 10 am-5 pm; closed Jan 1, Thanksgiving, Dec 25) **$$**

Stephen Phillips Trust House. *34 Chestnut St. Phone 978/744-0440.* (1804) Federal-style mansion with McIntire mantels and woodwork. Furnishings, rugs, porcelains reflect the merchant and seafaring past of the Phillips family. Also carriage barn with carriages and antique automobiles. (Late May-Oct, Mon-Sat) **FREE**

Witch Dungeon Museum. *16 Lynde St. Phone 978/741-3570.* Reenactment of witch trial of Sarah Good by professional actresses; tour through re-created dungeon where accused witches awaited trial; original artifacts. (May-Nov, daily) **$$**

Witch House. *310 1/2 Essex St. Phone 978/744-0180.* (1642) Home of witchcraft trial judge Jonathan Corwin. Some of the accused witches may have been examined here. (Mid-Mar-Nov, daily) **$$**

Special Events

Haunted Happenings. *Various sites. Phone 978-744-0004.* Psychic festival, historical exhibits, haunted house, costume parade, contests, dances. Entire month of Oct.

Heritage Days Celebration. *Phone 978-744-0004.* Band concerts, parade, exhibits, and ethnic festivals. Mid-Aug.

Hotel

★ ★ **HAWTHORNE HOTEL.** *18 Washington Sq W (01970). Phone 978/744-4080; toll-free 800/729-7829; fax 978/745-9842. www.hawthornehotel.com.*

89 rooms, 6 story. Pets accepted, some restrictions; fee. Check-out 11 am. TV; cable (premium). In-room modem link. Laundry services. Restaurant. In-house fitness room. Health club privileges. **$**

B&B/Small Inns

★ **COACH HOUSE INN.** *284 Lafayette St (Rte A1A) (01970). Phone 978/744-4092; toll-free 800/688-8689; fax 978/745-8031. www.salemweb.com/biz/coachhouse.* 11 rooms, 9 with bath, 9 A/C, 3 story. No room phones. Complimentary continental breakfast. Check-out 11 am, check-in 3 pm. TV. Built in 1879. Totally nonsmoking. **$**

★★★ **SALEM INN.** *7 Summer St; Rte 114 (01970). Phone 978/741-0680; toll-free 800/446-2995; fax 978/744-8924. www.saleminnma.com.* With individually appointed rooms and suites, many of which feature Jacuzzis, kitchenettes, and fireplaces, this inn provides comfort and luxury without assaulting your wallet. Season packages available. 33 rooms, 4 story. No elevator. Pets accepted; fee. Complimentary continental breakfast. Check-out 11 am, check-in 3 pm. TV; cable (premium). In-room modem link. **$**

Restaurants

★★ **GRAPE VINE.** *26 Congress St (01970). Phone 978/745-9335; fax 978/744-9335. www.grapevinesalem.com.* American, Italian menu. Closed some major holidays; also Super Bowl Sun. Dinner. Bar. Outdoor seating. Totally nonsmoking. **$$$**

D

★★★ **LYCEUM.** *43 Church St (01970). Phone 978/745-7665; fax 978/744-7699. www.lyceumsalem.com.* One of the area's best restaurants, this comfortable, elegant dining room is located in the building where Alexander Graham Bell made his first phone call in 1877. Chef James Harvey's specialty is New American cuisine. Don't miss the portabella appetizer. Closed Thanksgiving, Dec 25. Lunch, dinner, Sun brunch. Bar. Built in 1830. Totally nonsmoking. **$$**

D

★★★ **RED RAVEN'S LIMP NOODLE.** *75 Congress Ave (01970). Phone 978/745-8558.* This quirky North Shore restaurant (one of two in town) is known for a menu that blends foods from around the world with a sense of humor and an offbeat setting. The door to the women's room is indicated with a brassiere. Need we say more? Eclectic menu. Closed Mon, Sun; also most major holidays. Dinner. Bar. Turn-of-the-century Victorian décor; paintings. **$$**

D

★ **STROMBERG'S RESTAURANT.** *2 Bridge St (01970). Phone 978/ 744-1863. www.strombergs.com.* American, seafood menu. Closed Mon. Lunch, dinner. Bar. Children's menu. Casual attire. Outdoor seating. **$$**
[D]

★ **VICTORIA STATION.** *86 Wharf St (01970). Phone 978/745-3400; fax 978/745-7460. www.victoriastationinc.com.* Seafood menu. Closed Dec 25. Lunch, dinner. Bar. Children's menu. Outdoor seating. **$**
[D]

Stockbridge and West Stockbridge

2 hours 12 minutes; 130 miles from Boston

Settled 1734 **Pop** 2,276 **Elev** 842 & 901 ft **Area code** 413 **Zip** Stockbridge, 01262; West Stockbridge, 01266

Information Stockbridge Chamber of Commerce, 6 Elm St, PO Box 224; 413/298-5200; or visit Main St Information Booth

Web www.stockbridgechamber.org

Established as a mission, Stockbridge was for many years a center for teaching the Mahican. The first preacher was John Sergeant. Jonathan Edwards also taught at Stockbridge. The town is now mainly a summer resort but still has many features and attractions open year round. West Stockbridge is a completely restored market village. Its Main Street is lined with well-kept storefronts, renovated in the style of the 1800s, featuring stained glass, antiques, and hand-crafted articles.

What to See and Do

Berkshire Botanical Garden. *Rtes 102 and 183. 2 miles NW, at junction MA 102, 183 in Stockbridge. Phone 413/298-3926.* Fifteen-acre botanical garden; perennials, shrubs, trees, antique roses, ponds; wildflower exhibit, herb, vegetable gardens; solar, semitropical, and demonstration greenhouses. Garden shop. Herb products. Special events, lectures. Picnicking. (May-Oct, daily) **$$$**

Berkshire Hills. *www.berkshires.org.* This western Massachusetts resort area is just south of Vermont's Green Mountains, but has neither the ruggedness nor the lonesomeness of the range to its north. The highest peak, Mt. Greylock (elevation: 3,491 feet), is cragless and serene. Farms and villages dot the landscape. The area is famous for its variety of accommodations, culture, and recreation. There are also countless summer homes and camps for children by the lakes, ponds, and brooks. Berkshire County is about 45 miles long from north to south, and half that from east to west. It has 90 lakes and ponds, 90,000 acres of state forest, golf courses, ski areas, ski touring centers, numerous tennis facilities, and campsites. The area first became famous when Nathaniel Hawthorne wrote *Tanglewood Tales,* and it has since become distinguished for its many summer cultural activities, including the Tanglewood Music Festival at Tanglewood (see LENOX) and the Berkshire Theatre Festival (see STOCKBRIDGE & WEST STOCKBRIDGE).

Chesterwood. *284 Main St. 2 miles S of junction MA 102 and MA 183, in Stockbridge. Phone 413/298-3579.* Early 20th-century summer residence and studio of Daniel Chester French, sculptor of the "Minute Man" statue in Concord and of Lincoln in the Memorial in Washington, DC. Also museum; gardens, woodland walk; guided tours. A property of the National Trust for Historic Preservation. (May-Oct, daily) **$$$**

Children's Chimes Bell Tower. *Main St, in Stockbridge.* (1878) Erected by David Dudley Field, a prominent lawyer, as a memorial to his grandchildren. Carillon concerts (June-Aug, daily).

Merwin House "Tranquility." *14 Main St, in Stockbridge. Phone 413/298-4703.* (circa 1825) Brick house in late Federal period; enlarged with a "shingle"-style wing at the end of the 19th century. European and American furniture and decorative arts. (June-mid-Oct, Tues, Thurs, Sat, Sun) **$$**

Mission House. *Main and Sergeant sts, on MA 102. Phone 413/298-3239.* House built in 1739 for the missionary Reverend John Sergeant and his wife, Abigail Williams; now a museum of colonial life. Collection of colonial antiques; Native American museum; gardens and orchard. Guided tours. (Memorial Day weekend-Columbus Day weekend, daily) **$$**

Naumkeag. *1 Sergeant St. Prospect Hill in Stockbridge. Phone 413/298-3239.* Stanford White designed this Norman-style "Berkshire cottage" (1886); the interior has antiques, Oriental rugs, and a collection of Chinese export porcelain. Gardens include terraces of tree peonies, fountains, a Chinese garden and birch walk. Guided tours. (Memorial Day weekend-Columbus weekend, daily) **$$$**

★ **Norman Rockwell Museum.** *9 Glendale Rd (01262). MA 183, in Stockbridge. Phone 413/298-4100.* Maintains and exhibits the nation's largest collection of original art by Norman Rockwell. (Daily; closed Jan 1, Thanksgiving, Dec 25) **$$$**

Special Events

Berkshire Theatre Festival. *Berkshire Playhouse. 6 E Main St, in Stockbridge (01262). Entrance from US 7, MA 102. Phone 413/298-5536.* Summer theater (Mon-Sat); Unicorn Theater presents new and experimental plays (Mon-Sat in season); children's theater (July-Aug, Thurs-Sat). Late June-late Aug.

Harvest Festival. *Phone 413/298-3926.* Berkshire Botanical Garden. Celebrates the beginning of the harvest and foliage season in the Berkshire Hills. First weekend in Oct.

Stockbridge Main Street at Christmas. *6 Elm St (01262). Phone 413/298-5200.* Events include a re-creation of Norman Rockwell's painting. Holiday marketplace, concerts, house tour, silent auction, sleigh/hay rides, caroling. First weekend in Dec.

B&B/Small Inns

★ ★ ★ THE INN AT STOCKBRIDGE. *Rte 7 N (01262). Phone 413/298-3337; toll-free 888/466-7865; fax 413/298-3406. www.stockbridgeinn.com.* This classic bed-and-breakfast offers a warm reception. Fireplaces and whirlpools are options in most of the rooms, and guests can enjoy the company of others over wine and cheese served in the afternoon. 16 rooms, 2 story. Children over 12 years only. Complimentary full breakfast. Check-out 11 am, check-in 2 pm. TV; VCR available. Outdoor pool. 1906 building on 12-acre estate. Totally nonsmoking. **$$**

D ⌸ ◹

★ ★ RED LION. *30 Main St (01262). Phone 413/298-5545; fax 413/298-5130. www.redlioninn.com.* 108 rooms. Check-out noon, check-in 3 pm. TV; VCR. Restaurant, bar; entertainment. Room service. In-house fitness room, massage. Pool. Historic resort inn, established in 1773. Victorian décor. Free transportation. **$$$**

D ⌸ ⌸ ◹

★ ★ ★ THE TAGGART HOUSE. *18 W Main St (01262). Phone 413/298-4303. www.taggarthouse.com.* This lovingly restored and renovated country house fronts the Housatonic River in the Berkshires. It is elegant, luxurious, sophisticated, intimate, and replete with the finest of antiques and sumptuous furnishings throughout. 4 rooms. No room phones. Closed Jan-Apr. Children over 18 years only. Complimentary full breakfast. Check-out noon, check-in 3 pm. In-room modem link. Game room. Built in the late 1800s; country manor house. Totally nonsmoking. **$$$**

◹

★ ★ ★ WILLIAMSVILLE INN. *MA 41 (01266). Phone 413/274-6118; fax 413/274-3539. www.williamsvilleinn.com.* A perfect way to escape and get away to the Berkshires. This is an ideal spot to enjoy many of the annual festivals. Breakfast is served daily by the fireplace; for added charm, enjoy afternoon storytelling, held during the summer. 16 rooms, 1-3 story. No room phones. Complimentary full breakfast. Check-out 11 am, check-in 2 pm. Restaurant (see WILLIAMSVILLE INN). Bar. Outdoor pool. Outdoor tennis. Downhill, cross-country ski 8 miles. Lawn games. Built in 1797. **$**

◹ ⌸ ⌸ ◹

Restaurants

★ ★ MICHAEL'S. *5 Elm St (01262). Phone 413/298-3530.* Continental menu. Closed Dec 25. Lunch, dinner. Bar. Children's menu (dinner). **$$**

◨

★ ★ ★ THE RED LION. *30 Main St (01262). Phone 413/298-5545; fax 413/298-5130. www.redlioninn.com.* The candlelit dining room of this

historic inn is filled with antiques, colonial pewter, and crystal. The contemporary New England menu emphasizes local, seasonal produce and offers several vegetarian options. Seafood menu. Breakfast, lunch, dinner. Bar. Pianist weekends. Children's menu. Jacket required. Outdoor seating. Contemporary New England menu. **$$**

D

★ ★ **TRUC ORIENT EXPRESS.** *1 Harris St (01266). Phone 413/232-4204.* Vietnamese menu. Closed Thanksgiving, Dec 25; also Tues, Nov-Apr. Lunch, dinner, brunch. Bar. Outdoor seating. **$$**

D

★ ★ ★ **WILLIAMSVILLE INN.** *MA 41 (01266). Phone 413/274-6118; fax 413/274-3539. www.williamsvilleinn.com.* This cozy inn dining room has an open fireplace and plenty of candlelight. The walls are lined with bookshelves, and you may feel as if you are dining in someone's home—only the food is better. The continental menu includes meat and poultry, salads, seafood, and other standard fare. Closed Mon-Wed (Nov-mid-June). Dinner. Bar. Reservations required. **$$**

SC

Side Trips Overnight Stays

If you are in need of some relaxation and just feel like hanging out on the beach, then Martha's Vineyard and Nantucket Island await you. In a few hours, you could be strolling in and out of little boutiques or sipping on some iced tea while lounging on the beach.

Bangor, ME

4 hours; 234 miles from Boston

Settled 1769 **Pop** 31,473 **Elev** 61 ft **Area code** 207 **Zip** 04401

Information Bangor Convention and Visitors Bureau, PO Box 1938 04402

Web www.bangorcvb.org

In 1604, Samuel de Champlain sailed up the Penobscot River to the area that was to become Bangor and reported that the country was "most pleasant and agreeable," the hunting good, and the oak trees impressive. As the area grew, these things remained true. Begun as a harbor town, as were many of Maine's coastal areas, Bangor turned to lumber when the railroads picked up much of the shipping business. In 1842, it became the second-largest lumber port in the country.

Bangor received its name by mistake. An early settler, Reverend Seth Noble, was sent to register the new town under its chosen name of Sunbury; however, when officials asked Noble for the name, he thought they were asking him for the name of a tune he was humming, and replied "Bangor" instead. Today, the city is the third largest in Maine, and is a trading and distribution center.

What to See and Do

Bangor Historical Museum. *159 Union St at High St. Phone 207/942-5766.* (Thomas A. Hill House, 1834) Tour of the first floor of a Greek Revival house; a second-floor gallery features changing exhibits. (Tues-Sat, June-Dec) **$**

Cole Land Transportation Museum. *405 Perry Rd. Phone 207/990-3600. www.colemuseum.org.* The Cole Museum takes great pride in depicting the history of transportation in the American Northeast. The museum houses one of the largest collections of snow removal equipment found in one place anywhere in the country, as well as a cache of military vehicles. A great place to take children, more than 20,000 visitors go through the turnstiles each year to see the museum's permanent collection, including local railroad pieces and cars and trucks, uniquely designed to traverse the streets of Bangor. Historic photographs of Maine are also on display. (May-early Nov, daily) **$$**

Monument to Paul Bunyan. *Main St in Bass Park.* A 31-foot-tall statue commemorating the legendary lumberjack. **FREE**

Special Events

Band concerts. *Paul Bunyan Park, 647 Main St. Phone 207/947-1018.* Tues evenings, July-Aug.

Bangor Fair. *100 Dutton St. Phone 207/990-4444.* One of the country's oldest fairs. Horse racing, exhibits, stage shows. Late June-first week in Aug.

Kenduskeag Stream Canoe Race. *647 Main St. Phone 207/947-1018.* Mid-Apr.

Motels/Motor Lodges

★ ★ **BEST INN.** *570 Main St (04401). Phone 207/942-1234. www.bestinn .com.* 50 rooms, 2 story. Pets accepted, some restrictions. Complimentary continental breakfast. Check-out 11 am. TV. Restaurant, bar. **$**
D ⬚ ⬚ SC

★ ★ **BEST WESTERN WHITE HOUSE INN.** *155 Littlefield Ave (04401). Phone 207/862-3737; fax 207/862-3737. www.bestwestern.com.* 66 rooms, 3 story. Pets accepted, some restrictions; fee. Complimentary continental breakfast. Check-out 11 am. TV; VCR available (movies). In-room modem link. Bar. Sauna. Outdoor pool. Downhill, cross-country ski 4 miles. Lawn games. **$**

★ **COMFORT INN.** *750 Hogan Rd (04401). Phone 207/942-7899; fax 207/942-6463. www.comfortinn.com.* 96 rooms, 2 story. Pets accepted, some restrictions; fee. Complimentary continental breakfast. Check-out noon. TV; cable (premium). In-house fitness room. Game room. Outdoor pool. Cross-country ski 10 miles. Free airport transportation. **$**

★ **DAYS INN.** *250 Odlin Rd (04401). Phone 207/942-8272; toll-free 800/329-7466; fax 207/942-1382. www.daysinn.com.* 101 rooms, 2 story. Pets accepted; fee. Complimentary continental breakfast. Check-out 11 am. TV; cable (premium), VCR available. In-room modem link. Room service. Game room. Indoor pool, whirlpool. Downhill, cross-country ski 12 miles. Free airport transportation. **$**

★ **ECONO LODGE.** *327 Odlin Rd (04401). Phone 207/945-0111; toll-free 800/393-0111; fax 207/942-8856. www.econolodge.com.* 128 rooms, 4 story. Pets accepted; fee. Check-out 11 am. TV; cable (premium). In-room modem link. Laundry services. Downhill, cross-country ski 7 miles. **$**

★ **FAIRFIELD INN.** *300 Odlin Rd (04401). Phone 207/990-0001; fax 207/990-0917. www.fairfieldinn.com.* 153 rooms, 3 story. Complimentary continental breakfast. Check-out noon. TV; cable (premium). In-room modem link. Sauna. Indoor pool, whirlpool. Downhill ski 7 miles, cross-country ski 5 miles. **$**

★ ★ **FOUR POINTS BY SHERATON.** *308 Godfrey Blvd (04401). Phone 207/947-6721; toll-free 800/228-4609; fax 207/941-9761. www.fourpoints.com.* 101 rooms, 9 story. Pets accepted, some restrictions; fee. Check-out noon. TV; cable (premium). In-room modem link. Restaurant, bar. Outdoor pool. In-house fitness room. Downhill, cross-country ski 7 miles. Airport transportation. Business center. Enclosed walkway to airport. **$**

Hotels

★ ★ **HOLIDAY INN.** *500 Main St (04401). Phone 207/947-8651; toll-free 800/799-8651; fax 207/942-2848. www.holiday-inn.com/bangor-civic.* 121 rooms, 4 story. Pets accepted, some restrictions. Check-out noon. TV; cable (premium). In-room modem link. Restaurant, bar; entertainment. Room service. Health club privileges. Outdoor pool. Downhill ski 10 miles. Free airport transportation. Opposite Civic Center. **$**

★ ★ **HOLIDAY INN.** *404 Odlin Rd (04401). Phone 207/947-0101; toll-free 800/914-0101; fax 207/947-7619. www.holiday-inn.com/bangor-odlin.* 207 rooms, 3 story. Pets accepted, some restrictions. Check-out noon. TV; cable (premium), VCR available. In-room modem link. Restaurant, bar; entertainment. Room service. Health club privileges. Indoor pool, outdoor pool, whirlpool. Downhill ski 15 miles, cross-country ski 10 miles. Free airport transportation. **$**

D ◄ ⌖ ⩶ ✈ SC

B&B/Small Inn

★ ★ **THE LUCERNE INN.** *Rte 1A Bar Harbor Rd (04429). Phone 207/843-5123; toll-free 800/325-5123; fax 207/843-6138. www.lucerneinn.com.* 30 rooms, 3 story. Complimentary continental breakfast. Check-out 11 am, check-in 2 pm. TV; cable (premium). Fireplaces. Dining room. Room service. Outdoor pool. Colonial-style farmhouse and connecting stable, established as an inn in 1814. **$$**

D ⩶ ⩹

Restaurants

★ **CAPTAIN NICK'S SEAFOOD HOUSE.** *1165 Union St (04401). Phone 207/942-6444; fax 207/947-8630.* Seafood menu. Closed Thanksgiving, Dec 25. Lunch, dinner. Bar. Children's menu. **$$**

D SC

★ ★ **MILLER'S.** *427 Main St (04401). Phone 207/945-5663; fax 207/942-2245.* Closed Dec 25. Lunch, dinner, Sun brunch. Children's menu. **$$**

D SC

Martha's Vineyard

2 hours 30 minutes; 92 miles from Boston

Settled 1642 **Pop** 12,690 **Elev** 0-311 ft **Area code** 508

Information Chamber of Commerce, Beach Rd, PO Box 1698, Vineyard Haven 02568; 508/693-0085

Web www.mvy.com

This triangular island below the arm of Cape Cod combines moors, dunes, multicolored cliffs, flower-filled ravines, farmland, and forest. It is less than 20 miles from west to east and 10 miles from north to south.

There was once a whaling fleet at the island, but Martha's Vineyard now devotes itself almost entirely to being a vacation playground, with summer houses that range from small cottages to elaborate mansions. The colonial atmosphere still survives in Vineyard Haven, the chief port; Oak Bluffs; Edgartown; West Tisbury; Gay Head; and Chilmark.

Gay Head is one of the few Massachusetts towns in which many inhabitants are of Native American descent.

What to See and Do

Aquinnah Cliffs. *State Rd, Aquinnah (02535).* These cliffs—a national landmark—are the most popular and most photographed tourist attraction on Martha's Vineyard because of the stunning view they offer. The 150-foot, brilliantly colored cliffs were formed over millions of years by glaciers; today, the cliffs are owned by the Wampanoag Indians, who hold them sacred. (Previous names of the cliffs include Dover Cliffs, so named by settlers in 1602, and Gay Head Cliffs, a name that originated from British sailors. Gay Head was the official name of this part of Martha's Vineyard until 1998.) On top of the Cliffs stands Aquinnah Light lighthouse, which was commissioned by President John Adams in 1844 to protect ships from the treacherous stretch of sea below and built with clay from the cliffs. (Apr-Nov)

Chicama Vineyards. *Stoney Hill Rd, West Tisbury (02545). Phone 508/693-0309. www.chicamavineyards.com.* Martha's Vineyard was once awash in winemaking; today Chicama Vineyards is reviving the practice. The European grapes are used to produce a variety of wines, including Merlot, Chardonnay, and Cabernet. You'll also find other foodstuffs for sale, including vinegars and salad dressings, mustards and chutneys, and jams and jellies. Tours and wine tasting are available, but hours vary with the day and season. (Hours vary; call ahead) **FREE**

East Beach. *Chappaquiddick Rd, Chappaquiddick Island (02539). Take your four-wheel drive car on the On Time ferry from Martha's Vineyard to Chappaquiddick Island. From the ferry dock, take Chappaquiddick Road until a sharp right turn, where the road becomes Dike Bridge Road. Park near the bridge or obtain an oversand vehicle permit to drive on the beach. Phone 508/627-7689.* East Beach is the popular name for two adjoining beaches: Wasque Reservation and Cape Pogue Wildlife Refuge. You'll go to a lot of trouble to get to this rustic beach that has no restrooms or concessions, but the quiet, beautiful stretch of shoreline makes the preparation and trip worthwhile. Chances are you'll have this stunning beach all to yourself. (Daily) **$$**

Edgartown. The island's first colonial settlement and county seat since 1642 is the location of stately white Greek Revival houses built by whaling captains. These have been carefully preserved, and North Water Street has a row of captains' houses unequaled anywhere. Edgartown is also home to an astounding number of art galleries. Located here is

Vineyard Museum. *8 Cooke St (02539). Phone 508/627-4441.* Four buildings dating back to pre-Revolutionary times join together to form the Vineyard Museum. Thomas Cooke House, a historic colonial home, specializes in antiques and folk art; Foster Gallery displays exhibits from the whaling industry; Pease Galleries specializes in Native American exhibits, and Gale Huntington Library is a useful tool for genealogy. A Cape Cod museum wouldn't be complete without displaying a huge Fresnel (lighthouse) lens—view it just outside the front doors. **$**

Felix Neck Sanctuary. *Three miles from Edgartown off Edgartown-Vineyard Haven Rd. Phone 508/627-4850. www.massaudubon.org/Nature_Connection/ Sanctuaries/Felix_Neck.* This 350-acre wildlife preserve is a haven for kids and bird lovers alike. Six miles of trails (guided or self-guided) meander through the sanctuary's meadows, woods, salt marshes, and beaches. The visitors center, which offers unique exhibits along with a more traditional gift shop, is open daily 8 am-4 pm (closed Mon from Oct to May). In the summer, consider enrolling the kids in Fern & Feather Day Camp at the Sanctuary. (Daily) **$**

Hyannis-Martha's Vineyard Day Round Trip. *Phone 508/778-2600.* Passenger service from Hyannis (May-Oct).

Menemsha Fishing Village. *North St, Menemsha (02552). Take a shuttle bus or bike ferry from Aquinnah.* Menemsha is a picturesque fishing village, which means you'll see plenty of cedar-sided fishing shacks, fishermen in waterproof gear, and lobster traps strewn about. The movie *Jaws* was filmed here, and if you saw it, you may have haunting flashbacks while you're here! You'll find quaint shopping areas in the village, as well.

Mytoi. *Dike Rd (02539). Phone 508/693-7662 or 508/627-6789.* Although Martha's Vineyard may not be a logical location for a Japanese garden, Mytoi has won praises for its breathtaking mix of azaleas, irises, dogwood, daffodils, rhododendron, and Japanese maple for nearly 50 years. You'll spy goldfish and koi swimming in a pond that's the centerpiece of the garden; you can visit the small island at the pond's center via the ornamental bridge. Take an easy 1-mile hike that weaves through the gardens and into forested area and salt marshes. Allow from an hour to a half-day. (Daily) **FREE**

Oak Bluffs. In 1835, this Methodist community served as the site of annual summer camp meetings for church groups. As thousands attended these meetings, the communal tents gave way to family tents, which in turn became wooden cottages designed to look like tents. Today, visitors to the community may see these "Gingerbread Cottages of the Campground."

Flying Horse Carousel. *33 Circuit Ave (02557). Phone 508/693-9481.* Whether you're traveling with a youngster who loves horses (but is too young to ride them for real) or want to hop on for yourself, Flying Horse Carousel is a treat not to be missed. This carousel, the oldest in the country and a national historic landmark, looks nothing like modern carousels you may have seen in malls or shopping centers. Instead, Flying Horse features gorgeous, hand-carved, lifelike horses that glide to festive music. Try to grasp the brass ring in the center to earn your next ride free.

Recreation. **Swimming.** *Phone 508/693-3057 or 508/693-0600 (Mink Meadows).* Many sheltered beaches, among them public beaches at Menemsha, Oak Bluffs, Edgartown, and Vineyard Haven. Surf swimming on south shore. **Tennis.** Public courts in Edgartown, Oak Bluffs, West Tisbury, and Vineyard Haven. **Boat rentals** at Vineyard Haven, Oak Bluffs, and Gay Head. **Fishing.** Good for striped bass, bonito, bluefish, weakfish. **Golf** at Farm Neck Club.

Steamship Authority. *1494 E Rodney French Blvd (02744). Phone 508/477-8600 or 508/693-9130. www.steamshipauthority.com.* New Bedford-Martha's Vineyard Ferry. Daily passenger service (mid-May-mid-Sept) to New Bedford. Same-day round-trips available. Also bus tours of the island. Schedule may vary. **$$$$**

⭐ **Vincent House.** *Pease's Point Way (02539). Main St in Edgartown. Phone 508/627-4440.* The oldest known house on the island, built in 1672, has been carefully restored to allow visitors to see how buildings were constructed 300 years ago. Original brickwork, hardware, and woodwork. (June-early Oct, daily; rest of year, by appointment) **FREE** Also on Main St is the

> **Old Whaling Church.** *89 Main (02539). Phone 508/627-4442.* Built in 1843, this is a fine example of Greek Revival architecture. Now a performing arts center with seating for 500.

Vineyard Haven. *Phone 508/693-0085. www.mvy.com.* Vineyard Haven is where most of Martha's Vineyard's year-round residents live, so its shops are a bit less upscale than those in ritzy Edgartown, where you could spend an afternoon or even an entire day. In both areas, you'll find clothing (both casual and upscale), books, jewelry, home-decorating items, and goodies to eat (fudge, candy, and jams). Vineyard Haven is perhaps best known as the location of the Black Dog General Store (along with the Black Dog Bakery and Black Dog Tavern) that sell T-shirts and other goods bearing the logo of its now-famous black Lab.

Woods Hole, Martha's Vineyard & Nantucket Steamship Authority. *Phone 508/477-8600. www.steamshipauthority.com.* Conducts round-trip service to Martha's Vineyard (all year, weather permitting).

The Yard. *Middle Rd (02535). Phone 508/645-9662. www.dancetheyard.com.* For 30 years, The Yard has hosted dance performances throughout the summer. The theater is intimate, with just 100 seats available, and makes its home in a renovated barn nestled in the Chilmark woods. The Yard also offers community dance classes, and free performances for children and senior citizens. (Mid-Oct-mid-June) **$$$**

Hotels

★ ★ ★ **HARBOR VIEW HOTEL OF MARTHA'S VINEYARD.** *131 N Water St, Edgartown (02539). Phone 508/627-7000; toll-free 800/225-6005; fax 508/627-8417. www.harbor-view.com.* Built in 1891, this resort is a prime example of the heritage of Martha's Vineyard. Overlooking Egartown Harbor, guests can relax in a rocking chair on one of the verandahs, stroll among the beautifully maintained gardens, enjoy a swim in the heated outdoor pool, or practice their backhand at a game of tennis. 124 rooms, 1-4 story. Check-out 11 am. TV; cable (premium). Fieldstone fireplace in the lobby. Restaurant (see COACH HOUSE), bar. Outdoor pool, poolside service. Outdoor tennis. Concierge. View of lighthouse. In operation since 1891. Beach opposite. **$**

D 🛒 🏖 🏄

★ ★ ★ **KELLEY HOUSE.** *23 Kelly St, Edgartown (02539). Phone 508/ 627-7900; fax 508/627-8142. www.kelley-house.com.* Built in 1742 and originally a tavern that offered a welcomed respite for weary sea-faring sailors, this enchanting inn still offers a respite from weary occupations but now includes warmly-appointed guest rooms, a central fireplace to cozy up in front of, and friendly, attentive service that makes the weary sailor in all of us feel like we've come home. Ideally perched near the waterfront in downtown Edgartown, this inn has managed to maintain its Early American charm as well as its historic pub. 53 rooms, 1-3 story. No elevator. Complimentary continental breakfast. Check-out 11 am. TV; cable (premium). Outdoor pool. Concierge. In operation since 1742. **$$**

Resort

★ ★ **ISLAND INN.** *Beach Rd, Oak Bluffs (02557). Phone 508/693-2002; toll-free 800/462-0269; fax 508/693-7911. www.islandinn.com.* 51 rooms, 1-2 story. Check-out 11 am. TV. In-room modem link. Laundry services. Restaurant, bar. Outdoor pool. Outdoor tennis. Bicycle path adjacent. Near beach. **$**

B&B/Small Inns

★ ★ **THE ARBOR INN.** *222 Upper Main St, Edgartown (02539). Phone 508/627-8137; toll-free 888/748-4383. www.mvy.com/arborinn.* 10 air-cooled rooms, 2 story. No room phones. Closed Nov-Apr. Children over 12 years only. Complimentary continental breakfast. Check-out 11 am, check-in 2 pm. Concierge. Built in 1880; antiques. **$$**

★ ★ **ASHLEY INN.** *129 Main St, Edgartown (02539). Phone 508/627-9655; toll-free 800/477-9655; fax 508/627-6629.* 10 rooms, 3 story. Children over 12 years only. Complimentary continental breakfast. Check-out 11 am, check-in 2 pm. TV. Fireplaces. Totally nonsmoking. **$**

★ **THE BEACH HOUSE.** *Pennacook and Seaview aves, Oak Bluffs (02557). Phone 508/693-3955. www.beachhousemv.com.* 9 rooms, 3 story. No room phones. Children over 10 years only. Complimentary continental breakfast. Check-out 11 am, check-in 1 pm. TV. Built in 1899; front porch. **$**

★ ★ ★ **BEACH PLUM INN.** *50 Beach Plum Ln, Menemsha (81432). Phone 508/645-9454; toll-free 877/645-7398; fax 508/645-2801. www.beachpluminn.com.* This Martha's Vineyard inn sits on a hilltop overlooking the ocean and boasts one of the island's most well-regarded restaurants. A stone drive and garden-like path lead to the main house, and several other cottages dot the 7-acre property. 11 rooms, 2 story. Complimentary full breakfast. Check-out 11 am, check-in 2 pm. TV; cable (premium), VCR (movies). In-room modem link. Restaurant. Tennis. Lawn games. Concierge. Built in 1890 from salvage of a shipwreck. **$$**

★ ★ ★ ★ **CHARLOTTE INN.** *27 S Summer St, Edgartown (02539). Phone 508/627-4751; fax 508/627-6452.* The Charlotte Inn extends open arms to guests seeking a quintessentially New England experience. This charming inn enjoys a central location among Edgartown's quaint streets and stately sea captains' homes. Convenient to the village, the Charlotte Inn is the perfect place to enjoy the many delights of Martha's Vineyard. A wrought-iron fence stands guard over the manicured grounds of this irresistible Colonial inn. Inside, a romantic English country style dominates the public and private rooms. Artwork, antiques, and other decorative objects lend a hand in creating a historical flavor in the bedrooms. Individually designed, some rooms feature four-poster beds. Spread throughout the main house, Carriage House, and Coach House, the rooms and suites are simply delightful. Light French cuisine enhanced by American and French wine is served in the restaurant, where candlelit dinners are particularly unforgettable. 25 rooms. Children over 14 only. TV; cable (premium), VCR available. Restaurant. Concierge. Afternoon tea. **$$**

★ ★ **COLONIAL INN OF MARTHA'S VINEYARD.** *38 N Water St, Edgartown (02539). Phone 508/627-4711; toll-free 800/627-4701; fax 508/627-5904. www.colonialinnmvy.com.* 43 rooms, 1-4 story. No elevator. Closed Jan-mid-Apr. Complimentary continental breakfast. Check-out 11 am. TV; cable (premium), VCR available (free movies). In-room modem link. Restaurant. **$**

★ ★ **DAGGETT HOUSE.** *59 N Water St, Edgartown (02539). Phone 508/627-4600; fax 508/627-4611. www.mvweb.com/daggett.* 31 rooms, 2 story. Check-out 11 am, check-in 3 pm. TV. Restaurant. Open hearth, antiques in dining room, part of a historic tavern (1660). Private pier. New England atmosphere. Totally nonsmoking. **$$**

★ ★ ★ **DOCKSIDE INN.** *Circuit Ave Ext, Oak Bluffs (02557). Phone 508/693-2966; toll-free 800/245-5979; fax 508/696-7293. www.vineyard.net/inns.* This gingerbread-style inn overlooks the harbor in the seaside village of Oak Bluffs and is walking distance to many attractions, miles of beaches, and shopping areas. 22 rooms, 3 story. Closed Dec-Mar. Complimentary continental breakfast. Check-out 11 am, check-in 2-7 pm. TV. In-room modem link. Game room. Concierge. Colorful gingerbread-style inn opposite docks. Totally nonsmoking. **$**

★ ★ **THE EDGARTOWN INN.** *56 N Water St, Edgartown (02539). Phone 508/627-4794; fax 508/627-9420. www.edgartowninn.com.* 12 rooms,

1-3 story. Closed Nov-Mar. Check-out 11 am, check-in 2 pm. TV in some rooms. Dining room. Historic (1798) sea captain's home. Inn since 1820; colonial furnishings and antiques in rooms. **$**

★ ★ **GREENWOOD HOUSE.** *40 Greenwood Ave, Vineyard Haven (02568). Phone 508/693-6150; toll-free 866/693-6150; fax 508/696-8113. www.greenwoodhouse.com.* 5 rooms, 3 story. Complimentary full breakfast. Check-out 10 am, check-in 2 pm. TV. In-room modem link. Lawn games. Concierge. Built in 1906. Totally nonsmoking. **$$**

★ ★ ★ **THE HANOVER HOUSE.** *28 Edgartown Rd, Vineyard Haven (02568). Phone 508/693-1066; toll-free 800/339-1066; fax 508/696-6099. www.hanoverhouseinn.com.* Set on a half acre of land, this cozy bed-and-breakfast is walking distance to the ferry, shopping, restaurants, and the library. Shuttles are available for travel to Edgartown and Oak Bluffs. Guest rooms are individually decorated. 15 rooms, 2 story. No room phones. Complimentary continental breakfast. Check-out 10 am, check-in 2 pm. TV. Built in 1920; gardens, enclosed sitting porch. Totally nonsmoking. **$$**

★ ★ ★ **HOB KNOB INN.** *128 Main St, Edgartown (02539). Phone 508/627-9510; toll-free 800/696-2723; fax 508/627-4560. www.hobknob.com.* Welcoming guests with a warm country ambience and personalized service, this remarkable inn offers timeless tranquility. Charmingly furnished guest rooms, fireplaces that ensnare guests with their warmth, and fine food add to the historic ambience. 16 rooms, 3 story. Complimentary full breakfast. Check-out 11 am, check-in 2 pm. TV. In-room modem link. In-house fitness room, massage, sauna. Bicycles. Concierge. Inn built in 1860; many antiques. Totally nonsmoking. **$$**

★ ★ **LAMBERT'S COVE COUNTRY INN.** *Lamberts Cove Rd, Vineyard Haven (02568). Phone 508/693-2298; fax 508/693-7890. www.lambertscoveinn.com.* 15 rooms, 2 story. No room phones. Complimentary full breakfast. Check-out 11 am, check-in 2 pm. TV in sitting room. Dining room (public by reservation). Outdoor tennis. **$$**

★ ★ ★ **MARTHA'S PLACE B&B.** *114 Main St, Vineyard Haven (02568). Phone 508/693-0253. www.marthasplace.com.* This Greek Revival home offers the perfect location: across from Owen Park Beach overlooking Vineyard Haven Harbor and just one block from the ferry, restaurants, and shops. All guest rooms feature down comforters and Egyptian cotton linens. 7 rooms, 2 story. No room phones. Complimentary continental breakfast. Check-out 10 am, check-in after noon. TV in some rooms. Built in 1840. Totally nonsmoking. **$$**

★ ★ ★ **THE OAK HOUSE.** *Seaview and Pequot aves, Oak Bluffs (02557). Phone 508/693-4187; fax 508/696-7385. www.vineyard.net/inns.* This authentic Victorian bed-and-breakfast was built in 1872. Each of the rooms is furnished with period antiques. Most rooms have views of the Sound. Afternoon refreshments are offered daily. 10 rooms, 9 with shower only, 3 story. No elevator. Closed mid-Oct-mid-May. Children over 10 years only. Complimentary continental breakfast. Check-out 11 am, check-in 4 pm. TV; VCR available. Street parking. Was the summer home for Massachusetts governor. Totally nonsmoking. **$$**

🖼

★ ★ **OUTERMOST INN.** *171 Lighthouse Rd, Chilmark (02535). Phone 508/645-3511; fax 508/645-3514. www.outermostinn.com.* 7 rooms, 2 story. No A/C. Children over 12 years only. Complimentary full breakfast. Check-out 11 am, check-in 2 pm. TV. Dining room. Concierge. Picture windows provide excellent views of Vineyard Sound and Elizabeth Islands. Totally nonsmoking. **$$**

🖼

★ ★ **PEQUOT HOTEL.** *19 Pequot Ave, Oak Bluffs (02557). Phone 508/693-5087; toll-free 800/947-8704; fax 508/696-9413. www.pequothotel.com.* 29 rooms, 25 with shower only, 3 story. No elevator. No room phones. Closed Nov-Apr. Complimentary continental breakfast. Check-out 11 am, check-in 3 pm. TV in some rooms. Street parking. Built in the 1920s. **$**

D 🖼

★ ★ **POINT WAY INN.** *104 Main St, Edgartown (02539). Phone 508/627-8633; toll-free 888/711-6633; fax 508/627-3338. www.pointway.com.* 14 rooms, 1-3 story. Pets accepted, some restrictions; fee. Complimentary continental breakfast. Check-out 11 am, check-in 2 pm. TV. Laundry services. Totally nonsmoking. **$$**

D 🐾 🖼

★ ★ **SHIRETOWN INN.** *44 N Water St, Edgartown (02539). Phone 508/627-3353; fax 508/627-8478. www.shiretowninn.com.* 35 rooms, 1-3 story. Some A/C. Closed mid-Oct-Apr. Complimentary continental breakfast. Check-out 11 am, check-in 2 pm. TV. Dining room, bar. 18th-century whaling house. **$**

🖼

★ ★ ★ **THORNCROFT INN.** *460 Main St (02568). Phone 508/693-3333; toll-free 800/332-1236; fax 508/693-5419. www.thorncroft.com.* Secluded on a tree-lined, 3-acre peninsula, this charming, white-shuttered home houses 14 romantic guest rooms, some with hot tubs and fireplaces. A full country breakfast can be enjoyed in the dining room or requested for breakfast-in-bed delivery. 14 rooms, 2 story. Complimentary full breakfast. Check-out 11 am, check-in 3-9 pm. TV. In-room modem link. Totally nonsmoking. **$$$**

D 🖼

Restaurants

★ ★ ★ **COACH HOUSE.** *131 N Water St, Edgartown (02539). Phone 508/627-7000; fax 508/627-8417. www.harbor-view.com.* Part of the Harbor View Hotel, this spacious dining room has beautiful views of the harbor. The menu features updated classics. New England cuisine. Breakfast, lunch, dinner, Sun brunch. Bar. Children's menu. Totally nonsmoking. **$$$**

[D]

★ ★ **HOME PORT.** *512 North Rd, Mehemsha (02552). Phone 508/645-2679; fax 508/645-3119.* Seafood menu. Closed mid-Oct-mid-Apr. Dinner. Children's menu. Reservations required. **$$$**

[D]

★ ★ **THE NAVIGATOR.** *2 Lower Main St, Edgartown (02539). Phone 508/627-4320; fax 508/627-3544.* Seafood menu. Closed mid-Oct-mid-May. Lunch, dinner. Bar. Children's menu. Outdoor seating. **$$$**

[D]

★ ★ **SQUARE RIGGER.** *225 State Rd, Edgartown (02539). Phone 508/627-9968; fax 508/627-4837.* Seafood menu. Dinner. Bar. Children's menu. Totally nonsmoking. **$$**

[D] [SC]

★ ★ **WHARF & WHARF PUB.** *Lower Main St, Edgartown (02539). Phone 508/627-9966.* Seafood menu. Closed Thanksgiving, Dec 24-25. Lunch, dinner. Bar; entertainment Wed-Sun. Children's menu. **$$**

[D]

Nantucket Island

4 hours 20 minutes; 102 miles from Boston

Settled 1659 **Pop** 9,520 **Elev** 0-108 ft **Area code** 508 **Zip** 02554

Information Chamber of Commerce, 48 Main St; 508/228-1700. General information may also be obtained at the Information Bureau, 25 Federal St; 508/228-1700

Web www.nantucketchamber.org

This is not just an island; it is an experience. Nantucket Island is at once a popular resort and a living museum. Siasconset (SCON-set) and Nantucket Town remain quiet and charming, despite heavy tourism. Nantucket, with 49 square miles of lovely beaches and green moors inland, is south of Cape Cod, 30 miles at sea. The island was the world's greatest whaling port from the late 17th century until New Bedford became dominant in the early 1800s. Whaling prosperity built the towns; tourism maintains them.

There is regular car ferry and passenger service from Hyannis. If you plan to take your car, make advance reservation by mail with the Woods Hole,

Martha's Vineyard, and Nantucket Steamship Authority, PO Box 284, Woods Hole 02543; phone 508/477-8600. A great variety of beaches, among them the Jetties, north of Nantucket Town (harbor), and Surfside, on the south shore of the island (surf), offer swimming. Tennis, golf, fishing, sailing, and cycling can be arranged.

What to See and Do

Actors Theatre of Nantucket. *2 Centre St (02554). Phone 508/228-6325. www.nantuckettheatre.com.* The Actors Theatre of Nantucket has staged comedies, dramas, plays, and dance concerts since 1985. Both professionals and amateurs make up the company, which offers between six and ten performances during the summer. When purchasing tickets, ask whether family matinees are offered for that performance. **$$$$**

Altar Rock. *Off Polpis Rd to the south on unmarked dirt road.* Climb up Altar Rock, which rises 90 feet above sea level, and you're afforded stunning views of Nantucket and the surrounding Cape. Go at dawn or dusk for the best views. The Moors surrounding Altar Rock offer a chance to hike on the trails or two-track dirt roads. Few tourists make the trek, which makes for unexpected solitude on Nantucket.

Barrett's Tours. *Phone 508/228-0174.* Offers 1 1/2-hour bus and van tours (Apr-Nov).

Bartlett's Ocean View Farm. *33 Bartlett Farm Rd (02584). Phone 508/228-9403. www.bartlettsoceanviewfarm.com.* Nurturing Nantucket's largest farm, the Bartlett family has tilled this land for nearly 200 years. Stop by for fresh vegetables, milk, eggs, cheese, freshly baked bread, and cut flowers. If you're looking for prepared dishes, taste the farm kitchen's salads, entrées (including several that are vegetarian), pies, snacks, jams, chutneys, and other farm delights. Also visit the East Coast Seafood market, less than a mile away, for fresh fish and seafood to complete your meal. (Daily 8 am-6 pm)

Bass Hole Boardwalk and Gray's Beach. *End of Centre St (02675). Take Route 6A to Church St. Bear left onto Centre St and follow to the end.* This honest-to-goodness elevated boardwalk—stretching 860 feet—offers delightful scenery as it meanders through one of Cape Cod's finest marshes to the beach. Kids enjoy playing on the beach or adjoining playground; the whole family can walk the beach and into the bay at low tide.

Boat Trips. Hyannis-Nantucket Day Round Trip. *22 Channel Point Rd (02601). Phone 508/778-2600.* Summer passenger service from Hyannis. **$$$$**

Cisco Brewers. *5 Bartlett Farm Rd (02584). Phone 508/325-5929. www.ciscobrewers.com.* If you enjoy beer, visit Cisco Brewers and taste the delicious locally made brews. From Whale's Tales Pale Ale and Bailey's Ale to Moor Porter, Cap'n Swain's Extra Stout, Summer of Lager, and Baggywrinkle Barleywine, just about every variety of beer is represented at Cisco. Stop by for the daily guided tour ($10; times vary) that includes a walk through the brewery (including taste testing), as well as a tour of the Triple Eight Distillery and Nantucket Vineyard next door. Allow one-and-a-half hours for the entire tour. (Summer: Mon-Sat 10 am-6 pm; fall-spring: Sat 10 am-5 pm) **FREE**

Claire Murray. *11 S Water St (02554). Phone 508/228-1913. www.claire murray.com.* Even if you've seen Claire Murray's delightful rug designs elsewhere in the country, visit the store where she got her start. Nantucket winters don't bring many visitors, and Claire Murray, who used to run a bed-and-breakfast, started hooking rugs to pass the time during these months. She soon began designing and selling rugs full-time around the world. Today, her store in Nantucket sells both finished rugs and kits and also offers classes. Around the Cape, look for other locations in West Barnstable, Osterville, Mashpee, and Edgartown (on Martha's Vineyard). (Mon-Sat 10 am-9 pm, Sun 11 am-7 pm)

⭐ **Endeavor Sailing Adventures.** *Straight Wharf (02554). Phone 508/228-5585. www.endeavorsailing.com.* US Coast Guard Captain James Genthner built his sloop, named the *Endeavor,* and has been sailing it for over 20 years. Take a 90-minute sail around Nantucket Sound and let the good captain and his wife, Sue, acquaint you with Nantucket's sights, sounds, and history. No sailing experience is necessary, and you can bring a picnic lunch. A special one-hour kids tour sails at 11:30 daily. (May-Oct; closed Nov-Apr) **$$$$**

First Congregational Church & View. *62 Centre St (02554). Phone 508/228-0950.* Also called Old North Church, the First Congregational Church offers Nantucket's best view of the island and surrounding ocean. Climb 94 steps to the 120-foot-tall steeple, and you're amply rewarded with a view from the top of the world. While you're at the church, take in the historical display that shows photos of the church as it has looked throughout its long history. (Mid-June-mid-Oct, Mon-Sat) **$**

Gail's Tours. *Phone 508/257-6557.* Narrated van tours (approximately 1 3/4 hours) of area. Three tours daily. Reservations recommended. Tours depart from Information Center at Federal and Broad streets.

Jetties Beach. *Take North Beach Rd to Bathing Beach Rd; from there, take a shuttle bus (Mid-June–Labor Day), walk, or bike, the distance (just over a mile) to the beach.* You won't find better amenities for families with kids than Jetties Beach. Besides the convenient rest rooms, showers, changing rooms, and snack bar, the beach employs life guards, offers chairs for rent, provides a well-equipped playground, maintains volleyball and tennis courts, and offers a skateboarding park. You can also rent kayaks, sailboards, and sailboats through Nantucket Community Sailing (phone 508/228-5358), which maintains an office at the beach. Look for occasional concerts and a July 4 fireworks display. (Daily)

The Lifesaving Museum. *158 Polpis Rd (02554). Phone 508/228-1885. www.nantucketlifesavingmuseum.com.* The building that houses the museum is a re-creation of the original 1874 lifesaving station that was built to assist mariners from the oft-times deadly seas. Museum exhibits include lifesaving surfboats, large and intricate lighthouse lenses, historical objects from the *Andrea Dorea* (which sank off the coast of Nantucket Island), demonstrations, stories of rescues, and action photos. **$**

Loines Observatory. *59 Milk St (02554). Phone 508/228-8690. www.mmo.org.* Part of the Maria Mitchell Association (MMA)—named for the first professional female astronomer—the Loines Observatory gives you a chance to peek through a fine old telescope and view the magnificent, star-filled Cape Cod skies. Also visit the MMA's other observatory on Vestal Street, which includes an outdoor true-to-scale model of the solar system, an astronomy exhibit, and a sundial. Kids may prefer the attractions at The Vestal Street Observatory, which is noted for its work with young scientists. (Mon, Wed, Fri evenings in summer, Sat evenings year-round; closed Tues, Thurs, Sun in summer, Sun-Fri year-round) **$$**

⭐ **Main Street.** *15 Broad St. Phone 508/228-1894. www.nantucket.com.* Paved with cobblestones, lined with elegant houses built by whaling merchants, and shaded by great elms, this is one of New England's most beautiful streets. The Nantucket Historical Association maintains the following attractions (June-Oct, daily; spring and fall, limited hours).

1800 House. *Mill and Pleasant sts. Phone 508/228-1894.* Home of the sheriff, early 19th century. Period home and furnishings; large, round cellar; kitchen garden.

Folger-Franklin Seat & Memorial Boulder. *Madaket Rd, 1 mile from W end of Main St.* Birthplace site of Abiah Folger, mother of Benjamin Franklin.

Hadwen House. *Main and Pleasant sts.* (1845) Greek Revival mansion; furnishings of whaling period; gardens. **$$**

⭐ **Jethro Coffin House (Oldest House).** *16 Sunset Hill Ln (02554). N on North Water to West Chester, left to Sunset Hill. Phone 508/228-1894.* Built in 1686, Oldest House is, true to its name, one of the oldest houses you'll ever visit in the United States, and the oldest on Nantucket. The house was a wedding present given to the children of two feuding families (the Gardners and the Coffins) by their in-laws, who reconciled after the happy event. In 1987, after lightning struck Oldest House, it was fully restored to its original beauty. This colonial saltbox and its spare furnishings exude classic Nantucket style and charm. (Seasonal; call for dates and times) **$**

Museum of Nantucket History (Macy Warehouse). *2 Whalers Ln (02554). Straight Wharf. Phone 508/228-1894.* Exhibits related to Nantucket history; diorama; craft demonstrations. **$$**

Old Fire Hose Cart House. *Gardner St off Main St.* (1886) Old-time fire-fighting equipment. **FREE**

Old Gaol. *Vestal St. Phone 508/228-1894.* (1805) Unusual two-story construction; used until 1933. **FREE**

Old Windmill. *On Mill Hill, off Prospect St.* (1746) Built of wood from wrecked vessels, with original machinery and grinding stones. Corn ground daily during summer. **$**

Research Center. *Broad St, next to Whaling Museum. Phone 508/228-1655.* Ships' logs, diaries, charts, and Nantucket photographs; library. (Mon-Fri)

Whaling Museum. *12 Broad St (02554). Broad St, near Steamboat Wharf. Phone 508/228-1736.* Outstanding collection of relics from whaling days; whale skeleton, tryworks, scrimshaw, candle press. **$$**

Murray's Toggery. *62 Main St (02554). Phone 508/228-0437. www.nantucketreds.com.* Murray's Toggery was the first store in Nantucket to sell Nantucket Reds—casual red pants that eventually fade to a decidedly pink hue—a product that defines both Cape Cod and the preppy look. Murray's also sells oxford shirts, sweaters, shoes, hats, coats, and jackets for both men and women. (Mon-Sat 9 am-7 pm, Sun 10 am-6 pm; winter: Mon-Sat 9 am-5 pm; closed Sun in winter)

Nantucket Gourmet. *4 India St (2554). Phone 508/228-4353. www.nantucket gourmet.com.* Nantucket Gourmet offers a well-balanced blend of cookware and other culinary tools, and condiments to take back home with you (including marmalades, jams, mustards, and vinegars), and ready-to-eat deli foods for your lunch on the island. You'll find great gifts for any food-lover. (Summer: daily 10 am-6 pm; winter: Mon-Fri 10 am-4 pm; closed holidays)

Nantucket Maria Mitchell Association. *1 Vestal St. Phone 508/228-9198 or 508/228-0898 in summer. Combination ticket available for museum, birthplace, and aquarium.* The birthplace of the first American woman astronomer; memorial observatory (1908). The scientific library has Nantucket historical documents, science journals, and Mitchell family memorabilia. Natural science museum with local wildlife. Aquarium is at 28 Washington Street. (Mid-June-Aug, Tues-Sat; library also open rest of year, Wed-Sat; closed July 4, Labor Day) **$$**

Nantucket Town. *The areas between Main, Broad, and Centre sts. Phone 508/228-1700. www.nantucketchamber.org/directory/merchants.* Nantucket Town is a shopper's dream, with narrow cobblestone streets that wind past hundreds of shops. You'll find items for your home (furniture, rugs, throws and blankets, baskets, prints, soaps, and so on), your boat (including all manner of weather-predicting equipment), and yourself (from preppy and upscale clothing, hats, shawls, jewelry, and everything in between). In about 20 stores, you'll find the famous Nantucket baskets (also called lightship baskets), which are handmade through a time-consuming process. You'll also come across numerous art galleries, antiques shops, and craft stores.

Nantucket Whaling Museum. *13 Broad St (02554). Phone 508/228-1894. www.nha.org.* To really understand Nantucket, you have to understand whaling, the industry that put Nantucket on the map. The Nantucket Whaling Museum—housed in a former factory that produced candles from whale oil—shows you a fully rigged whale boat (smaller than you may think), rope and basket collections, scrimshaw (whale-bone carving) exhibits, a huge lighthouse Fresnel lens, a skeleton of a finback whale, and maritime folk art. Enjoy one of three daily lectures offered by the museum staff. Visit in December to see the Festival of Trees, which includes 50 decorated Christmas trees. **$$**

Old Mill. *South Mill and Prospect sts (02554). Phone 508/228-1894.* This Dutch-style windmill is impressive in its beauty and sheer size (50 feet high), but it was built for function—to grind grain brought by local farmers—and it remains functional today. Believed to be the oldest windmill in the United States, it was built in 1746 with salvaged oak that washed up on shore from shipwrecks and, after many owners, eventually came to belong to the Nantucket Historical Society. (Daily June-Aug; call for off-season hours) **$**

Rafael Osona Auctions. *21 Washington St (02554). At the American Legion Hall. Phone 508/228-3942.* If you like antiques, you'll love Rafael Osona. The auctioneers host estate auctions on selected weekends (call for exact dates and times) that feature treasured pieces from both the US and Europe. If an auction isn't planned while you're in town, visit the two dozen other antique stores on the island, plus many more around Cape Cod. (Late May-early Dec)

Siasconset Village. *E end of Nantucket Island (02554).* The Siasconset Village lies 7 miles from Nantucket Town, and can be traveled by bicycle or shuttle bus. This 18th-century fishing village features quaint cottages, grand mansions, restaurants, a few shops, and a summer cinema. Visit Siasconset Beach and the paved biking path that meanders through the area.

Something Natural. *50 Cliff Rd (02554). Phone 508/228-0504. www.something natural.com.* If you're looking for a casual breakfast or lunch—perhaps even one to take with you on a bike ride or island hike—check out Something Natural for healthy sandwiches, breads and bagels, salads, cookies, and beverages. The eatery has also established a second location at 6 Oak Street (508/228-6616). (May-Oct)

The Straight Wharf. *Straight Wharf (02554). On the harbor, next to the ferry* Built in 1723, the Straight Wharf is Nantucket's launching area for sailboats, sloops, and kayaks, but it's also a great shopping and eating area. Loaded with restaurants and quaint, one-room cottage shops selling island fare, the wharf also features an art gallery, a museum, and an outdoor concert pavilion.

Strong Wings Summer Camp. *PO Box 2884 (02584). Phone 508/228-1769. www.strongwinds.com.* Open for just one month every year, the Strong Winds Summer Camp offers more excitement and activity for kids than you're likely to find anywhere else on the Cape. Kids ages 5 to 15 attend three-day or five-day sessions, where they explore the natural attributes of the area, mountain bike, hike, kayak, snorkel, rock climb, and boogie board (as appropriate for each age group). Older kids even learn search-and-rescue techniques. (Daily, late June-late Aug; closed Sept-mid-June) **$$$$**

The Sunken Ship. *12 Broad St (02554). Phone 508/228-9226. www.sunken ship.com.* The Sunken Ship is a full-service dive shop that offers lessons and rentals. When the *Andrea Doria* sank off the coast of Nantucket in the middle of the last century, the area invited divers from around the world to investigate the sunken ship, hence the name of this shop. The general store offers an eclectic array of dive and maritime goods. (Daily; call for closures) **$$$$**

Windswept Cranberry Bog. *Polpis Rd (02554).* Cranberries are an important industry to Nantucket; in town, you can purchase jars of cranberry honey, and Northland Cranberries harvests berries from Nantucket to make its well-known juices. To see how cranberries are grown and harvested, visit this 200-acre cranberry bog during the fall harvest (late September through October from dawn to dusk), when bogs are flooded so that machines can shake off and scoop up the individual berries. (Mid-October also brings the Nantucket Cranberry Festival.) Even at other times of year, the bog is peaceful and beautiful—a good place to walk and bike and spend half a day. Another nearby cranberry bog is the Milestone Bog (off Milestone Road west of Siasconset). (Daily dawn-dusk)

Special Events

Christmas Stroll. *Phone 508/228-1700.* First weekend in Dec.

Daffodil Festival. *Siasconset Village (02564). Phone 508/228-1700. www.nantucket.net/daffy.* The Daffodil Festival celebrates the budding of millions of daffodils on the main roads of Nantucket. A parade of antique car classics kicks off the well-attended event, which also includes open houses, garden tours, and a lively picnic that offers great food and live entertainment. Late Apr. **FREE**

Harborfest. *Phone 508-228-1700.* Early June.

Nantucket Arts Festival. *Various venues (02554). Phone 508/325-8588.* This week-long festival celebrates a full range of arts on the island: films, poetry and fiction readings, acting, dance performances, and exhibits of paintings, photography, and many other art forms. Look for the wet-paint sale in which you can bid on works completed just that day by local artists. Early Oct. **FREE**

Nantucket County Fair. *Tom Nevers Navy Base (02554). Phone 508/325-4748.* Looking for an old-fashioned county fair? Head to Nantucket for down-home family fun and entertainment. At the Nantucket County Fair, an event that began over 150 years ago, you'll find pies, breads, pastries, jams, jellies, fresh fall fruits, and concessions of all types. You'll also see and experience tractor displays and rides, a petting zoo and pet show, a flea market, quilt displays and sales, hay rides, concerts, and square dancing. Third weekend in Sept. **$$**

Nantucket Film Festival. *Various venues (02554). Phone 508/228-6648. www.nantucketfilmfestival.org.* Like other film festivals worldwide, Nantucket's festival screens new independent films that may not otherwise garner attention. You'll be joined by screenwriters, actors, film connoisseurs and, occasionally, big-name celebrities at the festival's seminars, readings, and discussions. A daily event called Morning Coffee showcases a panel of directors, screenwriters, and actors participating in Q&A with festival-goers, who sip coffee and munch on muffins. Mid-June. **$$$$**

Nantucket Wine Festival. *Phone 508/228-1128. www.nantucketwine festival.com.* This is a wine festival like no other: take in a wine symposium, a variety of food and wine seminars, a wine auction, and many other events. The Great Wine in Grand Houses event allows you to visit a private mansion, sip fine wines drawn from nearly 100 wineries, and dine on food prepared by some of the world's finest chefs. Reservations are required and should be made as soon as you know you'll be visiting the island. Mid-May. **$$$$**

Sand Castle Contest. *Phone 508/228-1700.* Third Sat in Aug.

Motel/Motor Lodge

★ ★ **HARBOR HOUSE VILLAGE.** *S Beach St (02554). Phone 508/228-1500; toll-free 866/325-9300; fax 508/228-7639. www.nantucketislandresorts.com.* 104 rooms, 2-3 story. No elevator. Check-out 11 am, check-in 3 pm. TV; cable (premium). In-room modem link. Restaurant, bar; entertainment. Room service. Outdoor pool, poolside service. Concierge. Public beach opposite. **$**

D ⌷ ⌷

Hotels

★ ★ ★ **VANESSA NOEL HOTEL.** *5 Chestnut St (03554). Phone 508/228-5300. www.vanessanoel.com.* 8 rooms, 3 story. Complimentary continental breakfast. Check-out 11 am, check-in 1 pm. TV; cable (premium). Internet access. Restaurant, bar. Room service. **$$$**

D ⌷

★ ★ ★ **WHITE ELEPHANT RESORT.** *50 Easton St (02554). Phone 508/228-2500; toll-free 800/475-2637; fax 508/325-1195. www.whiteelephantresort.com.* Step back in time for a game of croquet on a sweeping, manicured lawn at this harbor-front resort. Visitors to the expansive property can stay in one of 58 guest rooms or 12 cottages. 70 rooms, 1-3 story. No elevator. Closed Nov-Apr. Check-out 11 am, check-in 3 pm. TV; cable (premium). In-room modem link. Restaurant, bar; entertainment. Beach nearby; boat slips for guests only. Concierge. **$$$**

D SC

B&B/Small Inns

★ ★ **CARLISLE HOUSE INN.** *26 N Water St (02554). Phone 508/228-0720; fax 781/639-1004. www.carlislehouse.com.* 17 rooms, 3 story. No room phones. Closed early Dec-Mar. Children over 10 years only. Complimentary continental breakfast. Check-out 11 am, check-in 2 pm. Street parking. Restored whaling captain's house (1765). Totally nonsmoking. **$**

⌷

★ **THE CARRIAGE HOUSE.** *5 Ray's Ct (02554). Phone 508/228-0326. www.carriagehousenantucket.com.* 7 rooms, 2 story. No A/C. Complimentary continental breakfast. Check-out 11 am, check-in 1 pm. Victorian décor. Center of old historic district; near ferries. Totally nonsmoking. **$**

⌷

★ ★ ★ **CENTERBOARD GUEST HOUSE.** *8 Chester St (02554). Phone 508/228-9696. www.nantucket.net/lodging/centerboard.* This sparkling-white Victorian home was built in 1886 and offers seven guest rooms, including one two-room suite with a fireplace, canopied bed, and marble bath. The historic district location is steps from ferries, restaurants, and beaches. 8 rooms, 3 story. Closed Jan-Feb. Complimentary continental breakfast. Check-out 11 am, check-in 3 pm. TV. In-room modem link. Street parking. Restored Victorian residence (1885). Totally nonsmoking. **$**

★ ★ **CENTRE STREET INN.** *78 Centre St (02554). Phone 508/228-0199; toll-free 800/298-0199; fax 508/228-8676. www.centrestreetinn.com.* 14 rooms, 3 story. No room phones. Closed Jan-Apr. Children over 8 years only. Complimentary continental breakfast. Check-out 11 am, check-in 3 pm. Concierge. Colonial house built in 1742; some antiques. Totally nonsmoking. **$**

★ ★ **COBBLESTONE INN.** *5 Ash St (02554). Phone 508/228-1987; fax 508/228-6698.* 5 rooms, 3 story. Closed Jan-Mar. Complimentary breakfast. Check-out 11 am, check-in 2 pm. TV. Fireplace in library. Lawn games. Concierge. Built in 1725. Totally nonsmoking. **$**

★ ★ ★ **JARED COFFIN HOUSE.** *29 Broad St (02554). Phone 508/228-2400; fax 508/228-8549. www.jaredcoffinhouse.com.* Experience 19th-century style with modern amenities at this quaint inn. Built in 1845, the red-brick, three-story main house is crowned with a cupola affording guests splendid harbor views. Jared's beautiful dining room offers a wonderful, seasonal menu. 60 rooms, 3 story. Check-out 11 am, check-in after 3 pm. TV. In-room modem link. Restaurant, bar. Concierge. Historical objets d'art. **$**

★ ★ **MARTIN HOUSE INN.** *61 Centre St (02554). Phone 508/228-0678. www.nantucket.net/lodging/martinn.* 13 rooms, 3 story. No A/C. No elevator. No room phones. Closed Jan-Feb. Complimentary continental breakfast. Check-out 11 am, check-in 3 pm. TV in common room; cable (premium). In-room modem link. Restaurant. Street parking. Built in 1803. Totally nonsmoking. **$**

★ ★ **ROBERTS HOUSE INN.** *11 India St (02554). Phone 508/228-0600; toll-free 800/872-6830; fax 508/325-4046. www.robertshouseinn.com.* 45 rooms, 3 story. Complimentary continental breakfast. Check-out 11 am, check-in 2 pm. TV. Concierge. Built in 1846; established in 1883. **$**

★ ★ **SEVEN SEA STREET INN.** *7 Sea St (02554). Phone 508/228-3577; fax 508/228-3578. www.sevenseastreetinn.com.* 11 rooms, 2 story. Children over 5 years only. Complimentary continental breakfast. Check-out 11 am, check-in 3 pm. TV; VCR. Whirlpool. View of Nantucket Harbor. Totally nonsmoking. **$$**

★ ★ ★ **SHERBURNE INN.** *10 Gay St (02554). Phone 508/228-4425; toll-free 888/577-4425; fax 508/228-8114. www.nantucket.net/lodging/ sherburne.* This 1835 inn, located in the heart of Nantucket, has a rich history, as it was once the location of the Atlantic Silk Company. The guest rooms are individually decorated. 8 rooms, 3 story. Children over 6 years only. Complimentary continental breakfast. Check-out 11 am, check-in 2 pm. Street parking. Concierge. Period antiques, fireplaced parlors. Totally nonsmoking. **$**

★ ★ **SHIPS INN.** *13 Fair St (02554). Phone 508/228-0040; fax 508/228-6254. www.nantucket.net/lodging/shipsinn.net.* 12 rooms, 4 story. No A/C. Closed Nov-Apr. Complimentary continental breakfast. Check-out 10 am, check-in 2 pm. TV. Dining room, bar. Built in 1831 by a sea captain; many original furnishings. Totally nonsmoking. **$$**

★ ★ **TUCKERNUCK INN.** *60 Union St (02554). Phone 508/228-4886; toll-free 800/228-4886; fax 508/228-4890. www.tuckernuckinn.com.* 20 rooms, 2 story. Check-out 11 am, check-in 3 pm. TV; cable (premium), VCR. Laundry services. Dining room. Lawn games. Totally nonsmoking. **$**

★ ★ ★ ★ **THE WAUWINET.** *120 Wauwinet Rd (02584). Phone 508/228-0145; toll-free 800/426-8718; fax 508/228-6712. www.wauwinet.com.* Nearly 30 miles out to sea, the idyllic island of Nantucket is a place where crashing waves wash away everyday cares. The Wauwinet embodies the perfect getaway on this magical island. Tucked away on a private stretch of beach, The Wauwinet leads its guests to believe that they have been marooned on a remote island, yet this delightful hotel remains close to the town's charming cobblestone streets, a complimentary jitney ride away. Built in 1876 by ship captains, The Wauwinet's rooms and suites have a sophisticated country style blended with the services of a posh resort. Private beaches fronting the harbor and the Atlantic Ocean are spectacular, and clay tennis courts challenge guests to a match. Whether diners choose to arrive by foot or by sunset cruise on the 26-foot *Wauwinet Lady,* Topper's restaurant (see) promises to be an exceptional event. With a 20,000-bottle wine cellar and an impressive menu, it is an epicurean's delight. *Secret Inspector's Notes:* One of the most enjoyable ways to enjoy the fabulous Nantucket sunsets is with a signature pitcher of martinis or a glass of champagne on the outdoor terrace at the back of the hotel or in an Adirondack chair at the base of the lawn. 36 rooms, 1-3 story. Closed Nov-early May. Complimentary full breakfast. Check-out 11 am, check-in 4 pm. TV; VCR (movies). In-room modem link. Dining room. Room service. Outdoor tennis. Lawn games. Bicycles. Sailboats, rowboats. Totally nonsmoking. **$$$$**

Restaurants

★ ★ ★ **21 FEDERAL.** *21 Federal St (02554). Phone 508/228-2121; fax 508/228-2962.* Seafood menu. Menu changes daily. Closed Jan-Mar. Dinner. Bar. Outdoor seating. **$$$**

★ ★ ★ **AMERICAN SEASONS.** *80 Center St (02554). Phone 508/228-7111; fax 508/325-0779.* Regional American menu. Closed Jan-Apr. Dinner. Bar. Outdoor seating. **$$$**

D

★ **ATLANTIC CAFE.** *15 S Water St (02554). Phone 508/228-0570; fax 508/228-8787. www.atlanticcafe.com.* American, seafood menu. Closed late Dec-early Jan. Dinner. Bar. Children's menu. **$$**

D

★ ★ **BLACK EYED SUSAN'S.** *10 India St (02554). Phone 508/325-0308.* Eclectic/International menu. Closed Sun; also Nov-Apr. Breakfast, dinner. Casual attire. Outdoor seating. **$$**

★ ★ **BLUE FIN.** *15 S Beach St (02554). Phone 508/228-2033. www.nantucketbluefin.com.* Eclectic/International menu. Closed Jan-Apr. Dinner. Bar. Children's menu. Casual attire. **$$**

D

★ ★ ★ **BOARDING HOUSE.** *12 Federal St (02554). Phone 508/228-9622; fax 508/325-7109. www.nantucketrestaurants.com.* Contemporary American menu. Dinner. Bar. Outdoor seating. **$$$**

★ ★ ★ **CHANTICLEER.** *9 New St (02564). Phone 508/257-6231; fax 508/257-4154. www.thechanticleerinn.com.* Owner/chef Jean-Charles Berruet delights his guests with expertly prepared food and perfectly professional service. The main dining room is cozy and romantic, with a crackling fireplace, fresh flowers, and a view of the famous rose garden. Take a stroll through the rose and herb gardens during a visit here and drink in all the beauty of the place. French menu. Closed Mon; also late Oct-mid-May. Dinner. Bar. Reservations required. Outdoor seating. **$$$**

D

★ ★ ★ **CLUB CAR.** *1 Main St (02554). Phone 508/228-1101. www.theclubcar.com.* Lunch and dinner at the Club Car are elegant, but the atmosphere remains casual. The Club Car lounge is housed in a renovated club car from a train that used to run between Steamboat Wharf and Siasconset Village, so the décor is fascinating. The restaurant offers seats for people-watching along Main Street and the waterfront, and a pianist performs nightly. French, continental menu. Closed Nov-late May. Dinner. Bar. Turn-of-the-century décor. Reservations required. **$$$**

★ ★ ★ **COMPANY OF THE CAULDRON.** *7 India St (02554). Phone 508/228-4016.* Eclectic/International menu. Closed Mon; also mid-Dec-May. Dinner. Harpist Wed, Fri, Sun. Totally nonsmoking. **$$$**

D

★ ★ ★ **LE LANGUEDOC.** *24 Broad St (02554). Phone 508/228-2552; fax 508/228-4682. www.lelanguedoc.com.* The upstairs of this French spot features a romantic setting. Downstairs is a fun, casual café. French, American menu. Closed Feb-Mar. Dinner. Bar. Early 1800s building in the heart of the historic district. Outdoor seating. **$$$**

★ ★ ★ **ORAN MOR.** *2 S Beach St (02554). Phone 508/228-8655.* International menu. Closed Dec 25. Dinner. Bar. Casual attire. **$$**

D

★ **ROPE WALK.** *1 Straight Wharf (02554). Phone 508/228-8886; fax 508/228-8740. www.theropewalk.com.* Seafood menu. Closed mid-Oct-mid-May. Dinner. Bar. Children's menu. Outdoor seating. **$$**

D

★ ★ ★ **SUMMER HOUSE.** *17 Ocean Ave (02554). Phone 508/257-9976.* American menu. Closed mid-Oct-mid-May. Dinner. Bar. Children's menu. Casual attire. Outdoor seating. **$$**

D

★ ★ ★ **TOPPER'S.** *120 Wauwinet Rd (02554). Phone 508/228-0145; fax 508/325-0657. www.wauwinet.com.* Located near the Great Point Lighthouse in the Wauwinet Inn (see), this romantic, sophisticated restaurant is filled with flowers, art, and the island's upper-crust clientele. The food, service, and wine list are all first rate. American menu. Closed late Oct-early May. Dinner, Sun brunch. Bar. Outdoor seating. Totally nonsmoking. **$$$**

D

★ ★ **WEST CREEK CAFE.** *11 W Creek Rd (02554). Phone 508/228-4943.* Contemporary American menu. Closed Tues; also Jan 1, July 4, Dec 25. Dinner. Bar. Outdoor seating. Totally nonsmoking. **$$$**

Index

Notes

Notes

Notes

Notes

Notes

Notes

Notes

Notes

Notes